INTROSPECTION

Vinay Singh is a spiritual seeker, a lifelong experimenter, and a keen observer of human behaviour. A collector of real-life stories, he brings together experience, empathy, and insight in equal measure. He served in the Indian Air Force for 23 years, retiring as a Wing Commander, before moving into Strategic IT Consulting, where he led major national projects for the Comptroller and Auditor General (CAG) of India, the Election Commission of India, the Ministry of Defence, and two of Indian Railways' factories. He also led IT consulting projects for IIM Lucknow, IIFT, and several others. He contributed as a guest faculty at IIM Lucknow for a few years. Having stepped away from professional engagements, he now devotes his time to his spiritual practice and the study of ancient scriptures and various spiritual methods.

INTROSPECTION

Your Inner Superpower Revealed

Vinay Singh

hachette
INDIA

First published in paperback in 2026 by Hachette India
(Registered name: Hachette Book Publishing India Pvt. Ltd)
An Hachette UK company
www.hachetteindia.com

1

ISBN 978-93-5731-518-0

Hachette Book Publishing India Pvt. Ltd
4th & 5th Floors, Corporate Centre
Plot No. 94, Sector 44, Gurugram – 122003, India

Typeset in Stempel Garamond LT Std 10.5/14.5
by Manmohan Kumar, Delhi

Printed and bound in India
by Manipal Technologies Limited

MIX
Paper | Supporting responsible forestry
FSC™ C043100

CONTENTS

PREFACE

In the ancient Indian education system, a student was taught at a *Gurukul* for holistic human growth – professional *vidya* as well as *brahma vidya*. While professional education equipped them to earn a living, *brahma vidya* taught them the purpose of life and *how to live*. Through introspection, meditation, and disciplined living, they were trained to regulate the mind, refine conduct, and harmonize thoughts, words, and action. The emphasis was on qualities that allowed one to engage fully in the world without becoming entangled by it.

Brahma vidya reminded every student that a truly meaningful life is not measured by possessions or position, but by one's **awareness, purpose, and capacity to live in harmony with others**. In essence, while the outer education prepared one for a profession, *brahma vidya* prepared one for life itself.

As of date, for a young professional, the key concerns remain: job, CTC, entertainment, and a suitable partner. However, there comes a time in our lives when uncomfortable moments or **patterns start repeating** themselves. It could be in our professional relationships, personal relationships, financial matters, or even health matters.

Our usual reaction in such difficult times is predictable: we try our best to change the circumstances. If that doesn't work, we expect the other person to change so that our expectations are met. When that too fails, many of us turn to God, seeking a favourable outcome. And when even divine negotiations seem unanswered, a few among us finally ask,

'Why me?'

But once in a while, a rare person approaches God with a different question:

'Please let me know if there's something for me to learn in this situation. I am open and willing to introspect, to learn my lesson – if any.'

That is when miracles begin to unfold.

In every conflict, difficulty (even if our own gaps are minimal), or even a period of great success, there is always scope for reviewing our own actions – our beliefs, thoughts, and behaviours. This simple act of Introspection (self-review) marks the beginning of our evolution journey.

Let's pause for a moment and ask: instead of waiting for extreme situations to push us towards introspection, could we not begin earlier? The answer is – Yes. Introspection gives us that power. It allows us to walk *ahead* of problems (most of the time). When we are aware of our own shortcomings and sincerely determined to refine ourselves, the need for extreme events diminishes.

This quiet invitation – to look within, to understand our patterns, reactions, and motives – is the true beginning of introspection. It is not an act of judgement, but of gentle curiosity.

This workbook was born out of that same curiosity. Over the years, I've noticed something fascinating – people spend enormous energy trying to 'fix' others, yet very little trying to understand themselves. We attend workshops to improve relationships, but seldom pause to ask: '*What is it in me that keeps creating the same kind of relationships?*'

As discussed, in the absence of a comprehensive education system, it becomes imperative that we learn to introspect and pass it on to the next generation from a young age.

This book, therefore, is not about changing others – it's about knowing and evolving ourselves. It invites you to sit with your own self to have an honest conversation, and to rediscover the art of being self-aware.

Each chapter offers 2 gifts: reflection and action. You will find relatable anecdotes drawn from everyday life – moments that reveal how our emotions, habits, tendencies, and conduct quietly shape our experiences. You'll also discover self-assessment tools, scoring guides, and reflection prompts to help you translate awareness into growth.

The aim isn't perfection – it's progress.

It isn't self-criticism – it's self-compassion.

And it isn't a medicine – it's a return, homeward, to the Heart.

And that is how this workbook was born – not as a manual, but as a mirror.

So, dear reader, I invite you to embark on this journey with a curious smile. Bring along your willingness, a notebook, and perhaps a cup of tea. As you read and reflect, you might begin to realize that the person you most needed to understand all along… was you.

May this workbook be your quiet companion, your compass for growth, and your bridge to more fulfilling relationships – with others, and most importantly, with yourself.

I also wish that education policy makers consider including the subject of introspection in colleges.

With warmth and gratitude,
Vinay Singh

INTROSPECTION:
THE CASE OF YASH AND THE MYSTERIOUS MANAGER

It was a bright and sunny morning – the kind that makes birds chirp louder, trees sway poetically, leaves look greener, and humans like Yash feel... slightly more miserable.

Yes, on that deceptively cheerful morning, Yash – an earnest 30-year-old IT professional with 5 years of experience and 2 freshly minted strands of grey – found himself praying sincerely. Not for world peace or spiritual awakening, but just to survive another week under his new manager.

Yash worked at a prestigious IT company in the heart of Silicon Valley. For the past 3 months, he'd been reporting to Daniel – a manager known for his punctuality, perfectionism, and an uncanny ability to find flaws even in birthday emails. Despite Daniel's regular one-on-one feedback sessions, Yash felt like he was starring in a slow-burning episode of *Survivor: Corporate Edition*.

To make things worse, the tech industry was in one of its seasonal existential spirals – layoffs, restructures, and enough uncertainty to keep therapists and yoga studios in business for years.

Over dinner, while pushing peas around his plate like philosophical burdens, Yash confided in his wife, Vaibhavi. She listened with the patience of a saint married to a man unravelling.

Then came the gold.

'Why don't you talk to that Keshav Uncle?' she said.

'He always looks like he's either meditating or smiling at some secret cosmic joke.'

The next morning, Yash jogged into the park, a little slower than usual – partly due to stress, partly due to a heavy breakfast of unresolved emotions. Right at the entrance, as if by divine appointment, stood **Keshav Uncle** – retired IT Consultant, part-time philosopher, and full-time observer of human folly. Keshav used to spend half of his time in the USA to help raise his grandchildren.

Keshav: 'Yash, you look like your laptop just crashed without saving. All okay?'

Yash: 'Honestly, uncle, I'm struggling. Work's been a mess. I need your advice.'

Keshav: 'Go on. I've got time – and tea.'

Yash: 'My boss Daniel keeps pointing out flaws in my work. At our last review, he gave me a long list of areas to improve. He even said those traits will help beyond work.'

Keshav: 'And how did that make you feel?'

Yash: 'Like crawling under my desk and staying there till retirement. I'm stressed, sleep-deprived, and my stomach's staging a daily protest.'

Keshav (nodding): 'As Dr. Bruce Lipton says in the book *Biology of Belief*, most health issues start with the noise in the mind. So, what's your solution?'

Yash: 'I honestly don't know. The more I think, the worse it feels. Even home feels tense.'

Keshav: 'Let's create a few options for understanding. Whatever comes to mind, just say it.'

Yash: 'Alright. Option 1: Daniel is the villain. Simple.'

Keshav (smiling): 'Keep going.'

Yash: 'Should I... look at my own gaps too? But Uncle, the problem *is* Daniel!'

Keshav: 'Ah, the classic defence: "It's not me, it's him." May work in breakups, not in self-growth.'

Keshav: 'So we're at a stalemate. Do you still think 100 per cent of the problem is him?'

Yash (pauses): 'No... maybe 80 per cent. The other 20 per cent could be me.'

Yash (half-joking): 'Maybe I should just pray he gets transferred to Antarctica.'

Keshav: 'Creative, but not elegant. You see, if we don't learn what life is trying to teach, the same lesson returns – louder, messier. So Option 2?'

Yash: 'Fine. I'll review my actions.'

Keshav: 'Excellent. Connect to your heart. Be a neutral observer of your past conversations with Daniel. You may want to list your traits that, if refined, could improve these dynamics. Let's talk tomorrow.'

Next morning...

Yash: 'Here's what I came up with: I struggle to disconnect from work after working hours. I want to do things *my* way, but I don't communicate the reasoning well. I'm sensitive to feedback. And... I really don't like Daniel pointing out my flaws.'

Keshav: 'That's introspection in action. You've crossed into Level 2: Owning your flaws. What if Daniel isn't your enemy, but a mirror – and you're just mad at the reflection?'

Yash paused. That stung. Like bitter *karela sabzi* (bitter gourd vegetable) – unpleasant, but somehow good for you.

Yash: 'That... makes sense.'

Keshav: 'Bravo. What's your next move?'

Yash: 'I'll make a list of actions to improve the relationship.'

Keshav: 'I'd love to hear it.'

2 days later...

Yash (smiling): 'Here's what I've got:

1. I'll listen to Daniel's feedback as an observer.
2. I'll put myself in his shoes before reacting.
3. I'll explain my ideas without getting attached to them.'

Keshav: 'Where did you get all this wisdom in 2 days?'

Yash: 'Looked within. And asked Vaibhavi.'

Keshav: 'Smart man.'

Yash: 'Uncle, how do *you* handle these situations?'

Keshav: 'When someone gives me feedback – spouse, colleague, or even a stranger on a bus – I treat it as a gift. I detach, revisit, and ask, 'What's my part in this?' Many times it helps me to find my own gaps. Over time, that became my superpower.'

Yash: 'You're right. Daniel said these changes will help even beyond work. Maybe... he's not my enemy. Maybe he's my accidental mentor.'

Keshav: 'Exactly. Sometimes, our greatest teachers come disguised as the most annoying people. Like coconuts – hard, annoying, but nourishing once cracked.'

Over the next few days, Yash stopped praying for Daniel's transfer to Antarctica. He began observing. Listening. He no longer saw Daniel as the villain in a badly written office drama – but as a mirror reflecting parts of himself he'd avoided.

Eventually, he did the unthinkable: He asked Daniel for informal feedback... and lived to tell the tale.

Three months later...

Yash jogged into the park, lighter – not in weight, but in spirit.

Yash: 'Uncle, I had that chat with Daniel. I even asked how I could grow – not just as an employee, but as a person. Things have changed. I'm more confident. Our interactions are better. And my stomach finally stopped sending distress signals.'

Keshav (smiling): 'Wonderful. That's the power of introspection. When you change the lens, the view changes.'

Key Takeaways

1. Sometimes, your worst boss is your best teacher.
2. Most of the time, feedback isn't an attack – it's a flashlight in a dark room.
3. And often, what feels like suffering is self-improvement in ugly packaging.
4. Also, always keep a Keshav Uncle in your life. They cost far less than therapy and come with a thermos full of tea.

'Knowing yourself is the beginning of all wisdom.' – **Aristotle**

'Wisdom is not knowing the answers but knowing where to find them – often within yourself.' – **Anonymous**

'Introspection is the art of seeing yourself without the usual excuses.' – **Author**

WHY INTROSPECTION MATTERS

For many years, it has been observed that while desiring self-improvement, the majority often don't priotitize introspection—examining the tendencies, habits, conduct, and emotions. The rich often say, 'Why should I look within? Everything is great. There is no need for introspection'. However, in crisis moments the usual question from most of us is 'God! Why me?'

This approach is more like ***walking behind the problem.***

By harnessing the superpower of introspection, ***We can walk ahead of most of the problems* in our lives.** Even in the unavoidable circumstances, after doing our 100 per cent effort, with enhanced acceptance and forgiveness, we can be at peace most of the time.

Yet, discussing the idea of regular self-assessment, especially with younger generations, often reveals a surprising level of excitement. People recognize the profound potential in periodically looking inward to refine themselves and achieve a more fulfilling life.

The challenge, however, often lies in ***knowing* what *to introspect*,** particularly when life seems to be flowing smoothly. This workbook addresses that very need by providing a structured framework for your self-exploration of 74 attributes.

Relationship: The Mirror of Our Inner World

As you embark on the profound journey of knowing yourself better through introspection, it's crucial to understand why this inner work holds such immense power for your external connections. Our relationships—with family, friends, colleagues, partners, and even strangers—are not merely external interactions; they are often direct reflections of our inner state. The qualities we nurture or neglect within ourselves inevitably ripple outward, shaping the very fabric of our bonds with others.

The title of the workbook is chosen for a reason. While the scorecard focuses on knowing where you stand for your chosen attributes, its goal is to transform your relational landscape. How does this alchemy occur?

'The yielding heart attracts grace, happiness,
Cheerfulness and joy, which in turn, build relationships' **– Daaji***

*Daaji aka Kamlesh D. Patel is a spiritual guide, an author, and the current global guide of Heartfulness

---

The Direct Link: Introspection and Improved Relationships

Introspection is the act of pointing a torch inward, revealing your hidden tendencies, unexamined emotions, and reactive patterns (habits and conduct). When you understand yourself better by knowing where you stand, you gain the clarity and capacity to chart out your enhancement journey. This process is like – to proceed on a journey, first ***we need to know where we are.***

With an enhanced self, you relate to others more effectively and authentically. Cultivating the attributes you are assessing in this workbook directly impacts the 4 pillars of healthy relationships:

1. Communication

Clarity (Attributes like Clarity, Ability to Listen, Empathy): When you are clear about your own thoughts, feelings, and intentions, your communication becomes more direct and less prone to misinterpretation. Introspection helps you articulate your needs and boundaries without ambiguity, fostering trust, and understanding.

Patience and Thoughtfulness (Attributes like Patience, Emotional Regulation, Overthinking): By understanding your triggers and practising emotional regulation (as explained in the Emotional Quotient section), you move from impulsive 'reaction' to thoughtful 'response.' This allows for calm, constructive dialogue, even in heated moments, preventing unnecessary conflict and hurt.

2. Empathy

Self-Awareness as a Foundation (Attributes listed in Chapter 2): The more you understand your own emotional landscape – your fears, insecurities, joys, and struggles – the better equipped you are to recognize and relate to these same emotions in others. *Introspection builds emotional intelligence, which is the bedrock of empathy.*

Acceptance and Non-Judgment (Attributes like Acceptance, Forgiveness, Prejudice): As you cultivate acceptance of your own imperfections and learn to forgive yourself, you naturally extend that compassion to others. This reduces your tendency towards 'fault-finding', 'dealing with criticism', or 'prejudice,' allowing you to approach others with an open heart and genuine understanding, seeing them not through the lens of your projections (own filters), but as they are.

3. Conflict Resolution

Courage and Non-Avoidance (Attributes like Courage, Confrontation, Avoidance of Conflict): Introspection helps you identify your patterns of 'succumbing to confrontation.' By recognizing and working on these, you gain the courage to address disagreements directly and constructively, rather than letting resentment fester. You learn to navigate difficult conversations with a focus on resolution, not blame.

Humility and Adaptability (Attributes like Humility, Adaptability and Flexibility, Acceptance): When you introspect, you cultivate the humility to acknowledge your own role in conflicts and the flexibility to consider different perspectives. This makes you less rigid in your positions and more open to finding mutually beneficial solutions, rather than insisting on being 'right.'

4. Deeper Connection

Authenticity and Vulnerability (Attributes like Shame, Fear, Guilt): As you shed layers of 'fear', 'guilt', and 'shame' through introspection, you become more comfortable being your true self. This authenticity allows for deeper vulnerability, which is the gateway to genuine intimacy and profound connection in any relationship.

Gratitude and Love (Attributes like Gratitude, Love, Compassion): By regularly assessing and cultivating attributes like 'Forgiveness', 'Praising Others', 'Gratitude', and 'Love', you shift your focus towards appreciation for others and the bonds you share. This positive energy is palpable and naturally draws people closer, fostering stronger, more fulfilling relationships built on mutual respect and affection.

In essence, every attribute you diligently examine and cultivate within yourself becomes a building block for more resilient, harmonious, and meaningful relationships. This workbook is your guide to not just understanding who you are, but to becoming the kind of person who enriches the lives of everyone around them.

How This Workbook Helps

This workbook is a tool to:

- **Build a habit of regular introspection:** Establish a consistent practice of self-reflection.
- **Deepen your awareness:** Guides you through a process of introspection that leads to greater observation and heightened awareness and consciousness.
- **Provide clear guidance:** Offers a comprehensive list of attributes for targeted self-assessment.

- **Serve as a quick reference:** A handy guide for anyone committed to personal development.

Attributes

Through interactions, particularly with young people keen for self-improvement, a comprehensive list of human attributes has been compiled, spanning tendencies, habits, conduct, and emotions. This workbook includes **74 attributes** categorised into 4 key areas:

1. **Key Attributes:** 19
2. **Emotional Quotient:** 30
3. **Tendencies:** 12
4. **Habits and Conduct:** 13

You'll have the opportunity to rate yourself on a scale of 0–5 for each applicable attribute. You may also add additional attributes to the scorecard, which you feel are important to you. A few indicative additional attributes are: Arrogance, Authenticity, Awareness (Self-Awareness), Creativity, Determination, Discipline, Generosity, Honesty, Integrity, Kindness, Leadership, Loyalty, Optimism, Perseverance, Resilience, Responsibility, Self-Control, Tolerance, etc.

Read one attribute at a time. Reflect. Don't rush.
Let the stories and scoring guidelines work quietly within.

Additionally, 21 attributes have been listed under the category: **Qualities applicable for spiritual seekers**. However, no scoring guide for this category has been provided since it's a far more specialized subject, and for many attributes, a scale doesn't fit in.

The true strength of this exercise lies in its iterative nature: by repeating it every 6 or 12 months or at any frequency best suited for you. By comparing scores, you gain invaluable insights into your personal evolution. This consistent approach yields several profound benefits:

- **Increased Self-Awareness:** Deepen your understanding of yourself through a continuous cycle of introspection and observation.

- **Motivation for Growth:** If you notice areas where little or no change has occurred after repeated exercises, you'll likely feel inspired to explore new methods for enhancing those attributes.
- **Support for Your Spiritual Journey:** For current spiritual practitioners, this comprehensive scorecard of attributes can significantly aid your spiritual journey.

Self-Assessment: Your Compass for Awareness and Growth

Take this as a conversation with yourself—one chapter at a time.

1. Anecdotes

'Stories are mirrors—look into them, and you may see yourself more clearly.'

This section is the starting point—the place where reflection meets real life. Here, you will find **anecdotes woven around 42 of the 74 attributes** included in the self-assessment (awareness). These anecdotes are not abstract theories but lived experiences, crafted to make each attribute easier to understand and apply.

Most of the anecdotes are based on true stories. However, to protect the privacy of individuals: **names, locations, and certain details have been suitably modified**. What remains untouched is the essence—the lesson, the insight, the spark that each story carries.

Think of these anecdotes as your **companions for introspection**. Just as a compass points north, these stories will help you orient yourself inward—guiding you to notice patterns, recognize strengths, and gently uncover areas for growth.

2. Self-Assessment (awareness) Scoring Guide

This section is the heart of the workbook and is designed to be your personal compass, guiding you through an honest and insightful evaluation of various attributes that shape your inner world and external relationships. ***It's not about judgment, but about awareness; not about perfection, but about progress.***

We encourage you to read through each score level carefully before assigning yourself a score. This granular detail is designed to help you identify not just if you possess a quality, but how it manifests in your daily life. Remember, this is a deeply personal exercise; be truthful with yourself, for true growth begins with honest self-perception.

3. Beyond the Score: The Power of Reflection Prompts

While assigning a score provides a snapshot of your current state, true insight comes from understanding why that score is accurate. Following each scoring guide, you will find a series of Reflection Prompts/Questions.

The goal is to guide the reader through a process of recall, analysis, emotional awareness, and insight. The reflection prompts are structured in the form of a few questions covering:

1. **Recall/Observation**: When did this attribute manifest? (Positive or negative instance)
2. **Context/Triggers**: What was happening around you? Who was involved? What caused it?
3. **Behaviour/Action**: What did you do or say? How did you react?
4. **Internal Experience**: What were you feeling, thinking, or sensing internally?
5. **Impact/Outcome**: What was the result of your behaviour on yourself and others?
6. **Alternative/Learning**: How could you have acted differently? What insight did you gain?

The benefits of reflection prompts are as follows:

- **Deeper Understanding**: They will help you recall specific situations, identify triggers, and connect your scores to real-life experiences.
- **Uncovering Patterns**: By exploring the 'why' and 'how' behind your actions, you'll begin to see recurring patterns in your thoughts, emotions, and behaviours.

- **Gaining Context**: The prompts encourage you to consider the circumstances surrounding your actions, offering a more compassionate view of your journey.
- **Paving the Way for Change**: The insights gained from these reflections are the foundation for the 'Tools for Change' that follow. They help you pinpoint exactly what needs your attention for growth and enhancement.

Take your time with each attribute. Answer the reflection prompts as candidly as possible, allowing your answers to reveal the nuances of your inner landscape. This combined process of scoring and reflective questioning will illuminate your path forward, helping you cultivate the self you aspire to become.

Guidelines for Self-Assessment (Awareness)

Life is a journey, and this scale can help you recognize your progress so far and areas for growth.

1. To understand how to score, please refer to the detailed, specific **scoring guidance provided** with each attribute.
2. You are welcome to **add additional attributes.**
3. You are not required to score every attribute; **you may skip any attribute.**
4. Please score each attribute on a scale of 0–5. Record the date of your assessment for future reference. Subsequent scores may be recorded after repeating this exercise at your chosen fixed interval (e.g., quarterly, half-yearly, or annually).
5. This self-assessment (awareness) is for your personal use and reflection only.
6. Alternatively, if you don't wish to refer to detailed scoring guidance, here's a scoring guide based on frequency, which you can use for various human attributes:

For positive qualities such as Courage, Hope, Love, etc.

Score 0: Never (The quality is virtually absent or never observed.)

Score 1: Rarely (The quality is present only on very few, isolated occasions.)

Score 2: Sometimes (The quality is present on occasion, but not consistently.)

Score 3: Frequently (The quality is present often, a regular part of your experience or behaviour.)

Score 4: Almost Always (The quality is present in nearly every relevant situation or time.)

Score 5: Always (The quality is consistently and invariably present.)

For negative qualities such as Anxiety, Fear, etc.

Score 0: Always (The quality is consistently and invariably present.)

Score 1: Almost Always (The quality is present in nearly every relevant situation or time.)

Score 2: Frequently (The quality is present often, a regular part of your experience or behaviour.)

Score 3: Sometimes (The quality is present on occasion, but not consistently.)

Score 4: Rarely (The quality is present only on very few, isolated occasions.)

Score 5: Never (The quality is virtually absent or never observed.)

Note: Remember, this is a personal reflection. Be honest with yourself about where you are today.

1

CORE ATTRIBUTES

This foundational category presents a selection of **core human attributes** that serve as the bedrock of our inner and outer life. They are not just desirable qualities but **vital nutrients of the mind and heart**, much like oxygen and water are to the body. Without them, our well-being weakens; with them, we thrive.

These *'Core Attributes'* represent fundamental qualities that anchor our **character, choices, and connections.** They act as invisible threads that weave together our inner peace and our ability to build meaningful outer relationships. For example, the **patience** we practise at work may ripple into harmony at home, while the **courage** we summon in personal trials often shapes how others perceive and trust us. Think of them as your inner Wi-Fi signals – sometimes strong, sometimes weak – but when aligned, everything in life connects better.

By understanding and consciously cultivating these core attributes, you lay down a strong **groundwork for deeper self-exploration.** Just as a builder must first ensure a solid foundation before raising the walls, so too must we strengthen these essentials before moving towards other attributes of refinement and transcendence.

Each attribute here offers a **unique lens of introspection** – sometimes acting like a mirror reflecting hidden tendencies, and at other times like a window opening to new possibilities. Together, they become stepping stones in your journey of self-discovery, allowing you to move from self-awareness to self-transformation, and eventually towards self-mastery. And if the mirror feels too honest some days, remember – it's not judging you; it's just showing you the parts your selfie filter skips.

In the chapters that follow, these attributes will not remain abstract concepts. Through **real-life anecdotes, reflective exercises, and practical scoring guidelines**, you will learn to see them in action – within yourself and others. The aim is not perfection but progress: the ability to pause, notice, and recalibrate. In doing so, you not only enhance your own growth but also **contribute to healthier, more fulfilling relationships** in every sphere of life. In short, this isn't a manual for becoming flawless – it's a guide to becoming slightly wiser than the person who hit 'snooze' this morning.

1. Introspection

Scoring Guide

Here's a scoring guide for the quality 'Introspection,' ranging from 0 to 5, with hints to help you rate yourself. When rating yourself, consider **how often you pause to truly examine your inner experiences**, how well you understand your own motivations, and how much you learn about yourself from your reflections.

This scale **focuses on your ability and tendency to look inward, reflect on your thoughts, feelings, and motivations, and understand your inner world.**

Score 0: Rarely or Never Reflects Inward

You **rarely or never take time to think about your own thoughts, feelings, or behaviours.**

You tend to react impulsively without considering why you feel or act a certain way.

You find it difficult to identify your own emotions or understand your motivations.

You often feel confused about why you did something or why you feel a certain way.

Score 1: Superficial or Crisis-Driven Reflection

You might **occasionally reflect, but usually only in response to a crisis, a major problem, or when directly asked.**

Your reflections are often superficial, focusing on external events rather than internal states.

You struggle to connect your feelings to underlying thoughts or beliefs.

You **tend to blame external circumstances or others** for your internal experiences.

Score 2: Fluctuating or Limited Introspection

You have moments of **inward reflection, but they are often inconsistent or limited in depth.**

You might identify basic emotions but struggle to explore their nuances or origins.

You can sometimes recognize patterns in your behaviour but find it hard to understand *why* those patterns exist.

You might intellectually understand the value of introspection, but don't consistently practice it.

Score 3: Growing Self-Awareness and Regular Reflection

You are increasingly able to **regularly engage in self-reflection**, even without a crisis.

You can identify a broader range of your emotions and begin to understand their triggers.

You're starting to connect your thoughts, feelings, and behaviours, gaining insights into your inner workings.

You actively seek to understand your motivations and **are open to uncovering your blind spots.**

Score 4: Consistent and Deep Introspection

You consistently **engage in deep and meaningful introspection as a regular practice.**

You have a strong understanding of your emotional landscape, thought patterns, and core beliefs.

You can effectively analyse your reactions and motivations, learning from your experiences.

This level of self-awareness allows you to make conscious choices aligned with your values.

Score 5: Profound Self-Understanding and Insight

You possess a profound and **integrated understanding of your inner world,** including your conscious and subconscious patterns.

Your introspection leads to consistent personal growth, emotional regulation, and clear decision-making.

You can observe your thoughts and feelings without judgment, gaining deep insights into the human condition through your own experience.

This level of introspection allows for a sense of inner wisdom and authenticity.

Reflection Prompts

1. How often do you consciously engage in introspection? What methods do you use (e.g., journaling, meditation, silent reflection)?
2. What insights have you gained about yourself through past periods of introspection?
3. Do you introspect after an unpleasant interaction to find your own gaps?

2. Courage: When Fear Knocked, Calmness Answered

In the lush rear garden of a home tucked away in the Bay Area of Silicon Valley, Vaibhavi often found solace on her favourite swing under the lime tree. The garden was alive with playful squirrels darting about, pausing mid-scamper as if they were debating stock options, before digging holes to stash away future snacks. Some of them had recently discovered the neighbour's loquat tree – which, for reasons only trees understand, had decided to grow mostly into Vaibhavi's backyard, like an extroverted relative who prefers your couch over theirs.

Evenings at her house had their own rhythm. As the sun dipped behind the hills, the grand old Oak tree in the front yard turned into a conference room for crows. They assembled like chatty executives, perched on crimson-tipped branches, cawing loudly as if presenting conflicting PowerPoint reports. Vaibhavi often listened to their lively board meetings with a half-smile and a steaming cup of tea warming her palms.

That evening, Yash was sprawled on a hammock, radiating the smug glow of someone who had just scored 5 goals against Messi's team – courtesy of his latest game conquest. His victory tale, complete with sound effects and enthusiastic commentary, was gathering dramatic momentum when a familiar figure strolled into view.

It was Keshav Uncle, the most beloved visitor in the neighbourhood. He had once served alongside Vaibhavi's father and was now visiting his son in the USA, staying in the same area as Vaibhavi's home. In his hands was a basket of freshly picked mulberries, their deep purple skins still glistening as if holding on to the last kiss of the afternoon sun.

Vaibhavi's eyes lit up. 'Mulberries! I haven't seen these since Hasimara, India. My dad was posted there. I used to climb a tree multiple times my height just for these!'

'Well,' Keshav chuckled, 'you had more courage than most cadets I trained.'

As the laughter died down, Yash – never one to miss a story opportunity – pounced.

'Uncle, you were in the Air Force! Tell us a real story of courage!'

Keshav smiled thoughtfully. 'I've seen many acts of courage – from pilots flying into war and storms to technicians fixing jets in hostile weather. But let me flip the script. How about *you* two tell me your stories?'

Yash shrugged, looking more interested in his remaining mulberries.

But Keshav had noticed something – a spark in Vaibhavi's eyes.

'Vaibhavi! You?'

She nodded, setting down her tea. 'Okay, here's one. When I was 15, I was scared of many things – especially insects. I'd see one, and suddenly the floor was lava, and I was a shrieking ninja. Any crisis? I'd run straight to my parents like they were my personal disaster management team.

But one night, something changed.'

She looked at Yash and continued.

'My dad tells it better, but here's the gist. It was almost midnight. The earth began to tremble – an earthquake. I woke up, heart pounding, and wanted to scream. But instead, I remembered something my dad once said:

'Stay calm even if you're scared. Connect to your heart for the guidance. The mind works better when you stop panicking.'

So I didn't scream. I woke Dad up quietly, told him there was an earthquake, and said, 'I'm going to wake Damini (my younger sister). Let's go outside.' That's it. No drama. Just action.'

Later, her father told the story with pride – and a little humour.

Her father's version:

'I was dreaming of flying in a Mirage-2000 over the Himalayas – very peaceful – when I was woken up by this calm but firm voice: 'Papa, there's an earthquake. I've got Damini. Let's go out of the house.'

I blinked at her, half-asleep, wondering who replaced my panicky teenager with this tiny Commander-in-Chief.'

Keshav Uncle smiled, deeply impressed. 'That, my dear, is courage – n ot the absence of fear, but wise action *despite* fear.

In your professional context – the ability to say 'no' to a senior colleague in a meeting when required, and the courage to apologise to a colleague far below your level are also examples of courage.'

Yash nodded slowly. 'And here I was thinking courage was only about jumping off planes or facing Messi's team.'

'Sometimes,' Keshav said, munching on a mulberry, 'it's about staying grounded – literally and emotionally.'

A few moments passed in silence as the sky dimmed into shades of cinnamon and dusk. Keshav added with a knowing grin,

'And now look at you, Vaibhavi – leading a team as a newly promoted **manager** in your company here in the Bay Area. That calm courage still shows up in how you handle things.'

Vaibhavi looked away for a second, half-embarrassed, half-glowing.

Key Takeaways

1. **Courage is not loud or dramatic.** Often, it appears in quiet, decisive actions.
2. **Fear is natural; panic is optional.** Learning to stay calm under pressure changes how we act and how others trust us.
3. **True courage often shows up in everyday life** – in parenting, in teams, in moments when no one is watching.
4. **Consistent inner work – like meditation and reflection – builds emotional resilience**, which is the bedrock of courage.
5. **Courage is remembered.** The calmest choices we make in difficult moments stay with us – and inspire others.

'It takes courage to act on the aspirations of the heart.
The courage to overcome temptations, overcome lethargy,
and do what is right.
Listening to the heart and following its guidance takes courage
and is not restricted to grand deeds alone.
Reaching for your highest potential by following the heart's guidance
requires courage every day'. – **Excerpt from the book**
'Spiritual Anatomy' by Daaji

'Courage doesn't always roar. Sometimes courage is the quiet voice at the end of the day saying, 'I will try again tomorrow."
– **Mary Anne Radmacher**

Scoring Guide

When rating yourself, take a moment to reflect on how you typically respond when faced with fear, discomfort, or uncertainty.

Score 0: Overwhelmed by Fear

You frequently **avoid situations or actions due to intense fear**, even when they're important for your growth or well-being.

You often choose the path of least resistance to avoid potential discomfort, conflict, or failure.

The mere thought of stepping outside your comfort zone fills you with significant anxiety or dread.

You rarely speak up or take a stand when it involves any personal risk or potential negative consequences.

Score 1: Hesitant, Rarely Acts on Courage

You recognize situations that call for courage, but you often **hesitate and back down** from taking action.

You might experience fleeting moments of bravery, but these are quickly overshadowed by fear.

You frequently regret not taking action later on.

You tend to prioritize safety and predictability over personal growth or upholding your values.

Score 2: Occasional Acts of Courage, Often with Apprehension

You **sometimes muster the courage to act**, especially when the stakes feel relatively low, but it's often accompanied by significant anxiety or self-doubt.

You might take a stand when directly challenged, but you don't proactively seek out opportunities to be brave.

You may still feel substantial fear before, during, or after courageous acts.

Your acts of courage are more reactive than intentional.

Score 3: Growing Courage and Intentional Action

You're increasingly able to **face your fears and take intentional action**, even when it's uncomfortable or challenging.

You might still feel fear, but you're actively learning to act despite it, rather than letting it paralyse you.

You're more willing to speak your truth, take calculated risks, or step into new challenges.

You recognize that courage is a skill you can develop, and you're actively working on strengthening it.

Score 4: Consistent Courage and Resilience

You consistently **demonstrate courage in various aspects of your life,** from navigating daily discomforts to making significant life decisions.

You approach new or difficult situations with a sense of resilience, trusting in your ability to face what comes.

You're generally not deterred by potential failure, criticism, or discomfort.

You proactively seek opportunities for growth that require you to step outside your comfort zone.

Score 5: Embodied Fearlessness and Boldness

You embody a profound sense of **inner conviction and boldness,** allowing you to pursue your purpose and values without significant hesitation.

You view challenges as inherent opportunities for growth and face adversity with a calm, determined, and often enthusiastic spirit.

You inspire others through your willingness to take calculated risks, speak truth to power, and stand up for what you believe in, even in the face of strong opposition.

Your **actions are consistently guided by deep inner conviction rather than external fears.**

Reflection Prompts

1. What are some areas of your life (personal, professional, relational) where you feel a lack of courage is holding you back?
2. What small step could you take this week to demonstrate a little more courage in a particular situation?

3. Clarity: Seeing Without Filters

By now, Vaibhavi and Yash had become seasoned consumers of Keshav Uncle's 'life lessons in story and discussion form.' Having already absorbed his thoughts on Introspection and Courage, they were hungry for more. In fact, they'd started treating these conversations as episodes in a private Netflix series – minus the subscription fee and with snacks included.

One sunny weekend, they strolled over to Keshav Uncle's place. The scene in the lawn was part circus, part battlefield. Keshav was in full mischief mode with his twin grandchildren. One tot was armed with a hosepipe, gleefully threatening to spray everyone in sight (including innocent passers-by), while the other was rolling on the grass in a fit of laughter. In the middle of it all, Keshav was hopping about with the agility of a 2-year-old – though not necessarily with the balance of one. It was genuinely hard to tell where the children ended and the grandfather began.

Before the visitors could be roped into the chaos, Ankit – Keshav's son – appeared like a well-timed rescue helicopter. Ankit worked in a senior role at Google and was respected as a brilliant researcher. Yet, his real claim to fame wasn't in Silicon Valley boardrooms but in his backyard – he had single-handedly remodelled and constructed his entire 2,000 sq. ft. house, with only his wife's guidance and occasional help in 3 years starting in March 2020 (Covid lockdown).

Behind the house stretched a kitchen and fruit garden, lovingly nurtured by the couple. Once everyone had settled into the shade, Vaibhavi wasted no time.

'Uncle, today we want to learn about the importance of 'Clarity' in life – especially in relationships, whether personal or professional.'

Keshav took his seat, the twins clambering into his lap as if he were a living armchair. 'Alright'.

Ashu's Story

A few years ago, a friend called me from Odisha. His friend's son, Ashu, needed help. Ashu's father was a respected doctor and social worker who ran a small hospital there. At 20, Ashu was in his third year of a prestigious undergraduate program in Delhi – ranked second in the country in its category. Bright, cheerful, and a college cricket player, he'd always been full of energy.

Then, a month back, Ashu dropped a bombshell at home: 'I don't want to study anymore.' No explanation, just 'I don't know'. His father rushed to Delhi and tried to talk to him, but Ashu's reply to every question was the same – 'I don't know.'

Worried, his father spoke to Ashu's friends for an update and then consulted a senior psychiatrist. Medicines were prescribed. When results seemed slow, they tried a yoga camp in Rishikesh. Still, no change. Finally. Then a holy pilgrimage was planned. During the same period on a friend's suggestion, they came to meet me.

When I met Ashu, I could see he was intelligent but tangled inside. 'I can't understand a single word in class,' he admitted. 'Even when I'm there, it's as if my mind is somewhere else.' From my experience, I sensed that his inner energy centres (chakras) were disturbed. So, I suggested that he may meet a spiritual trainer for introductory meditation sessions.

By the end of the third session, Ashu had his 'clarity moment.' He returned to his studies, graduated on time, and is now pursuing his Master's at a leading West Coast university.

What Really Happened

Vaibhavi tilted her head. 'That sounds too simple. What happened in those sessions?'

Keshav chuckled. 'To understand it fully, you may read *Spiritual Anatomy* by Daaji. But here's the essence: every repetitive thought – whether born of success, worry, or desire – leaves an energetic impression on us. Over time, these impressions solidify into what we call ***samskaras***. They cloud our perception.'

He went on to describe the first chakra and its sub-points – A, B, C, and D – and how different types of desires and attachments disturb them.

Yash interrupted, 'I'm still not clear on how exactly it helped Ashu.'

Keshav continued, '*Samskaras* are impressions that have accumulated over time – including past lives – formed by our strong likes and dislikes, emotions and attachments. When emotions are attached to our repetitive thoughts, it accelerates the formation of *samskaras*. These *samskaras* can also be understood as learnt behaviour. So it dictates how we think, react, and like or dislike.

When a similar situation arises in our life, these *samskaras* resurface and begin to influence our outlook.

We have 3 bodies: gross, astral, and causal. Let's try to understand this with an analogy: 'To understand this, imagine that as part of our astral body, we have a glass wall. On one side is the self, the living being; on the other side is a situation, a person, or an event. If the glass is clean, we can clearly see the situation for what it is, understand its needs, and see the person as they truly are. But if that glass wall gets covered with, let's say, a black filter called 'fear' – a *samskara* – and then another grey filter called 'attachment to our own or our parents' expectations,' our view becomes distorted. We can't see clearly, and we lose clarity on the issue. So *samskaras* are the invisible filters attached to us and through these we look at the world'.

'When this (lack of clarity) continues for a long time, more filters get added – frustration, stress, anxiety, and so on – further clouding our perception. That's exactly what happened to Ashu.'

He went on, 'During his sessions with the spiritual trainer, a special technique called 'cleaning' was used to remove these impressions from his chakras. Once these were cleared, the glass wall became relatively clean, and Ashu regained clarity about his goals and the actions needed to achieve them.'

Ashu himself reported that after the very first 30-minute session, for about 80 per cent of the time he felt as if his problems had simply disappeared. This improvement continued in the subsequent sessions. Despite this early success, the trainer advised Ashu to continue his medication, keep his doctor informed about his progress, and only reduce or stop the medication following the Doctor's recommendation.

Yash, looking impressed, muttered, 'So… clarity is not about thinking harder, it's about seeing without filters.'

'Exactly,' Keshav said. 'Reduce your inner complexities, and relationships – whether at home or at work – become easier to navigate.'

By then, the twins had fallen asleep on Keshav's lap, the sun dappling their faces through the leaves. Madhavi, his daughter-in-law, emerged with a plate of golden *puris*, pumpkin *sabzi* fresh from the garden, and a bowl of creamy *kheer* (pudding made in milk and rice). The lesson on clarity had been served – with dessert.

Key Takeaways

1. Clarity comes when inner filters – formed by fears, desires, emotions, and expectations, etc. – are cleaned away.
2. Sometimes, the solution is not adding more effort, but removing inner noise.
3. *Samskaras* can distort perception; self-work, cleaning, and meditation can restore balance.
4. In relationships, seeing people and situations *as they are* prevents misunderstanding and confusion.

'Clarity is not the absence of problems, but the ability to see them as they are – without the dust of our own expectations and filters.'

'A clear mind leads to a clear path.' – **Buddha** (attributed)

'Our mind is like water. When it's turbulent, it's difficult to see. When it's calm, everything becomes clear.' – **Prasad Mahes**

Scoring Guide

This scale focuses on clarity of thought, communication, and purpose. When rating yourself, consider how easily you understand things, how well you can explain them to others, and how clear your direction feels in life.

Score 0: Constant Confusion

Your thoughts often feel **muddled or chaotic**, making it difficult to focus or understand complex ideas.

You frequently struggle to articulate your thoughts or feelings to others, leading to misunderstandings.

Your goals or direction in life feel vague or non-existent.

You often feel overwhelmed by information and struggle to filter out what's important.

Score 1: Frequent Confusion, Occasional Glimpses

You often experience **confusion in your thinking or communication**, but you might have brief moments where things click into place.

You find it challenging to explain yourself clearly, and others often need to ask for clarification.

Your goals might exist, but they lack specific detail or a clear path to achieve them.

You struggle to make decisions due to a lack of clear understanding.

Score 2: Fluctuating Clarity

You experience periods of **relative clarity, but they are often interrupted** by moments of confusion, indecision, or difficulty expressing yourself.

You can communicate clearly on simple topics, but complex ideas still trip you up.

You might have a general idea of what you want, but the 'how' remains fuzzy.

You sometimes understand concepts intellectually but struggle to apply them practically.

Score 3: Growing Clarity and Intentional Communication

You generally have a **fair grasp of your thoughts and can express them clearly** to others most of the time.

You actively work to simplify complex information and present it understandably.

Your goals are becoming more defined, and you have a clearer sense of direction.

You're learning to identify and address sources of confusion in your thinking or environment.

Score 4: Consistent Clarity and Effective Communication

You consistently **think clearly, make well-reasoned decisions, and communicate effectively** in most situations.

You can articulate complex ideas with ease and adapt your communication style to your audience.

You have a strong sense of purpose and clear, actionable goals for your life.

You can quickly identify and resolve ambiguities, leading to efficient problem-solving.

Score 5: Profound Clarity and Visionary Insight

You embody a profound sense of **mental, emotional, and purposeful clarity.**

Your thinking is exceptionally clear, allowing you to grasp complex issues and discern core issues effortlessly.

You communicate with precision, eloquence, and often inspire others with your clear vision.

You possess a deep understanding of your purpose and can articulate a compelling future, both for yourself and potentially for others.

Reflection Prompts

1. How does a lack of clarity in your thoughts or communication impact your relationships or personal effectiveness?
2. What practice helps you achieve greater mental or emotional clarity (e.g., journaling, meditation, discussion, being free from accumulated daily impressions due to extreme circumstances)?

4. Strong Likes and Dislikes: Clinging, Complaining, and the *Samskara* Factory

Yash and Vaibhavi had a common friend, Vidya. One day, Vaibhavi felt a strong intuition – one of those sudden 'something's wrong' flashes – about Vidya's well-being. She called her, only to be met with sobs on the other end. Shocked, she and Yash rushed to see her.

They found Vidya going through a rough patch after a breakup with her boyfriend, Amar. Patiently, they listened as she told her side of the story. Vidya was adamant – *100 per cent of the fault was Amar's*. Yet, in between the complaints, she also replayed the good moments they had shared. Vaibhavi simply held her hand and listened, letting Vidya empty her emotional pockets. Keshav would later call this 'emotional detox' – except no yoga mat or green juice required.'

On their way back, Yash said, 'Keshav Uncle once spoke about ***samskaras***. I've also read about another variable – ***Bhoga*** – and something about **'life scripts we write before birth**.' Do you think any of these are playing a role in Vidya's suffering?'

They decided it was time to consult their go-to guide for untangling life's knots – Keshav Uncle.

The Interplay of Variables

At their next gathering, Keshav greeted them warmly and added a few more factors to Yash's list: likes and dislikes, a judgmental attitude, attachment to outcomes, and the emotions that bind us to both.

Likes and Dislikes, he explained, are hardwired into us. 'We naturally like some things, dislike others, and remain neutral to a few. That "something" could be a person, place, event, or someone's actions. The trouble starts when strong reactions lock us in place – replaying the same mental scene like a song on loop you can't delete. Most people don't realize they're running a mental playlist called 'Greatest Hits of My Grievances – Volume 1.'

Vaibhavi jumped in, 'That's exactly what's happening with Vidya.'

Keshav nodded. 'Yes. Most of us try to avoid unpleasant events and cling to pleasant ones. That's how repetitive thought patterns are born. In unpleasant situations, it might be revenge or despair – like in Vidya's case. In pleasant ones, it's clinging to past successes as if they were fresh every morning.'

He shared the story of a proud father whose daughter ranked 2nd in JEE Advanced and 4th in CBSE Class 12 in India. 'A wonderful achievement worth celebrating and thanking God for,' Keshav said. 'But for the next 3 years, every conversation, every WhatsApp DP, every Facebook post was the same. It's fine to be proud, but when your mental record is stuck on repeat, people eventually stop dancing to your tune. More importantly, such conscious repetition leaves deep energetic impressions – *samskaras* – and shrinks awareness, like trying to see the world through a drinking straw. Eventually, even relatives started hiding at weddings to avoid hearing the same 'rank story' again.'

Yash asked, 'So **strong likes and dislikes are one of the root causes of *samskaras*?**'

Keshav's warm smile was answer enough.

The Perceived Failure That Wasn't

Keshav continued with another story – this time about *failure*, or at least what seemed like one.

His friend Suresh's son, Ravi, was preparing for medical entrance exams, but also loved Economics. One day, Ravi announced he wanted to study Economics instead of Medicine. The family agreed – on the condition that he still sit for the medical entrance.

Ravi's results? Top 2,000 in medical merit, a perfect 100 in Economics, and 96 per cent overall in Class 12. But because of an 88 marks in English, he missed admission to SRCC, India's #1 for Economics – and even the top 20 colleges.

Suresh and his wife were crushed. Their dreams – SRCC, then maybe Civil Services or a foreign degree – vanished overnight. For weeks, they avoided friends. Even Keshav's weekly calls went unanswered until, finally, Suresh rang back, sounding low.

Keshav listened and then said, 'That's a fantastic result! Why not celebrate?'

Suresh sighed, 'Easy for you to say.'

Keshav chuckled. 'Let's look at this practically. Imagine the precious crystal passed down from your great-grandfather, one you cherish deeply. One day, your house help accidentally drops it while dusting. Irreplaceable. What do you do – sulk for a month, or feel grateful for having enjoyed it for so long? And since it wasn't intentional, you'd comfort the help, right?'

Suresh was silent for a moment. 'That… makes sense.'

'Exactly,' said Keshav. '**Acceptance, letting go, and gratitude** aren't just virtues – they're survival tools as well. Clinging to your 'ideal' outcome damages relationships, kills peace, and poisons the home atmosphere.'

Suresh admitted that in his case, peace at home, his productivity at work, and the family's overall mood had all been affected.

The Common Thread

Vaibhavi reflected aloud: 'In all 3 examples – Vidya, the proud father, and Suresh – repeatedly mulling over success or perceived failure damaged peace, productivity, and the home environment. And in Vidya's and Suresh's cases, forgiveness might also be needed to dissolve the emotional residue and prevent new *samskaras*.'

Keshav patted her back. 'Exactly. I am so proud of you, Vaibhavi. Any memory soaked in strong emotion will eventually spill into your conversations. Likes and dislikes make you judgmental, and judgment shrinks consciousness. Remember the 'glass wall' analogy?'

Vaibhavi grinned, 'Yes, Uncle. And don't be *too* proud of me – you might form a *samskara*.'

Keshav burst into laughter.

Yash added, 'Now I can see the web – **emotions, judgment, reactions, likes and dislikes, acceptance and *samskaras*** – all tangled together.'

Keshav nodded. 'And *Bhoga* and the life script... that's for another day.'

Key Takeaways

1. **Strong likes and dislikes cloud perception** – they shrink awareness and replay emotional loops like a stuck record.
2. **Clinging to pleasant experiences or brooding over unpleasant ones** creates *samskaras*.
3. **Acceptance, letting go, and gratitude** act as antidotes to obsessive clinging or judgment.
4. Every strong emotional memory eventually leaks into behaviour and conversations, shaping patterns of suffering or harmony.
5. True clarity comes when we can enjoy experiences without over-attachment and move on without resentment.

'We are disturbed not by what happens to us, but by our thoughts about what happens.' – **Epictetus**

'Likes and dislikes are like tinted glasses – they change how you see, not what is.' –**Author**

'Memories soaked in emotion become samskaras; letting go cleans the glass through which we see life.' – **Inspired by Heartfulness teachings**

Scoring Guide

When rating yourself, consider how strongly your opinions and preferences dictate your actions, your emotional reactions, and your openness to new or different experiences

Score 0: Extreme and Unyielding Preferences

Your **likes and dislikes are very rigid and absolute**. You love what you love intensely and hate what you hate just as strongly.

You find it extremely difficult to tolerate or engage with anything that falls outside your strong preferences.

Your strong opinions often lead to conflict or limit your experiences.

You may dismiss or judge others who don't share your intense preferences.

Score 1: Very Strong Preferences, Easily Triggered

Your **likes and dislikes are still very pronounced,** and you get easily upset or highly enthusiastic based on them.

You often express strong opinions, and your mood can be significantly affected by whether something aligns with your preferences.

You tend to stick to what you know and like, making it hard to try new things or adapt to different situations.

You might find yourself emotionally reacting to small things you dislike.

Score 2: Pronounced Preferences with Some Flexibility

You have **clear likes and dislikes**, and they influence your choices, but you can sometimes tolerate or engage with things outside your preferences, albeit with some effort.

You might verbally express your strong feelings, but you're not always completely consumed by them.

You can be persuaded to try new things, but it often requires convincing or a push.

You might still feel significant discomfort when encountering things you dislike.

Score 3: Balanced Preferences with Growing Openness

You have **discernible likes and dislikes, but they don't rigidly control your emotional state or choices.**

You can appreciate a wider range of experiences, even if they're not your top preference.

You're able to observe your strong feelings without being completely swept away by them.

You're becoming more open to exploring different options and perspectives.

Score 4: Flexible Preferences and Broad Appreciation

Your **preferences are flexible and don't dictate your happiness or interactions.**

You can genuinely find enjoyment or value in a broad spectrum of experiences, even those you might not naturally gravitate towards.

You can separate your personal taste from your ability to appreciate or respect something.

You are generally open-minded and adaptable, not easily bothered by minor dislikes.

Score 5: Minimal Attachment to Preferences, High Adaptability

You approach life with **minimal attachment to rigid likes or dislikes.**

You can find something to appreciate or learn from almost any experience, including unpleasant ones, people, or situations, regardless of your personal taste.

Your emotional state remains stable, unswayed by minor preferences or aversions.

You are highly adaptable, curious, and comfortable with a wide variety of inputs and experiences.

Reflection Prompts

1. How do your likes and dislikes influence your choices, your relationships, and your willingness to try new things?
2. Can you recall a time when a strong dislike prevented you from experiencing something potentially positive?
3. Is there a dislike you hold that you'd be willing to explore or challenge, even slightly, to broaden your perspective?

5. Acceptance: Effort is Ours, Outcome is His

A Gathering Begins

It was a pleasant weekend evening. Vaibhavi and Yash had decided to host a dinner for their friends. The menu was set, the lawn was ready, and the conversations were bound to spill into deep life topics.

Their friends had been listening with fascination from Yash and Vaibhavi to the 'real life stories' sessions with Keshav uncle. This time, they insisted on meeting *the* Keshav uncle himself – the man with more wisdom than Google, and far fewer pop-up ads.

Vaibhavi had already narrated the stories and the discussion to her friends on the previous topic, *'Strong Likes and Dislikes.'* But many of her friends were still curious about the story *'The Perceived*

Failure That Wasn't.' Since she and Yash couldn't answer all their questions, it was agreed that the conversation would continue once Keshav uncle arrived.

When Keshav finally walked in, the energy instantly lifted. Everyone gathered in the rear lawn. Chairs creaked, the swing swayed, and the soft glow of lights set the stage. Curious eyes watched as Keshav looked around, pleasantly surprised to see such a young and vibrant group – all between the ages of 25 and 32.

Acceptance of Results

After Vaibhavi recapped the earlier discussions, Sumit, one of the friends, spoke up:

'Uncle! The story of Suresh and his son Ravi really touched me. But I feel that many of us struggle to accept outcomes in relationships and careers. But does acceptance mean simply resigning to undesired results as 'destiny' – and making no effort at all?'

Keshav turned the question back to the group, inviting them to respond.

Ananya spoke up:

'We should put in our effort, then destiny will play its role. If we don't like the result, we need to work harder. I also feel: *'Acceptance is like downloading a software update – you may resist it at first, but life keeps reminding you until you press 'install'.'*

The Question of Effort vs. Destiny

'Well said, Ananya,' Keshav replied. 'I'll add just one thought. By design of Nature, humans have 100 per cent control over their effort, and even God does not interfere. Similarly, let's say God has 100 per cent control over the result. So if He doesn't interfere in our domain – effort – why should we interfere in His domain – result? That's where acceptance comes in.'

Ananya, 'I have observed that a few of my friends and relatives always blame others for any result, which is not to their liking'.

Keshav: 'In this regard, **St. Babu ji** ***in Complete Works of Ram Chandra Vol-V*** **says:**

'Complaining and blaming others are signs of non-acceptance. In one sense, the blame game turns us into helpless victims, while in another sense, it leads us to solicit someone else's agreement and sympathy through gossip, justifying why it is not our fault; We are not the ones who need to change. We avoid looking at ourselves by pointing fingers elsewhere.'

*Babu Ji (Shri Ram Chandra of Shahjahanpur was the second guide of Heartfulness meditation).

Sumit pressed further:

'Does that mean if we fail once, we shouldn't try again?'

Keshav explained:

'If you still have the option to try again, within reasonable limits of time and cost, of course, you must. But each result must be accepted as it comes, analysed for gaps, and used to strengthen the next attempt. For example, if you have only one shot at an exam like the Class 12 boards, then acceptance of the result is sensible. But even then, it doesn't stop you from learning from your effort and gaps (if any) and applying those lessons in future exams.'

Pre-written Life Script

Ananya leaned forward. 'Uncle, how does a pre-written life script play a role in such scenarios?'

Keshav replied, 'That's a very good question. I'll share my understanding – consider it a hypothesis, and you may verify it for yourself.

Creation of Soul and Purpose of Life

A soul, when created, was pure and divine, having originated from the Creator (call Him *Paramatma, Parabrahman*, Almighty, or by no name at all). It planned to enter the world and experience whatever it wished, for a duration of its choice. Yet, when the soul decides to return to its original home, it must be at the same level of purity as when it left.

In the beginning, since all souls had the same capacity and knowledge, there was no variety in experience. An experience is possible between humans when we have different personalities, perceptions, knowledge, experiences, etc. So different variables were created – primarily the *samskara.* Other key variables included:

- Sun, moon, stars, food, weather, animals, climate, river, mountains, sea, and so on were created.
- The 3 bodies were created: causal, astral, and gross. The living beings were designed within limitations of lifespan, hunger, procreation, etc.
- For human experience, consciousness (awareness) was needed, so it was packed into the astral body – consisting of ego (a sense of separate identity), mind, and intellect – and then equipped with the gross body of sense organs.

The soul was given freedom to choose and write its own life script before taking birth on the earth. A script needs to have variations, just as in the movies, and needs active participation of supporting actors too. Also, the two extremes of variability (Shall we call it *Maya*!) were also designed: hot and cold, high and low, success and failure, praise and insult, and so on.

One more rule was added: Once the soul takes human form, it needs to forget the script written by herself. If the script is known, the play is simple, and there would be no real experience, as the sequence of events and their variations are already known. And there will be no real learning from the experience. The very purpose of the script is thus defeated as it has become like a leaked examination paper.

In this regard, you may also refer to the book *Many Lives, Many Masters* by Dr. Brian Weiss and *Journey of Souls* and *Destiny of Souls* by Dr. Michael Newton.

Thus, experience became possible. To extend the variety further, the concept of *samskara* was introduced. Once formed, a *samskara* stays with us, influencing our responses until it is cleaned. Think of it as your soul's draft script – full of plot twists you didn't know you'd signed up for.'

At this point, Sumit interjected. 'Once a *samskara* is formed, how does it get cleared?' Keshav responded, 'Nature has designed a beautiful way to clear *samskaras* – this is *Bhoga.'*

Bhoga – The Cleaning Mechanism

As we've discussed earlier, repeated thoughts of an event, when loaded with extreme likes or dislikes, and experiences, create a memory. The emotions attached to that memory push it deeper in us when we mull over the experiences, crystallizing into a *samskara.*

Now we own this *samskara and it* becomes part and parcel of us. When we face a similar environment again at a later point in time, the earlier pattern of attraction or repulsion/experiences (which was present when the *samskara* got created) resurfaces. This has been observed, very often as the factor leading us to repeat a course of action taken earlier, which was not the best.'

Sumit asked, 'So what then is the best course of action?'

Vaibhavi piped in aloud:

'What I understood is, we need to undo these patterns by bringing in the **right understanding**. That's how a *samskara* could stop influencing us. For instance, when Suresh realized – after talking to Keshav uncle – that his reaction to his son's result was causing misery, he accepted the situation. This acceptance of the outcome of the situation changed it for him and dissolved its emotional hold.'

Keshav smiled, 'Exactly, Vaibhavi. That's a correct understanding.

We realize here that the correct thinking, right understanding, and correct approach to the situation becomes a vital part of the solution, which can help us eradicate the *samskara and* the misery thereof.'

Sumit continued, 'So what was the *Bhoga* in Suresh and Ravi's story?'

Keshav explained:

'Suresh's soul, while writing its script before this birth, knew it had to face situations to clean a specific past *samskara* of 'not accepting results.' So in its plan, it set up an intense challenge. This became his second chance – a test, really. He could either pass by choosing acceptance or fail again. This pre-written element coming alive in life is what we call *Bhoga.*'

Yash jumped in:

'But I always thought *Bhoga* meant only going through bad times.'

Keshav chuckled:

'*Bhoga* includes both good and bad experiences. Both are scripted opportunities to learn. For example, in another story of a proud father whose daughter topped an exam may need to learn humility. The script arranges for that too. The key is that whenever we face extremes (success, failure) in life, there is always a lesson waiting for us. Once we have learnt that lesson and corrected our response, thinking and understanding, then *Samskara* is cleaned and there is no need of further *Bhoga* on that subject.'

The Role of Samskaras

Sumit asked, 'Once a *samskara* is formed, does it play any constructive role?'

Keshav Beamed, 'Yes Indeed. For us to have varied experiences in life, there must be different characters – much like in a play. Someone has to be the hero, someone the villain, someone the advisor, and so on. In the beginning, all human beings were the same and had freedom to choose experiences, but no experience was possible since everyone was the same. So, it was *samskaras*, gathered over many lives, that created these differences and enabled us to become unique. Someone shall play the role of the villain and someone shall play the role of a hero, and so on. Then experience was possible.'

Sumit pressed further, 'So when can *samskaras* finally become zero?'

Keshav chuckled, 'As for your question, Sumit, why don't you all reflect on it and share your thoughts with me later? For today in summary, I would say that we are born for this purpose too and with the help of a spiritual practice, having the capacity to clean the *samskaras* can help. That is a subject for another day. All I can see right now is my *phirni* – I must undergo the *bhoga* of enjoying it!

The group burst into laughter, and Yash hurried off to fetch the dessert.

Key Takeaways

1. **Effort vs. Result** – Humans have full control over their effort; Let's say that God has full control over the result. Acceptance means respecting this boundary.
2. **Pre-Written Script** – Our lives carry patterns chosen by the soul before birth for its growth, hidden from us (after taking birth) to keep experiences authentic.
3. ***Samskaras*** – Past emotional impressions shape our behaviour and tendencies; they bind us until cleaned.
4. ***Bhoga*** – Life gives us chances (pleasant and unpleasant) to dissolve *samskaras* through right understanding and acceptance.
5. **Humour and Humility** – Even while grappling with profound truths, it helps to laugh, eat *phirni*, and stay grounded.

When faced with trials and tribulations in life, if you could go through them rather than trying to avoid them, precious time would be saved. – **Excerpt from the book *Spiritual Anatomy* by Daaji.**

'Happiness can exist only in acceptance.' – **George Orwell**

'Of course, there is no formula for success except perhaps an unconditional acceptance of life and what it brings.' – **Arthur Rubinstein**

'The first step toward change is awareness. The second step is acceptance.' – **Nathaniel Branden**

Scoring Guide

Remember, this is a tool for self-reflection, not judgment. Be honest with yourself, and know that acceptance is a practice that evolves over time.

Score 0: Strong Resistance/Denial

You actively **resist or deny reality**, especially when it's unpleasant or doesn't align with your expectations.

You often find yourself saying, 'This shouldn't be happening,' or 'It's not fair,' and dwelling on those feelings.

You struggle to acknowledge difficult emotions, circumstances, or aspects of yourself.

You might try to force situations to be different, even when it's clearly not possible.

Score 1: Occasional Acknowledgment, but Frequent Struggle

You can sometimes **intellectually acknowledge a difficult outcome,** but you frequently struggle emotionally to accept it.

You spend a lot of time wishing things were different or replaying events in your mind, trying to change the outcome.

You might accept certain aspects but intensely resist others.

Emotional distress related to non-acceptance is common for you.

Score 2: Fluctuating Acceptance

You have moments where you **feel a sense of acceptance**, but it's often fleeting, especially when under stress.

You're starting to understand that resisting reality causes more suffering, but you still fall back into old patterns of denial or struggle.

You might accept some things about yourself or your life, but actively judge or try to change others.

You're aware of the concept of acceptance but find it hard to consistently practice.

Score 3: Growing Acceptance

You're generally able to **acknowledge and accept reality** as it is, even when it's uncomfortable.

You experience fewer intense emotional reactions to things you can't change.

You're developing the ability to observe your thoughts and feelings without getting completely swept away by them.

You understand that acceptance doesn't mean resignation, but rather making peace with what is so you can move forward.

Score 4: Consistent Acceptance

You consistently **practice acceptance** in most areas of your life, including challenging situations.

You can acknowledge difficult emotions, thoughts, and circumstances without significant resistance or judgment.

You find yourself adapting more easily to change and unexpected events

You experience a greater sense of inner peace and freedom, even amidst external difficulties, because you're not fighting reality.

Score 5: Deep and Embodied Acceptance

You embody a deep sense of **unconditional and cheerful acceptance** of yourself, others, and life as it unfolds.

You can fully embrace both the pleasant and unpleasant aspects of existence without significant inner turmoil.

You respond to life's challenges with equanimity and a willingness to learn from all experiences.

This level of acceptance feels natural and deeply integrated into your being, leading to profound resilience and well-being.

Reflection Prompts

1. Describe something you are currently struggling to accept (about yourself, another person, or a situation). What resistance do you feel?
2. What are the benefits of accepting things as they are, even if they are not ideal?

3. What would it mean to truly accept one challenging aspect of your current reality, and what would that acceptance allow you to do differently?

6. Peace Within Myself: When Calm Becomes Your Superpower

In one of the gatherings, which by now had become a pleasant ritual, Vaibhavi fondly recalled a winter evening from when she was 19. It was spent in her grandfather's ancestral village, Senapur, in Uttar Pradesh. Her grandfather's uncle's family still lived there, and it was the 31 of December – a night so cold that even the stars seemed to be huddling together – that the respected elders of the village began assembling in the courtyard of the old haveli to welcome the New Year.

The courtyard was a living postcard of warmth and camaraderie. A campfire blazed at the center, crackling as if it were eavesdropping on the conversations and laughing along. The air was thick with the smoky, mouthwatering aroma of *Litti-Chokha*. Whole wheat dough balls, generously stuffed with spicy *sattu* (roasted gram flour), slowly roasted over charcoal and cow-dung cake fires – gaining that inimitable, earthy flavour that no gas stove can replicate. The *Chokha*, a rustic mash of roasted eggplant, potatoes, and tomatoes, was being seasoned with mustard oil, chopped onions, garlic, and green chillies. Every so often, someone would pour over a generous helping of melted ghee, bribing not just the taste buds but also the soul into complete surrender. That night, even the dietary control went off duty.

In the middle of this lively scene, Vaibhavi noticed her grandfather's uncle, Shyam Kanhaiya ji, seated on a simple wooden cot. Around him sat other village elders – retired professors, senior government officials, and doctors – each with an impressive city-worthy résumé. Yet, the man who drew the most quiet respect was this humble middle-level college teacher.

He sat with the poise of royalty – minus the crown, minus the sceptre – yet the calmness on his face was far more regal than any jewel-studded turban. And that calmness did not waver, even as conversations bubbled around him. He looked like the kind of man who could meditate even if the Wi-Fi went down during an India–Pakistan cricket match.

Later, curiosity got the better of Vaibhavi. She asked her grandfather why Shyam Kanhaiya ji was treated with such reverence when others in the group had far greater material achievements. Her grandfather smiled knowingly and said,

'Because he carries peace within him. You can see it in his face, hear it in his voice, and feel it in the way he treats people.'

When she probed further, he revealed the secret – Shyam Kanhaiya ji meditated daily and had devoted his life to giving, helping others without expectation. That night, as the fire crackled and the smoky scent of *Litti-Chokha* lingered, Vaibhavi understood something profound: some people are rich in a currency the world doesn't measure – but everyone values. And unlike the stock market or cryptocurrency, this one never crashes.

The Discussion That Followed

One of their friends asked, 'Alright, but **how does 'peace within myself' help me in my job or my personal life**?'

That question sparked an animated discussion. Vaibhavi, who had read 2 books on the mind's influence on health – *You Can Heal Your Life* by Louise Hay and *The Biology of Belief* by Dr. Bruce H. Lipton – jumped in first.

Effect on Health

'The book *Biology of Belief*,' Vaibhavi explained, 'shows that the mind is not just a storyteller – it's your body's chief broadcaster. When our minds are caught in loops of stress, fear, or confusion – what you can call 'mental noise' – our cells hear every broadcast. This isn't poetic fluff. Our T-cells, the soldiers of our immune system, are directly influenced by the tone of our inner dialogue.

Dr Lipton writes: '*Stunning new scientific discoveries about the biochemical effects of the brain's functioning show that all the cells of your body are affected by your thoughts.'* In simple terms, sustained inner turmoil makes your immunity pay a quiet but steady tax. It's like filing emotional tax – except this one drains energy, not your bank balance.

On the other hand, replacing fear-based thoughts with uplifting ones changes the body's internal chemistry. When the mind shifts from alarm to love, the cellular environment shifts too – making peace of mind not just a virtue, but a form of medicine.'

Vaibhavi added, 'In the book *You Can Heal Your Life*, there's a table of diseases with their 'probable causes' in thought patterns and suggested 'new thought patterns' for healing. Every time I've known someone battling illness, their mental habits matched the patterns in the book. That made me very conscious about keeping my thoughts constructive and positive.'

Though I must confess, she laughed, 'Sometimes I meditate more to save my stomach than enrich my soul!'

Keshav, sitting quietly in the corner, smiled appreciatively at the depth of the discussion.

Effect on Productivity

Damini, Vaibhavi's younger sister and a product manager who was based in Bengaluru and was visiting, shared her story:

'My first big test of this was during my Class 12 board exams. The maths paper that year was one of the toughest in a decade – newspapers confirmed it the next day. When I saw the paper, my confidence nosedived. But I used a tool my father had taught me – closing my eyes, connecting to my heart, and cleaning myself for 2 minutes. It worked. I regained clarity, wrote calmly, and scored 95/100 – the highest in my school.

One of my friends, who was expected to rank among the top 10 nationally, panicked instead. His mind froze, and he scored just 65/100. That fear was the only difference.'

Vaibhavi laughed, 'Same here! During my GRE, I bombed the first few questions and started panicking. I finally gave in and tried that tool (connecting to the heart and cleaning) I once dismissed as a waste of time. 2 minutes later, my mind cleared. I not only recovered but got into one of the top 5 US universities. Now I use it in tough work situations… and sometimes at home too.'

Keshav then shared his experience from years earlier. '2 decades back, during a health crisis of my father due to a heart stroke, I was in tears for most of the day. Fear had gripped me so tightly that even my shadow looked anxious. I still remember that feeling of helplessness. However, 6 years after this incident, I started meditation and also learnt the cleaning method.

Exactly a year later, my father suffered a more severe stroke, and the doctors decided to perform bypass surgery. This time, something had shifted in me. When the surgery was underway, I realized that for the past 3 days I had been absolutely calm – not out of ignorance, but out of inner steadiness. I was handling everything efficiently and even found myself giving confidence to my mother and sisters, who were scared most of the time.

In the first 48 hours after bypass surgery, disorientation is common. The ICU nurse, half surprised and half amused, told me, 'Whenever you come, your father calms down and seems at peace. But whenever your mother and sisters come, he gets restless and keeps asking for you.' That's when I understood that peace is contagious too – only this one doesn't spread through handshakes but through presence backed with meditation.

Later, my spiritual trainer explained that this happened because of the calm energy cultivated through meditation and the cleaning method. My mother and sisters, naturally carrying fear and worry, unknowingly passed it on to my father, whereas I had unknowingly become a walking tranquilliser. That realization left a deep mark on me.'

He continued, 'At work, my mental energy used to reduce considerably after 4–5 hours. A 5-minute cleaning technique followed by a 10-minute meditation during lunch break used to reset my mind to morning-level clarity. Over the years, my productivity soared, and the biggest factor was simple: peace within myself. It also helped me to have a better relationship with high-demanding clients as well as competitive colleagues. Apparently, peace is not just a virtue – it's also excellent corporate strategy.'

Key Takeaways

1. **Peace of mind is visible – and magnetic.** People sense it in your face, tone, and actions, and they respond to it with respect.
2. **Your thoughts affect your body.** Chronic mental noise undermines immunity; calm, constructive thinking supports healing.
3. **Clarity under pressure improves performance.** Simple practices to reset the mind can turn panic into peak output.
4. **Energy is contagious.** Your calm presence can influence others wherever you are.
5. **Inner peace is a long-term productivity tool.** It prevents burnout and sustains high performance in demanding environments.

'Peace comes from within. Do not seek it without.' – **Buddha**

'Calm mind brings inner strength and self-confidence, so that's very important for good health.' – **Dalai Lama**

'Peace is not the absence of problems, but the presence of calm amidst them.' – **Anonymous**

Scoring Guide

Remember, this is a personal reflection. Be honest with yourself about where you are today.

Inner peace is a journey, and this scale can help you recognize your progress and areas for growth.

Score 0: Constant Inner Turmoil

You feel a **near-constant sense of anxiety, agitation, or unease.**

Your mind is often racing, filled with worries, negative self-talk, or obsessive thoughts.

Small stressors feel overwhelming and easily disrupt your emotional state.

You rarely experience moments of genuine calm or contentment. Sleep may be difficult.

Score 1: Frequent Disquiet, Rare Moments of Peace

You experience **frequent periods of inner agitation or worry**, though not constantly.

Your peace is easily disturbed by external events or internal thoughts.

You might have fleeting moments where you feel a bit calmer, but they don't last long.

You often feel restless or unable to fully relax.

Score 2: Fluctuating Peace

You have periods of **relative calm, but they are often interrupted** by waves of stress, frustration, or sadness.

Your internal state tends to fluctuate significantly throughout the day or week.

You might find peace in specific activities (e.g., a hobby, nature) but struggle to maintain it in everyday life.

You are aware of the idea of inner peace, but find it hard to consistently achieve.

Score 3: Growing Inner Calm

You generally experience a **sense of calm most of the time**, even when facing challenges.

When stressed, you're able to recover your composure relatively quickly.

You're learning to observe your thoughts and emotions without being completely consumed by them.

You actively seek out practices or environments that support your inner peace (e.g., meditation, quiet time).

Score 4: Consistent Inner Peace

You maintain a **consistent and stable sense of inner peace** in most situations, including difficult ones.

You can navigate life's ups and downs with a grounded and calm demeanour.

Negative thoughts or emotions arise, but they don't derail your overall sense of well-being.

Score 5: Profound and Unshakeable Inner Peace

You embody a **deep, profound, and unshakeable inner peace** that feels independent of external conditions.

Your mind feels clear, calm, and present most of the time.

You experience a deep sense of serenity and acceptance, even in the face of significant adversity or uncertainty.

This level of peace is a core part of your being, allowing you to respond to life with wisdom and compassion.

Reflection Prompts

1. What daily activities or thought patterns tend to disrupt your inner peace?
2. How does your level of inner peace (or lack thereof) influence your interactions with others?
3. Have you explored tools (s) which can help you to remain peaceful even in the most challenging situations?

7. Reaction or Response: The Case of the Fiery Reply That Never Was

Samik, a friend of Yash, was a seasoned professional with battle scars from a decade in the corporate arena – and a reputation for having the reflexes of a warrior – in the middle of a sword fight.

Over the years, he had often reacted swiftly, sometimes *too* swiftly, especially when dealing with unfair clients or sharp-tongued colleagues. His retorts were sharp, his emails even sharper. And while his sense of justice was commendable, the *way* he responded often left behind a trail of regret and strained relationships. You could say his inbox had more scars than his résumé.

After one such email exchange that could easily qualify for inclusion in a corporate version of 'Epic Fails,' his yearly feedback included a gentle – but unmistakably clear – comment:

' Samik, your sword is sharp. But maybe... sheath it sometimes?'

Disturbed but honest enough to reflect, Samik turned to the trusted uncle of Yash – **Keshav.**

Keshav Uncle, as usual, offered 2 simple but profound solutions:

1. *'Unless it's a matter of life and death – or there's a literal fire – pause. Breathe. Take appropriate time, think, and then respond.'*
2. *'Clean the emotional residue of your day using a special cleaning technique. Reactions are often echoes of leftover emotional noise.'*
3. *'Connect to your heart when any unpleasant situation appears or an unpleasant conversation starts.'*

Taking the advice to heart, Samik began practising daily cleaning. Slowly, like dust settling after a storm, his tendency to instantly react started diminishing. He still got triggered sometimes, sure – but now mostly, instead of immediately charging into battle, he often paused, questioned, and occasionally even chuckled. He called it his 'new antivirus update' – detecting emotional malware before it crashed the system.

But old habits die dramatically.

One afternoon, he received a call from an important client, Jai. A junior team member, Jai, spoke brusquely to him – borderline rude. Samik spoke to him and got back to work.

One hour later, as he was sipping tea, the memory of Jai's tone resurfaced like a bad ad in the middle of a meditation video. 'Wait a minute,' he muttered. 'Did he just disrespect me?'

His old reflexes kicked in. Blood pressure rising, fingers flying, he drafted a scorching reply that would have made Jai consider a career change. He even reread it twice – because when anger writes, ego edits. Just as he was about to hit send, a message pinged on his phone:

'Dear Sir, I apologise for my tone earlier. I wasn't in the right state of mind, and I truly regret how I spoke to you. Can I call you?' – Jai

Samik paused, stunned. The arrow he was about to shoot evaporated mid-air.

He spoke to Jai, heard the apology, and accepted it. No drama. No burn bridges. No loss of dignity – for either side. And for once, HR could enjoy a peaceful day.

That evening, during his introspection walk, Samik reflected:

'Had I reacted instantly, I would have lost a sincere apology, a valuable client resource, and possibly harmed my own reputation. All because of 10 seconds of misplaced righteousness.'

Sometimes, he thought, a **delayed response isn't weakness. It's wisdom... disguised as patience.** After all, silence may not win arguments, but it definitely avoids sending emails that need to be unsent.

Key Takeaways

1. **A pause creates space for wisdom** – not every provocation deserves an instant reaction.
2. **Reactions are echoes of emotional residue**; clearing them daily prevents overflows.
3. **A sincere apology can be missed** if we rush to attack rather than wait to listen.
4. **Responding in place of reaction preserves dignity** – both yours and the other person's.
5. **Patience is not weakness**; it is power under discipline.

'Between stimulus and response, there is a space. In that space is our power to choose our response.' – **Viktor Frankl**

'Reaction is instinct; response is choice.' – **Author**

'Delayed and timely response isn't a weakness. It's wisdom disguised as patience.' – **Author**

Scoring Guide

This quality assesses how you typically react to situations, and how much regulation you feel you have over your emotional and behavioural output, particularly during challenging or unexpected situations.

Score 0: Highly Reactive and Out of Control

You often react impulsively and emotionally to situations, especially when stressed or surprised.

Your responses are frequently disproportionate to the event.

You struggle to pause or think before acting or speaking, often regretting your words or actions later.

You might find yourself yelling, shutting down, or engaging in other behaviours you later deem unhelpful or damaging.

You feel like your emotions or external circumstances completely dictate your responses.

Score 1: Often Reactive, With Some Glimpses of Control

You tend to react quickly and emotionally to many situations, though sometimes you can catch yourself.

Your initial responses are often driven by emotion (e.g., anger, fear, frustration).

You might recognize that your reaction wasn't ideal, but find it hard to change in the moment.

You may experience frequent arguments, misunderstandings, or internal turmoil due to your reactions.

You feel like you're often swept up by events rather than steering your own course.

Score 2: Mixed Reactions – Sometimes Controlled, Sometimes Reactive

Your responses vary. Sometimes you react impulsively, while other times you manage a more measured response.

You're becoming more aware of your triggers and patterns of reaction.

You might take a brief pause sometimes, but it's not consistent, especially under pressure.

You're working on improving, but old habits of reacting can still surface frequently.

You recognize the impact of your reactions and are actively trying to exert more control.

Score 3: Mostly Controlled and Thoughtful

You generally take a moment to process before responding, even in challenging situations.

Your responses are usually proportional to the event, and you aim for constructive outcomes.

You can identify your emotions without letting them completely derail your actions.

You're able to communicate your needs or concerns effectively without resorting to blame or aggression.

Score 4: Consistently Calm and Strategic

You **consistently respond to situations, rather than just reacting.**

You maintain composure even in high-stress or surprising circumstances.

You can effectively manage your emotions and choose responses that align with your values and goals.

You're proactive in de-escalating tension and finding solutions.

Score 5: Exceptionally Composed and Proactive

You embody a **remarkable level of composure and foresight in all situations.**

Your responses are not only controlled but often proactive, anticipating needs and preventing issues.

You can navigate highly volatile situations with grace, empathy, and clear strategic thinking.

Reflection Prompts

1. When was the last time you reacted instantly to a situation? What emotion drove that reaction, and what was its impact – on you and on others?
2. If you had paused before responding, even for a few breaths, how might the outcome – or your own state of mind – have been different?
3. What daily practice can help you stay anchored and calm, so that your future responses come from clarity rather than emotional residue?

8. Expectations

Case 1

By now, weekly gatherings had become a norm, and even if some of the usual participants could not come, they insisted on joining online. Before one such gathering, Sumit requested Keshav to hear about his brother Navin's issues. Navin, who had just entered college, was facing some struggles. He was added to the video call from back home in India. When Navin appeared on the screen, he wore the expression of someone carrying not just his exam stress but also the burden of India's trade negotiations with USA on his shoulders.

'What happened, Navin? It appears you're carrying the weight of the entire IIT-JEE syllabus on your head,' Keshav asked.

Navin sighed, 'It's exam season. I scored 76 on my test. Dad expected me to cross 90, like Sumit bhaiya used to score. Now he's upset, I'm upset, and even the neighbours will be upset. I don't know why my marks have suddenly become a national news bulletin!'

Keshav chuckled, 'You know, when I was your age, my father expected me to become an engineer. I expected to become a cricketer. My mother expected me to become a doctor. The neighbour aunty expected me to become her daughter's husband. Imagine the mess – I was one expectation away from needing ten lives!'

Navin laughed for the first time that evening.

Keshav continued, 'Expectations are like invisible contracts we never signed but are somehow held accountable for. The trouble begins when we mistake them for guarantees. Your father expects 90 – but that's his wish, not your binding reality. You gave your best, yes? Then accept the outcome and focus on where you can improve. In this regard, Steve Jobs said – '*Your time is limited, don't waste it living someone else's life*'.

The *only expectation you should always honour is the one you set with yourself – to grow a little more than yesterday*.'

Navin thought for a while and said, 'So you're saying expectations are like wish-list items, not mandatory assignments?'

'Exactly!' Keshav smiled. 'They are desires dressed in formal clothes. Keep them in perspective, and life will feel much lighter.'

That evening, Navin walked home with less weight on his shoulders. His marks hadn't changed, but his relationship with expectations had.

By the time the call with Navin was over, the usual group had gathered, and a campfire was lit at Keshav's place. Sumit told the group that he had been talking about expectations with Uncle.

Case 2

Namita jumped in, 'One of my friends was recently under a lot of stress. I asked her what was troubling her. She told me her husband doesn't take care of her. When I probed further, I found she had a very long list of expectations from him. I wondered – where's the problem in that? But on further probing, I discovered she had never actually shared her wishes with her husband. Gradually, she became unhappy, and fights on trivial matters with her husband have now become routine for the past 6 months.'

Vibhuti, who was happily married for a couple of years, threw her hat into the discussion ring: 'It's the job of a husband to know the wishes of his wife without being told – and he needs to fulfil them. My husband does that.'

Everyone laughed, partly at the statement and partly at the sheer confidence in her tone. The environment became lighter.

Vaibhavi finally spoke, 'Vibhuti's husband is sensitive, so he fulfils her wishes without being told. Namita! It seems your friend's husband is not as gifted. She may need to find other ways to drop bigger hints – maybe even billboard-sized ones! If that doesn't work, **she should simply share her wishes with him**. This way, the communication remains non-violent. On this subject, I recommend a book: *Nonviolent Communication: A Language of Life* by Marshall Rosenberg. Based on NVC, there is a free course: Heartfulness Communication as well.'

Yash asked Keshav to share his take on the subject.

Keshav said, 'All of you have already covered most of the points. But let me summarize it like this:

A wish → turns into a desire → becomes an expectation → is assumed as a right → but remains unspoken.

When remaining attached to the expectation, its **non-fulfilment means peace is gone → unhappiness grows → anger kicks in → confrontations begin**, often on trivial issues with the person expected to fulfil it.

Soon it **becomes a demand. After a few confrontations, it turns into violent words → peace of the home is lost → harmony vanishes → the productivity of everyone is affected → the health also gets affected.**

Later, when anyone involved introspects, they may fall in their own eyes. The heart whispers that the action was wrong, but the ego raises its head and stops corrective steps and tries to justify its own actions. If the pattern continues, it leads to self-isolation and guilt.'

After a few minutes, Vibhuti, grinning from ear to ear, said, 'My bua (my father's sister), who is 65 years old, recently told me that her husband is a fool. Curious, I asked why. She confessed that in her youth, just after marriage, she had a secret desire to wear a bikini like the famous actress Zeenat Aman and walk on a Goa beach. But her husband never got the hint – and here we are. I told her, 'Bua, come to the Bay Area, I'll take you to the lovely beaches here, and you can finally tick that item off your bucket list – if it's still there!' She gave me a solid whack on the back, but I could tell she was cool about it.'

The environment became light.

Key Takeaways

1. **Expectations are unspoken and assumed contracts** – they cause trouble when assumed as guarantees.
2. **Not all expectations are bad** – self-expectations for growth keep life meaningful.
3. **Expectations are like balloons** – fine to have, but they can pop if held too tightly.
4. **Communication is key**: expressing wishes openly prevents silent resentments.
5. **The moment you start living without expecting anything from anyone – not even the people closest to you – you take back your peace.**

'Expectation is the root of all heartache.' – **Shakespeare**

'Blessed is he who expects nothing, for he shall never be disappointed.' – **Alexander Pope**

'Low expectation is the key to happiness in life.' – **Christopher Miller**

'Expect Not' – **St. Chari ji***

*Chari Ji (Shri Parthasarathi Rajagopalachari was the third guide of Heartfulness meditation)

Scoring Guide

This scale focuses on how your expectations (of yourself, others, and life) impact your well-being and interactions. When assessing yourself, consider how often you feel disappointed, frustrated, or upset because things didn't go as you thought they 'should.' Also, reflect on how quickly you adapt when plans change.

Score 0: Rigid and Unrealistic Expectations

You hold very **fixed and often unrealistic expectations** of yourself, others, and how life *should* unfold.

You frequently experience significant disappointment, frustration, or anger when things don't go exactly as you anticipated.

You struggle to adapt when plans change or when people don't meet your unstated demands.

Your happiness is heavily dependent on specific outcomes.

Score 1: Frequent Disappointment from Unmet Expectations

You often set **high, sometimes implicit, expectations** that lead to frequent disappointment.

You struggle when others don't act as you predict or when situations deviate from your ideal.

You might blame yourself or others when expectations aren't met, leading to resentment or self-criticism.

You find it hard to go with the flow or embrace spontaneity.

Score 2: Fluctuating Awareness of Expectations

You are sometimes aware of your expectations influencing your feelings, but you still frequently get **caught up in disappointment** when they're not met.

You might intellectually understand the need for flexibility, but struggle to apply it emotionally.

You might have some realistic expectations, but also cling to several that are unhelpful or unattainable.

You sometimes articulate your expectations, but often only after you're already upset.

Score 3: Growing Flexibility and Conscious Expectations

You are increasingly able to **identify your expectations** and consciously adjust them when necessary.

You understand that unmet expectations are a source of suffering and actively work to cultivate more realistic or adaptable ones.

You're learning to differentiate between hopes and rigid demands.

You can recover more quickly from disappointment and embrace alternative outcomes.

Score 4: Balanced and Adaptable Expectations

You consistently hold **balanced and adaptable expectations** of yourself, others, and life.

You approach situations with a sense of hope and intention, but without rigid attachment to specific outcomes.

You can gracefully navigate changes and setbacks, viewing them as opportunities rather than failures.

You communicate your needs and desires clearly, reducing unstated expectations.

Score 5: Freedom from Limiting Expectations

You operate with a profound sense of **freedom from limiting expectations**, embracing life as it unfolds.

You have a deep understanding that true contentment comes from acceptance, not from demanding specific outcomes.

You approach life with curiosity and an open mind, genuinely appreciative of whatever arises.

Your happiness is largely independent of external circumstances or the actions of others, as you've released the need for things to be 'a certain way.'

Reflection Prompts

1. Think about a recent situation where your expectations (of yourself, others, or a situation) were either met or unmet. How did you feel?
2. How do unspoken or unrealistic expectations impact your relationships or your emotional well-being?
3. What is one expectation you currently hold that might be causing you unnecessary stress or disappointment?

9. Selfishness

In one of the usual weekly gatherings by now, Yash announced, 'Today's topic is Selfishness.' The group, in unison, turned to Keshav: 'Uncle, tell us about selfishness!'

Keshav, with a smile, countered, 'First, I would love to hear your own experiences.'

Ajit's Story

Ajit, a 28-year-old entrepreneur fresh from securing funding for his startup, jumped in first.

'Whenever my sister and I visit our parents during our holidays, it's our sacred time to seep in, meet friends, and devour every food joint we have been missing. Naturally, we end up waking around noon. But in our parents' home, the household comes alive at 6 a.m. sharp. Add the symphony of the doorbell and the whistle of the pressure cooker, and our dream of sleeping till noon goes straight out of the window. And my younger sister often yells at my mother, claiming nobody here respects 'holiday sleep hours'. This, naturally, turns into a full-blown soap opera between them. Sometimes, I wonder – is this selfishness?'

Many nodded since they have been through the same 'Parents vs visiting children' culture clash.

Yash offered his perspective.

'Yes, I think it's a little selfish. We're asking the household to disrupt its schedule for our convenience. My mother is a schoolteacher and has to leave by 7:30 a.m., with both breakfast and lunch packed. So, our cook arrives at 6 a.m. Initially, I used to get irritated too. But one day I realized – just as I seek my comfort, shouldn't I also respect my mother's needs and the household's rhythm? That's when I learnt to adapt. Flexibility, I realized, keeps both the peace and relationship and consideration for everyone at home.'

Keshav beamed. 'Bravo, Yash! That's maturity when you start seeing beyond your own convenience. This is how your consciousness expands and relationships flourish with most people you live or work with.'

Vaibhavi's Story

Vaibhavi then spoke of a recent divorce among their friends – a marriage that lasted barely a year.

'The root cause,' she said, 'was the husband's unwillingness to share any household work. Both were professionals, earning similar salaries. Yet, after work, he would play computer games or watch TV while she managed the cooking and chores alone. She complained to us several times, right in front of him, but nothing changed.'

Keshav's Story

'Alright,' Vaibhavi smiled, 'now it's your turn, Uncle.'

Keshav's eyes twinkled.

'I'll share 2 examples from the *Mahabharata*, which, to me, is the best script ever written. Tell me – what was Bhishma Pitamaha's selfish act?'

The group was puzzled. A few ventured guesses, but most said Bhishma's life was entirely selfless.

Keshav began. 'First, Dhritarashtra. His selfishness lay in his desire to see his own son crowned king, despite the elders and ministers – including Bhishma and Vidura – favouring the more eligible (as per bloodline) and capable Yudhisthir. Dhritarashtra's consciousness was limited to his immediate family, but as a king, his duty was to choose the most qualified successor, even if it was his brother's son.

'The ideal king treats all subjects as his children and chooses a successor from among them based solely on merit. In fact, Hastinapur once had such a ruler – King Bharata – who chose a sage's son, Bhumanyu, as his heir, despite having 9 sons of his own. This was a shining example of selflessness and prioritizing the kingdom's welfare over bloodline.'

'What about Bhishma?' Vaibhavi asked.

Keshav continued.

'Bhishma was unmatched on the battlefield, second only to Lord Rama in fairness and power. He had taken a vow to support the throne of Hastinapur according to bloodline succession. But when the kingdom's welfare was being undermined by Duryodhana's arrogance, Bhishma remained silent – even during Draupadi's humiliation.

'Before his death, Bhishma asked Lord Krishna, 'What was my mistake?' Krishna replied, 'Your vow was noble. But times changed, and your rigid attachment to it began harming the kingdom. You clung to your vow at the cost of the greater good. That was selfishness in disguise. You should have broken the vow when it conflicted with *dharma*.'

'And that, my friends, is why he was removed from the battlefield.'

Keshav concluded, 'The level of selfishness in a person is inversely proportional to their consciousness and vice versa.'

'Selfishness, when left unchecked, is like carrying a leaky bucket – you keep pouring in joy, love, and goodwill, but somehow it never stays. The hole is our self-centeredness, quietly draining relationships and trust. The irony? In chasing only our own gain, we end up with less of everything that truly matters. The moment we turn the bucket outward – thinking of others, sharing, contributing – we discover it fills faster and holds more. '

Everyone thanked Keshav and requested that he give time for more such discussions in the future – especially on the subject of consciousness.

Key Takeaways

1. **Selfishness narrows consciousness** – it limits us to see only our own comfort and blinds us to others' needs.
2. **Flexibility and consideration expand relationships** – adapting to others' rhythms prevents conflict and nurtures harmony.
3. **Selfishness in disguise** often hides under noble vows or traditions (like Bhishma's case) when we cling to them at the cost of the greater good.
4. **True maturity begins when we think beyond our own convenience** – valuing the welfare of family, community, or nation above personal desires.

5. **When selfishness shrinks, selflessness expands** – When we give, contribute, and share, we actually receive more peace, love, and respect in return.

'A man wrapped up in himself makes a very small bundle.'
– **Benjamin Franklin**

'It is not selfish to think for oneself, but it is selfish to think only of oneself.' – **Author**

'Great achievement is usually born of great sacrifice, and is never the result of selfishness.' – **Napoleon Hill**

Scoring Guide

This scale, for 'Selfishness (Self-Oriented vs. Others-Oriented),' focuses on the degree to which you prioritize the needs and well-being of others over your own. When reflecting on your score, consider your typical motivations and actions in various situations, especially when your own needs might conflict with those of others.

Score 0: Exclusively Self-Serving

Your actions are almost always driven by **personal gain, benefit, or comfort,** with little to no consideration for others.

You rarely consider the impact of your choices on anyone but yourself.

You find it difficult to understand or relate to the concept of sacrificing for others.

You might exploit situations or relationships for your own advantage without remorse.

Score 1: Primarily Self-Interested with Minimal Regard for Others

Your primary focus remains on your **own needs and desires,** though you might occasionally acknowledge others.

You might do something for someone else only if it's convenient or if you expect something in return.

You often feel put out or resentful if you have to prioritize someone else's needs.

Empathy for others' struggles is limited and rarely translates into action.

Score 2: Conditional or Superficial Consideration for Others

You can sometimes **consider others' needs, but often with conditions or expectations** attached.

You might help others, but you expect recognition, appreciation, or reciprocation.

Your willingness to help depends heavily on your mood, the effort required, or how much you like the person.

You might talk about helping others more than you actually do.

Score 3: Growing Willingness to Prioritize Others

You are increasingly willing to **prioritize the needs of others**, even when it requires some personal sacrifice or effort.

You actively seek opportunities to be helpful and contribute to the well-being of those around you.

You're learning to put yourself in others' shoes and understand their perspectives.

While not always effortless, you find satisfaction in acts of kindness and support for others.

Score 4: Consistent Consideration and Active Contribution to Others' Well-being

You consistently **demonstrate a genuine desire to serve and support others**, often putting their needs before your own.

You regularly engage in acts of generosity, kindness, and helpfulness, both big and small, without expecting anything in return.

You actively seek ways to make a positive difference in your community or for individuals.

You derive deep satisfaction from contributing to the happiness and well-being of others.

Score 5: Embodied Selflessness and Unconditional Service

Your life is characterised by a profound and **unconditional dedication to the well-being of others**, often at significant personal cost or sacrifice.

You instinctively prioritize collective good over individual gain, demonstrating deep compassion and empathy.

You view serving others as an intrinsic part of your existence, finding joy and purpose in giving without expectation.

This level of selflessness inspires others and creates a ripple effect of positive impact.

Reflection Prompts

1. How do you believe your level of self-focus (or self-neglect) impacts your closest relationships?
2. What does true 'self-care' mean to you, distinguishing it from selfishness?

10. Anger: The Case of the Inner Volcano and Mr Suri

Yash had witnessed a full-blown shouting match at his office. What began as a mild disagreement between2 colleagues snowballed into a verbal WWF match – complete with creative vocabulary, finger-pointing, and red faces. One of the participants later confessed to Yash, 'Anger is like instant coffee – quick to brew, bitter to taste, and often keeps you up at night.'

It left Yash wondering:

Is anger always destructive? Or does it come with a secret utility belt like Batman?

One day, Yash approached his ever-composed Keshav uncle with a question that had clearly been simmering inside him:

'Uncle, what used to be your reaction when you were really, really angry?'

Keshav uncle chuckled – the kind of chuckle that comes from surviving emotional landmines – and said, 'Ah, anger. In my early years in the Air Force, I could flare up like a Diwali rocket. Especially with people who consistently underperformed or played peekaboo with ethics.

And let me tell you – working in a military environment where 'Boss is always right' is great for discipline, but a disaster for anger management for a few. You suppress it till it ferments.'

He leaned back and added with a twinkle in his eye,

'But anger is like black coffee – sharp and energizing for a moment, but the bitterness lingers long after the buzz wears off.'

Keshav explained how the bursts of anger often left him with a tight chest, a ruined afternoon, and relationships that felt like bruised fruit. For over 2 decades, he dabbled in self-help books, motivational posters ('Keep Calm and Lead On'), and even tried deep breathing – usually after the shouting was done. Deep breathing, of course, is most effective *before* the eruption – something he discovered after several post-eruption sighs.

Nothing worked.

'I justified it,' Keshav confessed. 'Because I was professionally sound and mostly right. So I told myself – what's the harm in a little righteous thunder now and then?'

Things only started to shift when he took up meditation.

'It wasn't dramatic,' he said. 'There were no halos or floating in mid-air. Just one day, I noticed – I hadn't yelled at Mr Suri for more than a month.'

Now, **Mr Suri** deserves a special mention.

He was the undisputed grandmaster of procrastination. A walking encyclopaedia of excuses.

'If there were 1001 reasons why something couldn't be done,' Keshav said, 'Mr Suri had invented at least 723 of them, plus a few bonus ones that defied logic and grammar.'

But just as Keshav was savouring his calm streak, the universe decided it was time for a test.

'One fine morning, Mr Suri dropped another one of his signature pearls. And just like that – *boom!* – my inner volcano erupted. Loud, fiery, and quite unnecessary.'

The heaviness returned. But this time, it felt different. More personal. More intrusive.

'Earlier, the anger felt like a power move. This time, it felt like I had kicked over my own inner peace. The calm I had nurtured through meditation had vanished – and I felt like I had screamed into my own soul.'

That day, Keshav learned something he hadn't read in any management book:

Yes, anger can sometimes get results. But if it takes away your inner balance, it's a very expensive transaction.

He turned to Yash and concluded:

'Now, if I must use anger, I treat it like borrowing fire to light a lamp – not to burn down the house. Express it as a tool, if needed. But stay detached. Let it pass through you, not possess you.

Key takeaways

1. Anger, if used consciously, can sometimes be a tool – but if it disturbs your inner peace, it's a tool with a hidden cost.
2. True strength isn't in bottling anger or unleashing it – it's in mastering the space between stimulus and response.

'The real cause of anger is usually one's own refractory temperament. A stubborn nature cultivated by the effect enshrouds one's sense of judgement. The distinction between right and wrong having thus

been lost, he remains rigidly fixed upon his views and allows no accommodation to others' views.'

– Excerpt from the book *Spiritual Anatomy* by **Daaji**

'You will not be punished for your anger, you will be punished by your anger.'

– **Often attributed to Buddha** *(though apocryphal, still widely quoted)*

Scoring Guide

This scale focuses on how you experience, express, and manage anger, from extreme reactivity to calm self-regulation. When rating yourself, consider how often you feel angry, how intensely you react, and how quickly you can return to a state of calm.

Also, think about the impact your anger has on your relationships and your own well-being.

Score 0: Explosive and Uncontrolled Anger

You experience **frequent, intense outbursts of anger** that are difficult or impossible to control.

Your anger often leads to yelling, aggression (verbal or physical), or destructive behaviour.

You find it hard to calm down once you're angry, and the feeling lingers for a long time.

Your anger negatively impacts your relationships, work, and overall well-being.

Score 1: Frequent Irritability and Reactive Anger

You feel **irritable or annoyed much of the time**, and anger is easily triggered by minor provocations.

While not always explosive, your anger often manifests as snapping at others, passive aggression, or prolonged sulking.

You struggle to manage your initial angry reactions and often regret your words or actions later.

You frequently feel misunderstood or victimized, fuelling your resentment.

Score 2: Fluctuating Anger Management

You have moments where you can manage your anger, but you still experience **frequent episodes of frustration or anger** that you struggle to control.

You might try to suppress anger, but it often leaks out in unhealthy ways, or explodes unexpectedly.

You're aware of your anger issues but find it challenging to consistently apply coping strategies.

Your anger can still strain relationships and cause personal distress.

Score 3: Growing Awareness and Moderate Control

You are increasingly able to **recognize the onset of anger** and have some strategies to manage it before it escalates.

You might still feel angry, but you're less likely to lash out or engage in destructive behaviours.

You're learning to express your anger in more constructive ways (e.g., asserting boundaries, communicating calmly).

You're actively working on understanding the root causes of your anger and developing healthier responses.

Score 4: Consistent Self-Regulation of Anger

You consistently **manage your anger effectively** in most situations.

When anger arises, you can identify it, understand its triggers, and choose a constructive response.

You rarely experience uncontrolled outbursts or prolonged resentment.

You use anger as a signal to address underlying issues or communicate your needs clearly and respectfully.

Score 5: Profound Calm and Wisdom in the Face of Frustration

You embody a profound sense of **inner calm and wisdom** that allows you to navigate frustrating or challenging situations with remarkable equanimity.

Anger is a rare and fleeting experience for you, quickly transmuted into understanding, compassion, or productive problem-solving.

You approach conflict with a clear mind and a focus on resolution, rather than blame or aggression.

Your presence often helps de-escalate tension in others, and you model healthy emotional regulation.

Reflection Prompts

1. Recall a recent experience of anger. What specific event or comment triggered it?
2. What physical sensations do you experience when you get angry? What thoughts run through your mind?
3. What alternative ways could you have expressed or managed your anger in that situation to achieve a more constructive outcome?

11. Dealing with Criticism

Aditya was Keshav's batchmate in Engineering College. His son Ajay was a bright student who landed a job with Google's development team during campus placements. But Ajay chose a different path – launching a startup with one of his batchmates. Things went fairly well at first, but after a year, they felt the need for venture capital (VC) funding. That's when Ajay grew restless.

During pitches to VCs, Ajay was asked questions about his strategy, approach, and action plan. But he took every query as criticism and put on a defensive suit of armour. Naturally, he failed to convince any VC. In one meeting, when Ajay grew angry, the VC shot back, 'The problem with your generation is that you think you know it all.'

The dream start was quickly turning into a nightmare. At this stage, Aditya decided to intervene, but Ajay wasn't keen on hearing his father's advice. So Aditya suggested he speak with Keshav. Ajay was very fond of his 'Keshav Uncle' and often called him whenever he found himself at life's crossroads.

Keshav said, 'Ajay! Tell me about the startup arena. It's been many years since I retired, and I could use an update.'

Ajay sighed. 'Uncle, it's very fast-paced. But I'm facing some issues. I've become too sensitive – any advice feels like criticism, and I just can't take it.'

Keshav asked, 'Why is criticism so bad?'

Ajay replied, 'Uncle, it's easy for you to say. You worked in a structured environment. Things are different now.'

Keshav said, 'Let me share an experience. A colleague of mine, Navin, once headed large Strategic and IT Consulting projects. Our clients were bureaucrats who had cracked the Civil Services exams. They carried rich, diverse experience – but with success often comes ego, and theirs was never far behind.'

Keshav continued, 'In my office, there was a colleague named Manu, at the same level as Navin. We had all worked on a project for the Election Commission of India (ECI). Manu was an expert in talking – and in pointing out why plans wouldn't work. It took Navin and me time to establish the right approach for the ECI project. Manu was eventually sidelined, and he blamed Navin. Later, Navin led an ambitious project for the Ministry of Defence, which had the potential to save ₹400–800 crores a year for the government. For one important presentation, Navin invited all the vertical heads – including Manu.'

Navin had completed the study of the 'as-is' and 'to-be' documents and was ready with key recommendations, including business process reengineering for the Ministry of Defence. He explained the project in detail to the vertical heads and Senior Consultants; and asked us to vet his draft recommendations.

'Please wear the hat of a critic,' Navin said, 'and don't hesitate to criticize anything. ' Manu didn't need a hat – he'd been wearing the critic's crown for years.

The meeting was successful, and Navin received critical reviews from multiple vertical heads. The next day, he reported to the VP that the contribution of his colleagues was immense – and even mentioned Manu by name.

The VP asked, 'Navin! I thought you and Manu didn't get along. How come you're praising him now?'

Navin smiled. 'Sir, we all know Manu can't make a project succeed. But I trusted him because I knew he'd apply more than 100 per cent effort to find gaps in my work and somehow try to put my work down. True to my expectation, Manu spotted 20 flaws – most were useless – but 2 of them forced me to think harder. They led me to a better solution. The credit must go to Manu, too. It's important to know how to filter useful criticism from noise. Good leadership means using the strengths of even your critics to your advantage.'

The VP burst into laughter.

A couple of years down the line, the project became a success and went on to save the government huge sums of money, just as envisioned.

Keshav turned to Ajay. 'Tell me, what did you do when you were young and your parents gave you some advice?'

Ajay admitted, 'Most of the time, I defended my actions – and sometimes I even shouted at them.'

Keshav nodded. 'Navin used to say, 'It's better we find the gaps in-house than have the client find them. And clients are not kind, even about a missing comma or full stop in a presentation.' Shouldn't we apply the same principle to anyone who spends time and energy criticizing us?'

Ajay said slowly, 'That does appear logical.'

Keshav added, 'The best approach is to listen to your critic fully without interruption. Later, run through the gaps they point out. If there's merit, adopt it – and don't forget to thank them, even if it's someone like Manu. If not, just let it go.'

Ajay recalled, 'In our childhood, we were taught a verse on criticism by Saint Kabir. Now I finally understand it. But Uncle, whenever someone criticises me, I still feel uncomfortable.'

Keshav smiled. 'That's natural. Ego kicks in, makes us angry or defensive, and we feel hurt. But if you live by Kabir's wisdom, your relationships will flourish – and you'll succeed in your profession and relationships too.'

Key Takeaways

1. Criticism, when reframed, becomes constructive feedback for growth rather than a personal attack.
2. Good leaders use even their critics' energy to their advantage.
3. Listening without interruption allows us to extract value, even from flawed feedback.
4. Ego resists criticism; humility transforms it into learning.
5. Saint Kabir's teaching on keeping critics close remains timeless wisdom.

'Keep your critic close to you; give him shelter in your courtyard. Without soap and water, he cleanses your character.' – **Saint Kabir**

'The trouble with most of us is that we would rather be ruined by praise than saved by criticism.' – **Norman Vincent Peale**

'Criticism is necessary if you want to attain excellence in anything we do. For a person who has such an understanding, criticism will not appear negative; It will be a window of opportunity.' – **Daaji**

Scoring Guide: Dealing with Criticism

This scale focuses on how you receive, process, and respond to feedback, from a highly defensive stance to a constructive and growth-oriented approach.

Score 0: Highly Defensive and Unreceptive

You view criticism as a personal attack and react with immediate defensiveness, anger, or withdrawal. You're unable to see any validity in the feedback and will often argue, make excuses, or blame others.

Criticism, no matter how well-intended, damages your self-esteem and can lead to resentment towards the person giving it.

Score 1: Easily Offended and Reactive

You often take criticism personally and can become visibly upset or sullen. You might listen to feedback but internally dismiss it, focusing on the negative emotions it caused rather than the message itself. You may feign acceptance but rarely act on the advice given, and you often feel misunderstood or unfairly judged.

Score 2: Fluctuating Receptivity

You can sometimes accept criticism, but it depends heavily on your mood, who is giving the feedback, and how it's delivered. You might initially get defensive, but later reflect on the feedback, though you may still struggle to implement it consistently. You are aware that you should be better at handling criticism, but find it challenging to put that into practice.

Score 3: Growing Awareness and Moderate Control

You are increasingly able to separate your identity from the feedback you receive. You may still feel an initial sting, but you can usually take a moment to process the information without an immediate emotional reaction. You can ask clarifying questions and begin to identify the potential for growth. You're starting to see criticism as a tool for improvement, not a judgment of your worth.

Score 4: Consistent Receptivity and Action-Oriented

You consistently handle criticism with maturity and grace. When you receive feedback, you listen carefully, ask thoughtful questions, and thank the person for their input. You can identify which parts are valid and create a plan to implement the necessary changes. You actively seek out feedback and use it as a powerful tool for personal and professional development.

Score 5: Profoundly Growth-Oriented and Wise

You embody a profound understanding that all feedback, even if poorly delivered, contains a kernel of truth that can be used for growth. You actively seek diverse perspectives and constructive criticism, viewing them as gifts. You are a role model for others in how to receive and give feedback, and you use every critique as an opportunity for self-reflection and wisdom. Criticism rarely affects your emotional state, instead fuelling your desire to learn and improve.

Reflection Prompts

1. Recall a recent time you received criticism. What was the specific feedback, and how did you feel when you heard it?
2. Did your initial reaction help or hinder your ability to understand the feedback?
3. What is one specific, actionable step you can take based on the criticism you received?

12. Patience

Cambridge Dictionary defines patience as '*the ability to wait, or to continue doing something despite difficulties, or to suffer without complaining or becoming annoyed.*' Sounds simple on paper, but in real life, patience sometimes feels like waiting for the Wi-Fi to reconnect in the middle of an online exam.

One weekend, Vaibhavi approached Keshav to talk about patience. Manish, one of Keshav's old friends, also joined the conversation online, curious to hear what wisdom might unfold.

'Uncle,' Vaibhavi began, 'in my professional discussions, when I'm under a tight deadline and some colleagues offer the most creative excuses for not finishing their work, my patience runs thin. Is there even an upper limit to patience, or do we just keep stretching it like chewing gum?'

Keshav smiled. 'Let me take you back 3 decades. I was posted at Air Force Station Hasimara, known for its 4300 mm of annual rainfall spread across 8 months. Nestled near the Bhutan border, Hasimara was surrounded by tea gardens and tall elephant grass, with the hills forming a picturesque backdrop. During those 8 months, gardening was reduced to just cutting grass – sometimes daily! Wildlife sightings were so routine that pythons, monkeys, hog deers, and peacocks felt like neighbours, and on lucky days, one could even spot a Barasingha deer, wild elephant, or a panther. Driving inside the technical area often felt less like commuting and more like participating in a wildlife safari.'

Keshav paused, as though walking quietly down the lanes of his memories.

Keshav continued, 'Our daily routine began with a 7:00 a.m. briefing. In the Armed Forces, punctuality is sacred – arriving late is 1 of the top 3 sins. To be on time, I would start my Gypsy at 6:45 a.m. and reach the briefing hall in 5 minutes. Then came a twist: a senior officer had just been posted, his car hadn't arrived, and he asked me for a lift.

On the first day, he turned up at 06:52. On the second day, 06:51. Despite polite reminders, it became a habit. My patience wore thin, especially since in Hasimara one always needed a buffer – sometimes the road was blocked by a python stretched across the entire width, head at one end and tail at the other, taking its own sweet time to cross. Imagine explaining to your AOC: 'Sorry sir, delayed due to python traffic!'

One morning, while fuming inside, a thought struck me: *Maybe this officer was sent into my life just to enhance my patience.* The realization made me smile. The very next day, his car finally arrived, and my test of patience ended.'

Keshav's friend Manish nodded. 'In the medical profession, patience isn't optional – it's oxygen. Patients, especially elders, tend to repeat their story 3 or 4 times, partly from stress. Young patients, too, sometimes circle back again and again out of fear. For a doctor with a waiting room full of people, patience is tested constantly. Interrupt them once, and you either lose the patient's trust – or add to their ailments!'

Keshav added, 'In spiritual work, there is no fee, only sincerity. I once met Mishra ji, a senior police officer who was also a spiritual trainer. Early in my journey for a few years, I used to have endless questions – I challenged everything, debated for hours. Mishra ji never lost patience. Even after 4 hours of intense discussion, he remained calm.

In contrast, in professional meetings, if someone repeated a point twice, my impatience would spring up like a cobra. Mishra ji's patience reminded me of a saint – or perhaps a wise grandmother who never flinches even when the children seem to bring the sky down to earth.'

Manish chuckled. 'Parenthood is the greatest patience teacher – you don't need self-help books when you have toddlers.'

Vaibhavi laughed, adding, 'And of course, a nagging or stubborn spouse can also sharpen your patience skills faster than any corporate workshop!'

Keshav concluded, 'As St. Babuji beautifully writes in *Complete Works of Ram Chandra, Vol. 3*: '*It is good to be tormented. Home is the school for tolerance and endurance. Patience in such things is considered to be penance – and is superior to other kinds of penances.*"

Vaibhavi smiled gratefully. 'Thank you, Uncle. That helps. I also understand it in this way – Patience is like Indian traffic – everyone complains, yet it's the only way you'll eventually get home.'

Key Takeaways

1. **Patience is not passive** – it is active endurance, a conscious choice in difficult situations.
2. **Real-life tests of patience come in many forms**: colleagues, children, spouses – or even pythons!
3. **Patience is not weakness; it is inner strength**, and often the quietest form of courage.

'Patience is bitter, but its fruit is sweet.' – **Aristotle**

'Adopt the pace of nature: her secret is patience.'

– **Ralph Waldo Emerson**

'Patience is not the ability to wait, but the ability to keep a good attitude while waiting.' – **Joyce Meyer**

Scoring Guide

This scale for 'Patience' focuses on your ability to tolerate delays, challenges, or annoyances without becoming agitated or frustrated.

Score 0: Zero Tolerance for Delays/Frustration

You have **very little to no tolerance for delays, inconveniences, or obstacles.**

You frequently become agitated, irritable, or angry when things don't happen immediately or as planned.

You often interrupt others, rush tasks, or make impulsive decisions to avoid waiting.

Small frustrations easily derail your mood and productivity.

Score 1: Easily Annoyed, Frequent Impatience

You are **easily annoyed by delays or minor setbacks,** and impatience is a frequent emotional state for you.

You often sigh, fidget, or express frustration verbally when things aren't moving fast enough.

While you might not explode, you often feel simmering resentment or irritation when challenged.

You struggle significantly with waiting in lines, traffic, or for processes to unfold naturally.

Score 2: Fluctuating Patience

You have moments where you can be patient, but your **patience often wears thin under stress or prolonged waits.**

You might start calm but quickly become agitated if a situation extends beyond your comfort zone.

You are aware of your impatience but find it difficult to control your reactions consistently.

You might show patience in some areas of your life, but none in others.

Score 3: Growing Patience and Awareness

You are increasingly able to **tolerate delays and challenges without significant distress.**

You recognize when your patience is being tested and can often choose a calmer response.

You understand the value of waiting and allowing processes to unfold naturally.

You're actively practising techniques to improve your patience, like deep breathing or reframing thoughts.

Score 4: Consistent Patience and Resilience

You consistently **demonstrate patience in most situations**, even those that are inherently challenging or frustrating.

You can maintain a calm demeanour and a clear mind when faced with delays, obstacles, or difficult people.

You approach life with a more relaxed and resilient attitude, less prone to agitation.

You understand that good things often take time and are comfortable with the process.

Score 5: Embodied Serenity and Deep Patience

You embody a profound sense of **serenity and unshakeable patience** that allows you to navigate life's inevitable delays and difficulties with grace.

You rarely feel agitated or frustrated, approaching all situations with a calm and understanding presence.

You see waiting or obstacles as natural parts of life's flow, often finding peace or even opportunities for reflection within them.

Your deep patience serves as a source of strength and wisdom, influencing your interactions and decisions positively.

Reflection Prompts

1. How does impatience affect your decision-making, your relationships, or your overall stress levels?
2. What is one small practice you could adopt daily to cultivate more patience (e.g., deep breaths before responding, mindful waiting)?

13. Forgiveness: The Case of Arjun and the Three Ancient Schemes

It began almost comically. Keshav's friend Arjun – a man so simple-hearted he could lend you his umbrella and then stand in the rain, smiling – suddenly found himself at the center of a malicious plot. The conspirators? None other than a strange, imaginary trio plucked from history's darker corners: **Shurpanakha**, Ravana's fiery-tempered sister with a taste for drama; **Manthara**, the bent-backed maid whose whispers once exiled Lord Rama; and **Shakuni**, the master manipulator of the Mahabharata whose dice seemed loaded by destiny itself.

It was an odd evening in Keshav's dream – one of those rare, vivid ones that feel uncomfortably real. There, seated on 3 low stools under a dim lamp, were none other than **Shurpanakha, Manthara,** and **Shakuni** – a legendary trio whose collective résumé included derailing kingdoms, breaking families, and generally stirring the pot wherever possible.

This was no reunion for nostalgia's sake. They were on a fresh mission: dismantling the life of Arjun, Keshav's gentle, trusting friend. In this whimsical 'meeting of the minds,' they decided to turn their talents toward Arjun. Not because he had wronged them, but because – as they might say – *it is simply in our nature*.

The plotting began.

Shurpanakha tapped her long nails on the table. 'First, we attack the mind – make him doubt himself.'

Manthara snorted. 'That's child's play. I've been doing that since Ayodhya was still just a postal pin code.'

Shakuni, rolling his dice lazily, grinned. 'You two think small. I'll make sure even his friends suspect him. Suspicion spreads faster than the flu.'

Shurpanakha raised an eyebrow. 'And what if he fights back?'

Shakuni chuckled. 'Then we'll tell everyone that *that* proves he's guilty. Works every time.'

They laughed in the way only professional mischief-makers can – half in glee, half in anticipation.

And so, whispers became rumours, and rumours took the shape of 'facts,' and Arjun's spotless reputation was dragged through a mire of invented faults.

At first, Arjun laughed it off. But laughter metamorphosed into unease. Unease became sleeplessness. And soon, sleeplessness became a slow erosion of his peace.

The year that followed could be read like a weathered almanac.

- **Spring** brought the first sting – budding distrust in old friends.
- **Summer** burning with the heat of resentment, each imagined revenge scenario like a thunderstorm building on the horizon.
- **Autumn** carried a bittersweet chill; Arjun's health waned, appetite dulled, and joy slipped away like leaves from a tree.
- **Winter** was the coldest – long nights, heavy thoughts, and the frost of loneliness even in crowded rooms.

During this time, Keshav watched quietly, knowing no amount of 'practical advice' could uncoil the knot in Arjun's heart.

And then, one evening, Arjun read 3 lines that shifted everything:

'If you return evil for evil, you simply multiply it. Only love can dissolve it.'

'Forgiveness is not about the other person deserving it – it's about freeing yourself. Forgiveness frees the forgiver first.'

It dawned on him: expecting Shurpanakha to act without temper, or Manthara without gossip, or Shakuni without manipulation was like expecting the sea to have no waves. They had acted as per their nature. His suffering was his choice – one he could now unchoose.

When Arjun forgave them – not as a grand moral victory, but as a quiet release – the seasons in his mind shifted. It was spring again.

Had he chosen revenge, he might have won small skirmishes but lost the war within, feeding the very bitterness that had wounded him. Instead, by forgiving, he reclaimed his health, his peace, and his life. Forgiveness did not make him weaker – it made him untouchable.

Forgiveness is not a favour we do for the offender; it's a health plan for our own heart. The mind cannot heal while it's running a courtroom 24/7. When we accept that some people are merely playing their roles, we stop auditioning for theirs. In letting go and forgiving them, we don't change their nature – we reclaim our peace.

Epilogue: The Contrast

Months later, under that same dim lamp in Keshav's dream, the 3 villains were at it again – plotting against some new unfortunate soul. Their laughter was still sharp, their schemes just as venomous.

Meanwhile, in the waking world, Arjun was sitting in his garden, sipping ginger tea while the morning sun warmed his face. The air was fresh, the birds were chatty, and the only plotting he was doing involved which flower bed to water first.

The villains hadn't changed. But Arjun had – and that made all the difference.

Key Takeaway

1. **Forgiveness is freedom.** It releases us from the heavy burden of resentment and bitterness.

2. **People act according to their nature.** Expecting Shakuni not to manipulate, or Manthara not to gossip, is like expecting the sea to have no waves.
3. **Revenge multiplies pain; forgiveness dissolves it.** By letting go, we reclaim peace instead of feeding bitterness.
4. **Forgiveness is not approval.** It doesn't mean the offender was right; it means we refuse to let their actions dictate our inner state.
5. **Forgiveness strengthens.** It transforms us from victims of circumstance to masters of our peace.

'To err is human, to forgive divine.' – **Alexander Pope**

'Forgive others, not because they deserve forgiveness, but because you deserve peace.' – **Jonathan Lockwood Huie**

'Forgiveness is not forgetting. It's letting go of the hurt.' – **Mary McCarthy**

Scoring Guide

This scale encompasses forgiving others, forgiving oneself, and letting go of resentment. When assessing yourself, consider how long you hold onto hurt or anger, how easily you let go of past hurts, and your ability to extend compassion to those who have caused you pain (including yourself).

Score 0: Deep-Seated Resentment and Inability to Forgive

You hold onto **grudges and resentment indefinitely**, often replaying past hurts in your mind.

You find it extremely difficult, if not impossible, to let go of anger towards those who have wronged you (or yourself).

You may actively seek to punish or see suffering for those who hurt you.

The pain of past events continues to dominate your thoughts and feelings.

Score 1: Occasional Attempts, but Predominantly Unforgiving

You might occasionally *think* about forgiving, but you frequently **struggle to actually release resentment**.

You tend to revisit old wounds, and negative feelings often resurface, even after a long time.

You might forgive small transgressions but hold onto major ones firmly.

Forgiving yourself for mistakes is also a significant challenge.

Score 2: Conditional Forgiveness, Often with Lingering Bitterness

You can sometimes **forgive others (or yourself) under certain conditions**, but there's often lingering bitterness, distrust, or a 'but...' attached.

You might outwardly say you've forgiven, but internally, you still harbour resentment or a desire for the other person to suffer.

It takes you a very long time to move past offences, and full emotional release is rare.

You might hold onto past events as reasons to avoid future vulnerability.

Score 3: Growing Capacity for Forgiveness

You are increasingly able to **identify, process, and release resentment**, even for significant hurts.

You understand that forgiveness is for your own well-being and actively work towards it.

You might still feel pain, but you're able to prevent it from consuming you.

You're making progress in forgiving yourself for past mistakes and imperfections.

Score 4: Consistent Practice of Forgiveness

You consistently **practice forgiveness** in your life, both towards others and yourself.

You're able to release resentment and anger relatively quickly, preventing it from festering.

You understand that forgiveness doesn't mean condoning behaviour, but rather freeing yourself from the emotional burden.

You approach conflicts with a mindset that seeks resolution and healing rather than holding onto blame.

Score 5: Embodied Forgiveness and Release

You embody a profound and **unconditional sense of forgiveness** that allows you to move through life free from the burden of past grievances.

You approach mistakes (yours and others') with compassion and understanding, seeing them as opportunities for learning and growth.

Resentment rarely takes root within you, and you can quickly find peace and acceptance.

This level of forgiveness allows for deep inner peace, empathy, and healthy relationships.

Reflection Prompts

1. What impact does holding onto unforgiveness have on your inner peace and your relationships?
2. What would it take for you to begin the process of forgiving a lingering hurt?

14. Procrastination

The young friends of Keshav from the Bay Area of Silicon Valley had set up a weekly Saturday morning routine for discussions, ever since Keshav had returned to his hometown, Hyderabad. The usual group, and sometimes a few of Keshav's other friends, joined the video calls.

In one such session, Yash admitted to his tendency to procrastinate and requested Keshav's guidance to overcome it.

A friend of Keshav, Sai, happened to be visiting him. Keshav looked at Sai and said to the group, 'Sai has a powerful story on this very subject.'

Sai began, 'I met Richa, a school teacher in her early-30s, around 25 years ago. She was a colleague of my wife and was unmarried. Richa lived with her mother, her *Chacha* (father's brother), her *Bua* (father's sister), and her elder brother's family. Her brother was married with 2 children. Her mother, also a retired school teacher, had been widowed a few years earlier.

They all lived together in a sprawling 7-acre farmhouse, inherited from Richa's maternal grandfather – a senior bureaucrat who had passed away a decade earlier. The farmhouse was beautiful, dotted with trees and plants, and located in a prime area.

In time, Richa's *Mausi* (mother's sister) – a co-owner of the property – proposed selling it. Eventually, the family agreed, and the property fetched a handsome price. Richa's mother received half the share. They moved into a rented flat, intending to purchase a good property soon.

But here came the twist. Having seen luxury in childhood with her affluent father, Richa's mother's suppressed desires resurfaced. With newfound money, she indulged in frequent visits to 5-star hotels. Property decisions were postponed again and again. She rejected good options, comparing each to the farmhouse they once had. She was searching for a Taj. Ironically, she visited the Taj Hotel so often she could have bought a room there.

'Initially, they had enough money to buy 3 flats in a prime area – ample security for the family's future. But with each year of delay, as property prices rose and money was spent, their capacity shrank: from 3 flats, to 2, to 1. Still, Richa's mother insisted, 'What's the hurry?' diverting conversations to theatre performances or hotel dinners.

As years passed, both her *Chacha* and *Bua* died. Eventually, Richa's brother persuaded their mother to invest the remaining money in his business venture. It failed disastrously, and soon all the ancestral wealth was gone.

Tragedy struck harder: Richa's brother passed away, and her mother, unable to bear the shock, died within 2 months. The family, once comfortably placed, was reduced to uncertainty and grief. Richa spiralled into depression, her performance at school deteriorated, and despite her employer's patience, she eventually stopped attending altogether. Relatives drifted away, and even social friends vanished.

One day, Richa disappeared from her home. Later, it emerged that she had been taken to an NGO, where she slowly recovered. 5 years later, I saw a video on social media – Richa, smiling faintly, now working at that NGO, helping with office work and caring for others. In serving again, she had found healing.'

Yash asked, 'Uncle, why did the family keep delaying such obvious financial decisions? What was the core reason?'

Keshav replied, 'I can see the following reasons:

- The filter of disproportionate desires clogged decision-making.
- Living in the past, chasing lost pleasures.
- Avoiding the hard work of searching and finalising a property.
- Comparing every option to the farmhouse, rejecting even good ones.
- Preferring activities that temporarily made them 'feel rich.'
- Most importantly, procrastination had become their norm – 'What's the hurry?"

Keshav added, '*Procrastination is like credit cards – fun until the bill arrives.* I feel that one needs to find a way to finish important assignments ahead of time, introspect on this tendency, and create own process to overcome it. I am sure even your relationships must sometimes feel the effect of this habit.'

At this, Vaibhavi burst out laughing – perhaps remembering Yash's habit of replying to messages only after they had expired like milk cartons. In his defence, Yash called it 'marinating thoughts before replying.'

The group called it 'ghosting with grace.'

Key Takeaways

1. **Procrastination is not just delay – it is silent erosion.**
2. Small postponements may compound into life-changing consequences.
3. Living in the past blocks wise choices in the present.
4. Unchecked desires can hijack decision-making.
5. Overcoming procrastination requires awareness, process, and discipline.

'Procrastination is opportunity's assassin.' – **Victor Kiam**
'Procrastination is the thief of time.' – **Edward Young**
'You may delay, but time will not.' – **Benjamin Franklin**

Scoring Guide

When assessing yourself, consider the **frequency, impact, and types of tasks** you tend to postpone. Think about how often you delay work, how much stress it causes you, and whether it affects important aspects of your life.

Score 0: Overwhelming, Debilitating Procrastination

You are almost constantly postponing important tasks, often to the point of severe negative consequences (missed deadlines, poor performance, relationship issues, significant stress). You find it nearly impossible to start or complete tasks, even those that are urgent or simple, feeling paralysed by the thought of them. Your life is frequently in a state of chaos due to unaddressed responsibilities.

Score 1: Severe, Frequent Procrastination

You frequently put off important tasks, leading to regular last-minute rushes, increased stress, and sometimes missed opportunities or suboptimal results. You often feel overwhelmed by your to-do list and struggle significantly with initiating work, even when you know the benefits of getting it done. This significantly impacts your productivity and peace of mind.

Score 2: Moderate, Noticeable Procrastination

You experience noticeable procrastination periodically, especially with tasks you find unpleasant, difficult, or non-urgent. While you usually get things done eventually, you often experience mild to moderate stress from pushing tasks to the last minute. You might spend a fair amount of time avoiding tasks or getting easily distracted.

Score 3: Mild, Occasional Procrastination

You experience mild, fleeting moments of procrastination from time to time, usually with small, less critical tasks or when you're feeling particularly unmotivated. These instances are manageable, don't typically lead to significant negative consequences, and you are generally able to get back on track relatively quickly.

Score 4: Rare, Brief Procrastination

You very rarely procrastinate on important tasks. When you do, it's a brief and quickly overcome impulse. You are generally proactive and organized, preferring to tackle tasks well in advance. You might occasionally delay a very minor or non-essential item, but it doesn't cause stress or impact your productivity.

Score 5: Minimal or Absent Procrastination

You rarely procrastinate. You are highly proactive, organized, and disciplined, consistently tackling tasks promptly and efficiently. You derive satisfaction from completing work ahead of schedule and manage your time effectively, rarely experiencing the stress associated with delaying responsibilities. You maintain a strong sense of control over your workload.

Reflection Prompts

1. Does delaying your work consistently spoil your relationships: at home and at Office?
2. What kind of tasks or decisions do you most frequently not do on time? What feelings arise when you think about these tasks?
3. How does your procrastination impact those who depend on you, your own stress levels, productivity, and overall sense of accomplishment?

15. Adaptability and Flexibility

Damini was confused – rattled, perhaps – and it was difficult to say which. Damini had always been one of the brightest in her group. Sensitive, intelligent, and beautiful, she had grown into a sensible young woman who excelled both academically and professionally. After completing her engineering degree from one of Delhi's top colleges, she joined a leading US-headquartered investment banking firm, where she quickly made her mark. Work soon took her to Bengaluru.

Bengaluru, often called the Silicon Valley of India, has become home to the Indian headquarters of nearly every major global tech company. It was also the nation's startup capital, where billions of dollars flowed in each year. Stories of 20- and 30-somethings turning into millionaires – or even billionaires – were no longer breaking news; they had become routine. Slowly but surely, the city of dreams for ambitious youth was shifting from Mumbai, the financial hub, to Bengaluru.

It wasn't long before Damini, too, felt the pull of the startup world. But unlike many who jumped headfirst into the frenzy, she was cautious by nature and believed in calculated risks. Instead of launching her own venture immediately, she chose to join a mature startup.

All looked fine and great on paper, but in a world where 'fail fast, fail cheap' was more like a *Gayatri Mantra* chanted daily by youngsters, paper-perfect plans were bound to crumble. Damini discovered this truth much earlier than she expected.

One fine morning – or late at night, depending on one's age and mental makeup – around 3 a.m., Damini was startled by her flatmate Sneha's shouts of joy. Sneha was practically bouncing with excitement, as if she had just won the lottery. In a sense, she had. Breathless, she announced she had received a $5 million term sheet from a leading venture capital firm. It was a moment worth celebrating, and soon their friends were called over.

For Bengaluru's young dreamers, 3 a.m. was not too late for a party – especially when the next day was work-from-home. They danced and laughed until sunrise. And, of course, in startup circles, sunrise was not just the time of day but also a vague deadline for sending 'deck_v5-final-final-revised.pptx.'

Damini was genuinely excited for her friend. Both had brainstormed the idea just weeks back, and Damini, with her exposure to large corporates as well as startup culture, had helped her friend in a meaningful way. She had refined the pitch, moving it from DOA (dead on arrival) mode to 'getting a meeting' format. So, it would not have been unfair to say that without Damini, the whole idea didn't have a chance. Yet amid the excitement, a faint unease crept into her mind.

She pushed it aside for the moment and went to pack, as she was leaving for Hyderabad, her hometown. As luck would have it, her favourite uncle Keshav was coming that very week too.

In the rush of packing, taxi, and boarding her flight, she had no time to think. Bengaluru traffic – though often criticized by outsiders – is in fact a perfect meditation ground. It allows no thought other than traffic to enter the mind, ensuring travellers remain perfectly in the moment and fully focused on the vehicles around them. In fact, the city might patent it as the cheapest meditation program in the world – no app subscription required, just a scooter honking in your ear. But as the plane took off and she finally had a moment of stillness, the questions she had been suppressing came rushing back.

Is she wasting her life by moving too slowly? Should she launch her own startup? Why was she still in this job? What did she truly want to do? All these questions started staring at her once she settled into her flight. *What am I doing? Why am I doing it? What is the plan?*

Where am I going? Eternal questions with no easy answers – and ones that have changed the path of many individuals, and perhaps mankind itself – kept bothering Damini.

The ride home was smooth and hassle-free, thanks to the superior infrastructure Hyderabad had built. Her parents were excited to see her, and her mother had cooked her favourite food. Dinner was the usual affair – her parents asking about her job and routine, while she told them about her friends, Sneha's startup, its term sheet, and valuation. While all of that was interesting and mind-boggling, it was a little beyond her parents' grasp of the world. They were less interested in valuation numbers and more concerned about her personal and professional path. Her mother, as usual, dropped subtle hints about settling down and finding a suitable groom, and that – as usual – irritated Damini. This time, however, the irritation ran deeper. *Here, the world is changing, my friend is on the path to build a unicorn, and my parents are busy matchmaking,* Damini muttered to herself, visibly annoyed. Her father noticed and gently steered the conversation back to routine matters.

Post-dinner, as father and daughter sat in the balcony, Damini came out with all her lingering questions. Her father listened calmly and thought of giving advice, but paused. Years of parenting had taught him that unsolicited advice travels at the speed of light – and bounces back even faster, and parents' advice is often dismissed as 'yada yada' by their own children; better to seek counsel from others – since a prophet is seldom honoured in his own land. And yes, Keshav was coming tomorrow. He asked Damini to discuss her doubts with Keshav.

Damini, though fond of her uncle Keshav and often sharing her problems with him, was not so sure this time. She wondered aloud if Keshav would be the right person to discuss startups and VC ideas. Her father said, 'Just chat with him and see how it goes. Anyway, in the end, you must follow your own instincts.' That seemed like a fair proposition, so Damini agreed – little realizing the grilling that awaited her.

'So why do you want to start up? And what is the big idea?' Keshav asked, smiling calmly.

'Well, the monetary rewards are huge, and I can drive it at my own pace. I need not suffer my slow and dumb colleague or that irritating boss. In fact, it was I who validated Sneha's idea – so why shouldn't I start? I am more capable. If Sneha can get $5 million, why can't I? And then there are the advantages of freedom, being my own boss, and not working according to others' wishes. I get a dozen ideas a day – so I need to start ASAP.'

'Is that so?' Keshav asked. 'Being your own boss, independence, freedom – all are good. But won't you still be answerable to investors, customers, employees, and suppliers? And how will you hire the smartest people you want to work with?'

The company where she worked was a successful startup, poised for IPO listing, having raised more than $100 million so far and on track for profitability – a state rarer than the dodo. Yet despite being led by dynamic and respected founders, hiring was a huge challenge. There was chaos all the time, and every day felt like being thrown from frying pan to volcano – or to the deep sea, depending on which scenario you hated more. If HR ever wrote a survival guide, it would have read: 'Welcome to the jungle. Helmets optional.' While these situations were exciting and full of learning, they also created enormous stress. *If they are struggling to hire, how will I?* she thought. *And if my company bends backwards to accommodate unreasonable client expectations, then freedom and independence – well, not so much. And as for huge monetary rewards – the founders have been at this for 18 years and are yet to make big moolah.*

Damini searched for the right hooks to answer, but found none. Keshav repeated his question:

'What is the big idea you want to work on? What is the itch you want to solve? Another D2C brand? Another coffee shop? Another gifting idea? Another fintech?'

The truth was, Damini had not spent more than a few hours – let alone weeks or months – on any 1 idea.

Seeing the confusion on Damini's face, Keshav spoke softly yet firmly, calmness in his tone:

'Startups are exciting and game-changing, yes. But do you think it's wise to do something just because your friends are doing it and finding success? Their success and failure are their life, their earnings, and their karma. *One needs to live one's own life – don't live somebody else's dream*, as Steve Jobs famously said.

The truth is, probably you are not fully ready for a startup. That doesn't mean you'll never be ready. You'll be ready the day you find your own itch – the one that keeps you awake at night, drives you crazy, and refuses to let you go. Startups may look exciting from the outside, but inside, they are much harder work, with many lonely nights. In the words of Rudyard Kipling, *And so hold on when there is nothing in you / Except the Will which says to them: 'Hold on!'*

So if you act only out of envy at someone else's success, that's fine – envy can push you to improve. But if it turns into comparison or jealousy, it will create frustration and unhappiness. Then it won't be your idea, your itch – it will be driven by shiny objects outside you.'

Almost as if reading her mind, Keshav added:

'You need to realize that we all have a few purposes in life – and that purpose can be anything. It can be as simple as raising a family, as tough as scaling a mountain, or as ordinary as living in peace. There is nothing truly great or mundane – it is the purpose that chooses us most of the time. We need to find it ourselves, not chase mirages in the desert. Be calm, reflect on your strengths and weaknesses, and remember: timing is everything. Then take the call your heart agrees with. Listen to your heart, and you'll be on the right path.'

Damini, who had come with scepticism, now felt a sense of calm. She hugged him and said, 'Uncle, I know – that's why you are my favourite. You always help me gain clarity. But this isn't my only query – I'll be back with more.'

Keshav laughed and said warmly, 'Damini, you've shown a very positive quality of adaptability and flexibility in your outlook. I am so proud of you.'

And somewhere, Bengaluru traffic smiled – it had taught her patience all along.

Key Takeaways

1. Adaptability means openness to change without losing oneself.
2. True flexibility is adjusting to one's own truth, not imitating others' journeys.
3. Envy may push us forward, but comparison locks us in frustration.
4. Clarity emerges when we pause, reflect, and realign.
5. The right path is not copied; it arises from our own 'itch' or calling.

'It is not the strongest of the species that survives, nor the most intelligent. It is the one most adaptable to change.' – **Charles Darwin**

'Flexibility makes buildings stronger, imagine what it can do to your soul.' – **Carlos Barrios**

'Blessed are the flexible, for they shall not be bent out of shape.' – **Anonymous proverb**

Scoring Guide

Read the descriptions for each score and choose the one that best reflects your typical behaviour and mindset.

Score 0: Resistant to Change

You strongly prefer established routines and ways of doing things.

New ideas, unexpected changes, or shifts in plans cause significant stress or frustration.

You often voice opposition to changes, even minor ones.

You find it very difficult to switch tasks, priorities, or approaches once you've started in a particular direction.

You might feel overwhelmed or shut down when faced with ambiguity or uncertainty.

Score 1: Struggles with Change

You recognize that change is necessary, but you often struggle to adjust.

You may experience discomfort or anxiety when faced with new situations, but you eventually comply, often with some grumbling.

You prefer clear instructions and established processes, finding it hard to navigate situations without them.

It takes you a considerable amount of time and effort to accept and integrate new information or methods.

You might stick to less efficient methods simply because they are familiar.

Score 2: Tolerates Change, but Slowly

You can tolerate change, but you need time to process and adjust.

You might feel a bit uncomfortable initially, but you can eventually get on board if given clear reasons and support.

You can adapt to new circumstances, but it often requires explicit guidance or a step-by-step approach.

You generally follow new procedures or adopt new tools, but you might not fully embrace them or see their potential benefits quickly.

You are capable of shifting priorities when necessary, but it can disrupt your flow and require significant mental effort.

Score 3: Adapts Reasonably Well

You generally accept change as a normal part of work or life.

You can adjust your plans and actions when new information or circumstances arise.

You are open to trying new methods or approaches, especially when you understand the rationale behind them.

You can shift focus between different tasks or priorities without excessive difficulty, though you might prefer to complete one thing before moving to another.

You are able to function effectively even when there's some level of uncertainty or ambiguity.

Score 4: Adapts Proactively and Embraces Novelty

You not only accept change but often see it as an opportunity for improvement or learning.

You proactively seek out new information, methods, or perspectives to improve your work or approach challenges.

You are comfortable with ambiguity and can make decisions or move forward even when all information isn't available.

You can smoothly transition between tasks, priorities, and roles as needed, maintaining productivity.

You might even anticipate future changes and prepare for them in advance. You are a positive influence during times of change for others.

Score 5: Highly Agile and Inspires Adaptability

You thrive in dynamic, fast-paced, and uncertain environments.

You are a natural problem-solver who creatively adjusts strategies and plans when faced with obstacles or new information.

You actively seek out opportunities for innovation and are excited by new challenges and unforeseen circumstances.

You effortlessly pivot between multiple priorities and projects, maintaining high performance and focus.

You inspire and help others navigate change, serving as a role model for adaptability and resilience. You see setbacks as valuable learning experiences.

Reflection Prompts

1. When has your inability to adapt caused you stress or missed opportunities or drift in your relations?
2. What is one area in your life where being more flexible could significantly reduce your stress or improve an outcome?

16. Comparing Yourself with Others

Damini invited Keshav for a discussion and also roped in Vaibhavi and her friends over a video call. The topic was – *'Comparing yourself with others.'*

The session began on a serious note. The group touched upon global turmoil – the weaponization of trade and the impact of AI on the job market. But soon, it zoomed into the everyday battlefield: office politics and personal comparisons.

Damini was having an interesting time at her office, and she shared it, 'One of my colleagues spends half his energy comparing his work with mine. In meetings, he makes it a point to highlight how he is 'different' or 'better.' Honestly, his reputation is nose-diving faster than my mobile internet connection on a rainy day.'

Everyone laughed, but the point was clear.

Vaibhavi joined in:

'It's everywhere. Some openly compare, while the majority are skilled at hiding the comparisons going on in their heads. Like secret accountants, constantly auditing their lives against someone else's balance sheet. It appears that comparisons are like social media filters – designed to make someone else look better while you feel worse.'

Keshav, smiling:

'Have you ever considered **why this 'program of comparison' was designed by the Creator**?'

Yash, with curiosity:

'Maybe… to know where we stand as compared to others?'

Sumit nodded:

'True, but it has a flip side as well. When comparison makes us feel superior, we glow. When it makes us feel inferior, we sink. Either way, we are riding an emotional seesaw.'

Keshav added, '**Comparison combined with the Ego due to success may become a lethal combination**.'

Vaibhavi added, 'It can easily slide into jealousy. My father often told me about his maternal uncle, who spent his entire life comparing his children with others. He would always find faults, always highlight gaps in other children. In the end, even his own children and grandchildren distanced themselves from him. They got tired of the never-ending scorecard.'

Sumit chuckled:

'Sounds familiar! My uncle was the same. He could have made a career as a professional comparer. Maybe he missed his true calling. In another timeline, he'd be the CEO of CompareBazaar.com.'

'My aunt always tormented her daughter – 'Why second? Why not first? Why don't you dress like your friend?' It was like a lifelong subscription to the 'Why Not Channel."

The group turned to Keshav for clarity.

Keshav said calmly:

'Comparison was not meant to be an external yardstick. It was meant as an internal compass. We are supposed to compare '*our today*' with '*our yesterday*'. Are we better in skill, in conduct, in compassion, etc., than we were before? That was the original design.'

He paused, then added with a twinkle:

'But humans cleverly outsourced this feature. Instead of asking 'Am I better than yesterday?' they ask, 'Am I better than my neighbour with the BMW?"

Yash laughed:

'I've seen it in India and here too. People ask – 'Where do you stay? Which car do you drive?' It's like your zip code and car brand decide your worth.'

Damini nodded:

'In social circles, I've noticed people judging based on the brand of purse – Hermes, Chanel, Dior, Bulgari, Louis Vuitton, Valentino, Gucci … It's as if happiness comes with a price tag and authenticity card.'

Keshav concluded:

'The source of happiness should never be dictated by possessions or comparisons. If that's the case, our happiness will always be fragile. A truly happy person is one who remains happy under all circumstances. Comparison should only be applied inward – on ourselves.'

Key Takeaways

1. **Comparison as a tool** – Designed for self-growth, not for competing with others.

2. **External comparison breeds negativity** – Jealousy, insecurity, and fragile happiness.
3. **Internal comparison builds resilience** – When we measure progress against our own past self, growth becomes natural.
4. **Fragility of possessions** – Material comparisons may give fleeting joy but never lasting peace.
5. **True success** – Being consistently happy regardless of circumstances.

'Comparison is the thief of joy.' – **Theodore Roosevelt**
'Be yourself; everyone else is already taken.' – **Oscar Wilde**
'Happiness is found when you stop comparing yourself to others.'
– **Anonymous**

Scoring Guide

This guide assesses your internal experience of **comparison**, specifically your tendency to measure your own worth, progress, or happiness against that of others. This is not about the analytical skill of comparing 2 external things, but about the emotional and psychological habit of comparing your life to someone else's. The scores reflect a progression from being consumed by negative comparison to developing a sense of inner peace and self-acceptance.

Score 0: Consumed by Comparison

You constantly compare yourself to others in nearly every area of your life – career, relationships, appearance, and possessions.

This habit often leads to feelings of inadequacy, jealousy, or resentment. You feel 'less than' others and are rarely satisfied with your own life.

Your self-worth is highly dependent on how you perceive yourself relative to others, leading to a fragile sense of self.

You find yourself celebrating the failures of others or feeling threatened by their success.

Score 1: Frequent and Painful Comparison

You often compare yourself to others, especially in areas you feel insecure about.

While you have moments of feeling good about yourself, they are quickly overshadowed when you see someone who appears to be 'doing better.'

This cycle of comparison causes frequent anxiety and self-doubt. You might feel a need to prove yourself to others.

You are aware of this habit but struggle to stop it, finding it difficult to simply be content with your own path.

Score 2: Fluctuating Comparison

You still compare yourself to others, but it's not a constant state. You have periods where you can focus on your own journey.

When you do compare, you might feel a pang of inadequacy or envy, but you can usually recognize the feeling and move past it without it consuming you.

You are starting to understand that social media and external appearances don't tell the full story.

You can sometimes celebrate others' successes without feeling threatened, but it requires effort.

Score 3: Increasing Self-Focus

You are actively working on the habit of comparison and are making progress.

When a thought of comparison arises, you can identify it and consciously shift your focus back to your own goals and progress.

You understand that everyone's journey is unique and that your value is not tied to someone else's achievements.

You are building a stronger sense of self-worth that comes from within, rather than from external validation.

Score 4: Consistent Self-Acceptance

You rarely compare your life to others. Your focus is firmly on your own path, growth, and personal goals.

When you see others succeed, you can genuinely feel happy for them without it impacting your own sense of worth.

You are comfortable with your own strengths and weaknesses. You understand that your journey is your own, and you are running your own race.

This mindset leads to a more peaceful and stable sense of happiness and contentment.

Score 5: Profound Inner Peace

The habit of comparison has largely dissolved. It no longer holds any power over you.

Your sense of self-worth is deep and unshakable, completely independent of external factors or the achievements of others.

You feel a genuine connection with others' successes, seeing them as inspiration rather than a threat.

Your mind is free from the noise of 'keeping up,' allowing you to fully enjoy your own life and pursue your passions with a quiet, confident resolve.

Reflection Prompts

1. In what area of your life (e.g., career, finances, relationships) are you most likely to compare yourself to others? Why do you think that is?
2. Can you think of a time when someone else's success inspired you instead of making you feel bad? What was different about that situation?
3. When did the comparison last drain you?

17. Ego

Damini's director, Digvijay, sat 2 levels above her in the hierarchy. In a team meeting, he snapped, *'I know better than anyone in the industry. Don't waste my time – just do as I say.'* Damini couldn't help thinking that he truly lived up to his name: *Digvijay* – 'the conqueror of worlds.'

She was shocked that such words came from a senior professional trained at premier institutes. For 2 days, she replayed the moment in her mind, trying to decode the roots of such ego. Quietly, she made a note to herself: *When I reach the Director's chair, this is exactly what not to do.*

Curious to understand ego better, Damini organized a meet-up at Keshav uncle's place – some joining in person, others online, including Vaibhavi and her friends. Keshav, ever the connector, invited a couple of his old friends to enrich the discussion.

Damini narrated the office incident and turned to her sister and friends, *'Have you too come across such arrogant behaviour from colleagues?'*

Vaibhavi chipped in, *'Yes. I've met some IT professionals who behave as if they're God's special gift to humanity – knowing it all, and assuming that you don't.'*

Yash added, *'But then we also know people like Sachin Tendulkar. Despite being hailed as one of the greatest batsmen ever, he always spoke with humility. At the same time, I also meet colleagues who act like they're better than everyone else. I guess that's part of life.'*

Damini turned to Keshav uncle: *'Uncle, tell us – what really is ego?'*

Keshav reminded them, *'Do you recall our earlier conversation on acceptance, when we spoke about the creation of the soul and its purpose?'*

Vaibhavi opened her notebook: *'Yes. You had explained that for human experience, consciousness was packed into the astral body – made of ego (sense of separate identity), mind, and intellect – and then fitted with the sense organs in the gross body.'*

Keshav smiled, *'Excellent, Vaibhavi. As Daaji explains in Spiritual Anatomy, ego exists on a spectrum – arrogance, pride, confidence, presence, and humility. Based on my understanding, here's how it looks in real life.'*

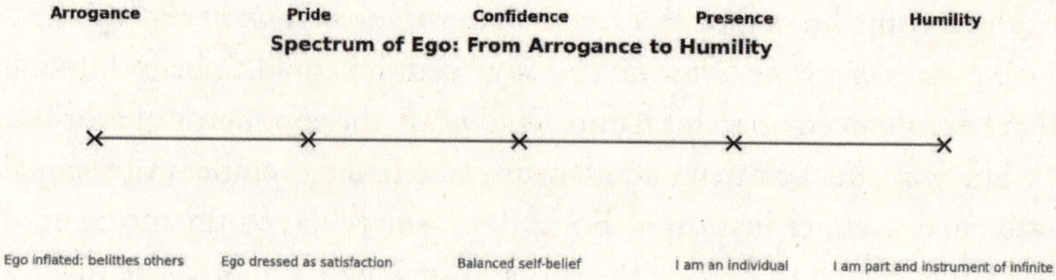

Examples:

1. **Arrogance**: Digvijay's statement in Damini's office is a textbook case.
2. **Pride**: A student tops the university exams and proudly says, *'My hard work paid off.'* Pride celebrates achievement, but if clung to, it can quietly morph into arrogance.
3. **Confidence**: Cricketer Ravindra Jadeja walks onto the pitch, calm and steady, telling himself, *'I've practised well; I can handle today's challenge.'* Here, Confidence is rooted in self-belief without needing to prove superiority.
4. **Presence**: *'My name is Ravindra Jadeja, and I play as an all-rounder in the Indian cricket team.'* It is a simple statement of fact, and in this regard, St. Babuji once said, *'Without ego – awareness of separate identity – we would be like vegetables.'*
5. **Humility**: Sachin Tendulkar, after winning the World Cup, said, *'This is because of team effort, support staff, and the wishes of 130 crore Indians.'* Humility safeguards us from pride and vanity.

Keshav continued, *'As Daaji says, 'ego often identifies with collectives: national pride, religious pride, even spiritual pride. You may think your country is the best – fair enough. But if you conclude that others are inferior, your ego has crossed the line."*

Yash asked, *'Isn't it natural to feel happy over success?'*

Keshav smiled, *'Of course. But remember, as long as the ego is present, we feel elated when praised and hurt when criticised. Ego fuels our progress, but it can also cause our downfall. Imagine Ravindra Jadeja scoring a century. His ego is thrilled. But if he starts gloating, feeling superior to teammates, the imbalance begins. The ego loves pampering and attention, especially from those we respect. If unchecked, it grows into arrogance.'*

Vaibhavi leaned forward, '*So what's the right mix of ego?*'

Keshav replied, '*Daaji explains beautifully:* ***What's needed is a flexible ego – able to rise to meet the task at hand and subside into humility when no longer needed. When ego loosens, reactivity subsides, and the heart becomes responsive.'***

Key Takeaways

1. Ego is not the enemy; it is a necessary sense of identity.
2. **Ego spectrum**: arrogance, pride, confidence, presence, and humility.
3. A healthy ego is flexible – rises to meet challenges, subsides into humility afterwards.
4. Left unchecked, ego blocks wisdom, hardens into arrogance, and hinders growth.
5. Practices like meditation, cleaning, and reflection help loosen the rigid ego.

'*The ego is not master in its own house.*' – **Sigmund Freud**

'*A dominant ego becomes unreceptive to the mind's inspirations.*
It shuts out guidance from intellect, clouds discrimination, and turns into arrogance.
And when that happens, self-improvement begins to decay.' – **Daaji**

Scoring Guide

Here, 0 represents a highly inflated ego and 5 represents a healthy, balanced ego.

Score 0: Overwhelming, Fragile Ego

Your ego is a dominant and consuming force, requiring constant external validation. You may be unable to accept criticism, quick to take offence, and frequently feel the need to prove your superiority. This often manifests as arrogance, a lack of empathy, and an inability to admit fault, leading to strained relationships and a resistance to personal growth.

Score 1: Significant, Inflated Ego

You frequently rely on your ego for a sense of self-worth. You may often feel a need to be right, to be the centre of attention, or to be seen as more important than others. While you might occasionally recognize these tendencies, they significantly impact your interactions, making you resistant to feedback and prone to defensiveness.

Score 2: Frequent, Impactful Ego

Your ego is a noticeable presence in your life, sometimes causing friction or discomfort. You may struggle with admitting mistakes or feel a competitive urge to one-up others. While you are generally able to function without constant validation, your ego can still influence your mood and choices, particularly in stressful or challenging situations.

Score 3: Moderate, Manageable Ego

You experience ego-driven moments periodically, particularly when you feel threatened or insecure. These feelings are noticeable but generally manageable. You can typically listen to others' opinions, accept constructive criticism, and admit when you're wrong, even if it feels uncomfortable. Your ego doesn't prevent you from having healthy relationships or from learning from your mistakes.

Score 4: Occasional, Fleeting Ego

You might experience brief, mild pangs of an ego-driven response on rare occasions, usually in very specific or unusual circumstances. These feelings are fleeting, easily dismissed, and don't lead to significant distress or impact your behaviour. You can quickly recognize and rationalize them away. You are generally secure in your self-worth and do not feel a constant need for external validation.

Score 5: Minimal or No Ego

You rarely, if ever, feel the need to assert your superiority or defend your sense of self-worth from external criticism. You are secure and confident, but also humble and empathetic. You can accept feedback gracefully, learn from your mistakes without being defensive, and genuinely value the contributions of others without feeling threatened.

Reflection Prompts

1. What situations or types of interactions typically trigger your ego?
2. How does your ego manifest in your thoughts or behaviours (e.g., defensiveness, a need to be right, seeking praise)?
3. What is one practice you can adopt to help you move from an ego-driven reaction to a more open, humble response?

18. Resisting Change

Damini was having a tough time implementing her new product designed for in-house efficiency. The current interesting situation – Imagine at this time when synonym of AI are making an impact everywhere, a successful startup planning to go for IPO, has resistance in implementing an automated system. The current system is manual and is managed using spreadsheets.

The battles in multiple meetings had baffled her. The root cause analysis was pointing to only one factor – **resistance to change**.

She requested the discussion group to throw more light on the subject.

Damini welcomed everyone and briefed them about the case of resistance to change at her office. She invited everyone's views.

Vaibhavi: 'My organization gave a mandate to my team to integrate AI tools with our software development platform. The mandate is to increase productivity by 25 per cent in one year. Initially, there was resistance from developers citing various reasons, including a few genuine ones as well. To understand the situation on the ground, I had to wet my hands again in coding. Finally, after a series of deliberations, we could implement it, and the goal of a 25 per cent increase in productivity is likely to be achieved ahead of time. I felt that in our case, resistance to change was at the individual level.

Time with AI has changed. Organization and individuals have to change, or else both shall lose their value.

All of you may remember what happened to BlackBerry, which refused to change with the times and lost its value.'

Damini: 'So, I see that in my organization's case, the resistance to change is more due to individual resistance and less is due to the Organization level.'

Yash: 'Why is it so difficult for individuals to change?

Tendency to Remain in Comfort Zone

Keshav: 'At a personal level, when we are struggling, we are open and willing to implement all the changes needed. However, when life is comfortable, we don't want to disturb our comfort zone and wish the good time to continue forever. And now changing our own tendencies, habits, behaviour, and thought process is the most difficult task.

Everyone is designed to function as per their own free will. So those who are powerful want others to change to meet their interest, and for that, if they have to use force (financial, physical, emotional, etc), they shall use it.

It's only at the moment of helplessness after trying all the tricks, we want to start opening and making changes in ourselves.

It's up to us to ***take the call when we want to change – before the problem or after***. Human beings are funny that way – we won't fix the roof until it starts raining.'

Damini: 'When did humans become so rigid?'

Keshav: 'The humans were always rigid in varying degrees. As discussed earlier, the greatest warrior of his time and a selfless person, Bhisma, also didn't want to change. He stuck to his vow, even when time had changed and it started being misused by Dhritarashtra and Suyodhana; and because of their actions, masses were being affected. In such extremes, Divinity had to intervene in the form of Lord Krishna. Similarly, other greats Dronacharya and Karna were also stuck to their own selfish interests, and all of you know what happened. They decided not to change even after the problems for themselves and millions of armed forces personnel. All 3 of the above great warriors and great persons (most of the time) were powerful, so a bit of **ego combined with resistance to change became lethal for themselves and the masses**, and as its result, millions died on the battlefield. In today's world, that would be like 3 top executives refusing to update the company's software – and crashing the entire system instead.

The case studies from the Mahabharata are one of the best case studies on human behaviour, and I feel that these case studies need to be part of the curriculum for students from class 10th till completion of their education.'

Yash: 'What are all the reasons that force us to offer resistance to change?'

Keshav: 'You would recall that we have discussed the **Purpose of our life, Pre-written life-script, and at a planned time, *Bhoga* manifests in the form of extreme events (success or failure) in our life** so that we learn that planned important lesson. However, when we are in an uncomfortable situation, many of us want to:

Step 1 – Make a sincere effort to handle the situation.

Step 2 (when step 1 fails) – Change others to fulfil my wish.

Step 3 (when step 2 fails) – Attempting to change the circumstances.

Step 4 (when step 3 fails or along with steps 1–3) – Pray to God to grant our wish and provide relief.

Most of the time, even after failure of step 1–4 with the passage of time, when discomfort becomes less – we continue being our old self.

Step 5 (when step 1–4 fails and discomfort increases) – willing to try anything that can reduce the discomfort.

Step 6 – A few decide to accept the outcome after making a sincere effort and become open to learn the lesson.

The cause of Resistance to Change at the Individual Level:

- **Samskaras**: Due to our samskaras, the complexities and impurities – inner resistance are created.
- **Loss of Familiarity:** People cling to habits and routines.
- **Fear of Failure:** Worry about not being able to adapt.
- **Ego Involvement:** Perceived threat to personal status, expertise, or past achievements.
- **Identity Conflict:** 'If I'm no longer the expert in this system, who am I?'
- **Emotional Overload:** Anxiety, stress, or feeling excluded from decisions.

The manifestations of resistance:

- Defensiveness or blaming others.
- Procrastination or avoidance.
- Constant complaints ('This new system won't work.').
- Reduced productivity.

Damini, 'What could be the reason for Resistance to Change at the Organizational Level?'

Keshav 'Some of the reasons are:

- **Fear of the Unknown:** Employees feel insecure about new systems, technology, or leadership.
- **Loss of Control:** Managers may resist because change threatens their authority.
- **Comfort with Status Quo:** 'We've always done it this way.'
- **Mistrust in Leadership:** Lack of transparency breeds scepticism.
- **Resource Constraints:** Belief that the organization lacks skills, time, or budget to implement change.

Manifestations:

- Passive resistance (missed deadlines, lack of enthusiasm).
- Open opposition (complaints, criticism, union pushback).
- High turnover or absenteeism.
- Formation of silos or cliques that block change.

Change is the only constant – but it is also the most resisted. At both organizational and individual levels, resistance can stall progress, create conflict, and drain energy. Understanding the roots of resistance is the first step in transforming it into acceptance and growth/evolution. Or, as someone once said in a corporate corridor:

'We love innovation – just not in our department.'

Key Takeaways

1. **Resistance often hides fear.**
   We resist change because of the fear of losing our comfort, identity, and control.
2. **Change resisted is suffering postponed.**
   The more we delay transformation, the harsher life's lessons become when they arrive.
3. **Awareness is the antidote.**
   The moment we observe our resistance rather than justify it, learning begins.
4. **Force can impose change, but reflection sustains it.**
   Real transformation happens when change aligns with understanding, not compulsion.
5. **The wise choose to change early.**
   It's up to us whether to learn before the storm or after it.

'Change is hard at first, messy in the middle, and gorgeous at the end.' – **Robin Sharma**

In order for us to change, we must know our current level, current mentality, current emotional state, our defects and our imperfections. We must notice them. Only then there is a possibility of change – **Daaji**

Scoring Guide

A higher score indicates greater adaptability and openness to change.

When scoring yourself, consider your **initial emotional and behavioural reaction to change**, the **frequency of your resistance**, and how **easily and effectively you adapt** to new situations, ideas, or environments.

Score 0: Overwhelming, Debilitating Resistance to Change

You are almost completely inflexible and consistently resist any form of change, no matter how minor or beneficial. The thought of new routines, technologies, or approaches causes significant anxiety, anger, or even panic. This extreme resistance severely limits your personal redundant relationships and professional growth, making it nearly impossible to adapt to evolving circumstances.

Score 1: Severe, Frequent Resistance to Change

You frequently and strongly resist change. You prefer established routines, methods, and comfort zones, and often react negatively to new ideas or shifts in plans. While you might grudgingly accept change eventually, it causes you considerable stress, discomfort, and a strong tendency to cling to the familiar, often expressing frustration or complaint.

Score 2: Moderate, Noticeable Resistance to Change

You periodically find yourself resisting change, especially when it involves significant unknowns, personal effort, or a departure from comfortable habits. While you understand the need for change intellectually, you often feel a noticeable internal pushback, leading to hesitation, delays in adoption, or a preference for the status quo.

Score 3: Mild, Occasional Resistance to Change

You experience mild, fleeting moments of resistance to change from time to time, usually when it's unexpected, inconvenient, or requires stepping far outside your comfort zone. However, these feelings are manageable, you can generally see the benefits of change, and you adapt relatively quickly without significant distress or prolonged hesitation.

Score 4: Rare, Brief Resistance to Change

You very rarely resist change. When you do, it's a brief, mild, and quickly overcome impulse. You are generally open-minded and see change as a natural part of life and an opportunity for growth. You might feel a momentary discomfort, but you quickly embrace new ways of doing things.

Score 5: Minimal or Absent Resistance to Change

You rarely resist change. You approach new ideas, shifts, and unexpected developments with remarkable openness, enthusiasm, and adaptability. You thrive on innovation and see change as an inherent part of progress and learning. You are a proactive agent of change, comfortable with ambiguity, and often help others embrace new realities.

Reflection Prompts

1. How did your resistance manifest (e.g., procrastination, complaining, avoidance, stubbornness), and what was the impact on yourself or others?
2. What might be the underlying belief about change that fuels your resistance (e.g., 'change is scary,' 'I can't handle it,' 'things will get worse')?

19. Love

Few pleasures in life are as underrated as the sound of gentle raindrops. There's something magical about the rain – the pitter-patter of drops, the smell of wet earth, paired with the aroma of freshly brewed coffee. Add a plate of sandwiches, and it feels as though heaven itself is hosting a picnic just for you.

Of course, if you ask Vaibhavi, she'd ditch the coffee in a heartbeat for adrak wali chai and a pile of garam-garam pakoras – crispy, spicy, unapologetically desi. But Yash, the self-proclaimed weight watcher, had already rebranded *pakoras* as 'fritters' and placed them on the no-fly list. Apparently, love handles don't deserve any more… well, love.

So there they sat, debating the subject that has confused poets, philosophers, and perhaps even people stuck in arranged marriages: *Does true love even exist?* You hear plenty about love between couples – compatibility, companionship – but does 'unconditional love' truly exist?

As if on cue, the rain gods sent them an answer in human form – Keshav Uncle. He tumbled out of an Uber, locked in mortal combat with his umbrella, looking like a retired James Bond who had misplaced the gadget manual. Wrestling heroically with the stubborn black umbrella, he finally made it to the porch – dripping wet but grinning ear to ear. His smile was big, warm, mischievous – the kind of smile that makes you feel answers are on their way.

'Uncle!' Vaibhavi called out, raising her cup as an invitation. Keshav shook the raindrops off his umbrella and settled into a chair like a king claiming his throne. 'Perfect timing. We were just wondering – does true love really exist?'

Keshav sipped the coffee Vaibhavi handed him, wiped a stray raindrop from his forehead, and leaned back. 'True love,' he began, 'is often confused with romance. People think it lives only in candlelight, violin music, or carefully curated playlists. But true love isn't about compatibility – it's about acceptance. And sometimes, life teaches this lesson the hard way.'

He paused, as though fishing a memory from deep waters. 'Let me share a story about my mother's cousin, Sudha. Not all children born to the same parents are destined for the same fate.'

Sudha, the eldest daughter, was married off while still in her teens – a common practice back then. Unlike her siblings, who pursued higher education, she barely completed her 10th grade before stepping into married life. Her husband, a handsome young man, was later sent to England for his studies – sponsored generously by Sudha's own parents.

Five years later, he returned with a degree – and a different heart. London had changed him. Exposure to a new world, culture, and freedoms made his old life feel small and outdated. He looked at Sudha, a simple, homely woman, and could no longer accept her for who she was. Yes, he provided for her – the house was comfortable, the children cared for. But his heart longed for a companion educated, modern, and dazzling enough to walk by his side in his newly acquired high-society world.

And he found her – in Anita. An artist, bold in thought, confident in presence. A woman who matched his new vision of life.

Keshav's voice softened. 'Sudha lived her days quietly, carrying out her duties, yet never truly seen. And yet she never crumbled. Instead, she poured her love into her children, ensuring they received the finest education – so they could belong in the very circles where their father now thrived.'

Anurag, her husband, rose high, eventually becoming governor of various states, his life adorned with achievements. His laurels, his reputation, every success was built on the foundation Sudha's parents had quietly laid. Yet not once did she speak of it. She never let her tongue carve wounds into his reputation or bitterness stain his image. Instead, whenever she spoke of him, her eyes sparkled with pride and admiration. Even if you searched her gaze for disappointment, you would find only devotion. The purest form of love – unconditional, uncomplaining, unshaken – lived in those eyes.

Keshav paused, his voice softer now. 'Sudha's story may not make it to poetry books nor the romance of candlelight or violins, but the rare courage to love without conditions – even when life gave her every reason not to.'

For a moment, silence wrapped the atmosphere – only the rain spoke, clapping against the ground as if in approval.

Then Vaibhavi, ever the mood lifter, broke the silence. 'So basically, true love is unconditional acceptance?'

Keshav, 'Yes. However, this topic is very vast, ranging from human affection to divine Love. What we have discussed today is a small part of the whole spectrum.'

She leaned back, smirking. 'Then someone please tell Yash to accept my *pakoras* unconditionally next time it rains.'

The whole porch erupted in laughter. The rain applauded harder, and even Yash – half guilty, half grinning – folded his hands in defeat.

Key Takeaways – Love

1. **True love is more than romance** – it is rooted in acceptance, not just compatibility.
2. **Unconditional love requires courage** – Sudha's strength was not in protest, but in quiet devotion without bitterness.
3. **Love builds dignity, not resentment** – protecting another's honour, even when hurt, is the higher form of love.
4. **Every day love is acceptance** – sometimes, it looks like embracing pakoras in the rain, or forgiving small differences.
5. **The essence of love is presence** – not who we fall for, but who we choose to keep standing with.

'True love begins when nothing is looked for in return.'
– Antoine de Saint-Exupéry

Scoring guide

This scale refers to a broad, compassionate love for humanity, not just romantic or familial love. When rating yourself, consider your thoughts, feelings, and actions towards people in general, not just those you know intimately.

This is about your broader sense of connection and care for the human family.

Score 0: Indifference/Apathy

You feel **little to no emotional connection or concern for others,** especially those outside your immediate circle.

You are primarily focused on your own needs and desires, with limited consideration for the well-being of others.

You may find it difficult to empathize with suffering or injustice in the world.

The struggles of others don't significantly impact you.

Score 1: Self-Centered with Occasional Consideration

Your primary focus is still on yourself, but you might show **occasional, superficial consideration for others** if it's convenient or directly benefits you.

You might feel fleeting moments of pity or sympathy, but they don't lead to action or sustained concern.

You struggle to see beyond your own perspective and rarely put yourself in someone else's shoes.

There's a noticeable lack of genuine warmth or connection with humanity as a whole.

Score 2: Developing Empathy, Limited Action

You are beginning to **feel empathy for others** and recognize the suffering in the world, but your actions are limited.

You might feel bad about injustices or difficulties faced by others, but you don't actively seek ways to help or connect.

Your compassion is often conditional or limited to specific groups you identify with.

You might intellectually understand the importance of human connection but struggle to embody it.

Score 3: Active Empathy and Willingness to Connect

You actively **feel empathy and compassion for a broad range of people,** including those different from yourself.

You are willing to step outside your comfort zone to connect with or understand others' perspectives.

You might occasionally engage in acts of kindness or support for others, even if they are strangers.

You recognize the interconnectedness of humanity and feel a growing sense of shared experience.

Score 4: Consistent Compassion and Active Contribution

You consistently **demonstrate deep compassion and a genuine desire for the well-being of others.**

You actively seek opportunities to contribute positively to the lives of individuals or to society.

You feel a strong sense of connection to humanity, and the joy and suffering of others genuinely affect you.

You practice forgiveness, understanding, and non-judgment towards others, even when it's challenging.

Score 5: Embodied Universal Love

You embody a profound and **unconditional love for all humanity,** seeing the inherent worth and dignity in every person.

Your actions are consistently guided by a deep sense of compassion, kindness, and a desire for collective well-being.

You naturally extend empathy, understanding, and support to all, without discrimination or expectation.

This love is a core part of your being, influencing your perspective on life and your interactions with the world. You see yourself as part of a larger human family.

Note: There are no reflection prompts since this topic is very elaborate.

2

EMOTIONAL QUOTIENT

'Emotions are messengers; listen before reacting.'

Case of Emotions Affecting Health

During one of her weekly sharing circles, Vaibhavi had a sparkle in her eyes. She had just come back from her sessions with her spiritual trainer and was eager to tell everyone – including the ever-curious Keshav uncle – about her discovery.

Vaibhavi began, 'For the past year, I kept getting this nagging pain in my shoulders and neck after sitting at work for 5–6 hours. Not every day, but enough to make me feel like my body was sending me a monthly subscription reminder – *'Pay attention to me!'*

She laughed and added, 'The doctor told me it was a postural imbalance. Apparently, my neck muscles were tight, my back and shoulder stabilisers weak – basically, my body was waging a small civil war. I did my best to fix my posture, and yes, the pain reduced… but it kept sneaking back like an uninvited guest at a wedding.'

Then she glanced playfully at Yash. 'One year into marriage, Yash and I had a disagreement – let's just say the '*honeymoon offer*' had expired. After a week of silent tension, guess what returned with full force? My old neck-and-shoulder pain! To cleanse the effects of tension, I went to my spiritual trainer for 4 days in a row to get sessions for meditation and cleaning. Though pain management was not on the agenda, on the third day – like magic – the pain just vanished. I shared my findings with the trainer, Lata ji.

Lata smiled knowingly, 'That's because emotions get stuck as negative energy in our body. They settle into our weak spots – like unwanted tenants. When cleaning is done, those tenants are finally evicted. If you want to dive deeper, you may read *The Emotion Code* by Dr Bradley Nelson. In short, the book states that: '*Much of our suffering is due to negative emotional energies that have become 'trapped' within us. Many people have found that when they free themselves of their trapped emotions, they are able to live healthier and happier lives. A single trapped emotion can create both physical and emotional problems.*'

Vaibhavi's face lit up with relief.

Keshav uncle leaned forward. 'So, what did you do after that? Other than forgiving poor Yash?'

Vaibhavi chuckled. 'I read the book, of course, and it made complete sense. To strengthen my neck and shoulders, I joined a gym. But here's the fun part – now, whenever that pain reappears, I don't run for a painkiller. I ask myself, '*Okay, Vaibhavi, who upset you this time?*' And usually the answer is waiting (emotions). And I do additional cleaning.'

She added, 'Dr Bruce Lipton's work and Louise Hay's affirmations confirmed what I felt – that our bodies whisper our emotions out loud. So now, whenever my shoulders feel heavy, I go back to Lata for an additional sitting. It's like emotional housekeeping. After all, who wants to carry unpaid emotional rent in their neck?'

Keshav: 'In addition to your experience, on the **linkage of Emotions to *samskaras***, Daaji says – '*Your likes and dislikes trigger your emotions, and your emotions create the blocks that affect the chakras. The unresolved emotional blocks create deep impressions with* *exceptionally vivid detail and long-lasting memory of the emotional turbulence. The yogis call these impressions samskaras*'.

Keshav: 'St. Babuji writes, following in the book *Complete Works of Ram Chandra Vol-2*:

- *The emotional blocks come up in our behaviour because they need resolution.*
  - o *Anger arises in everybody's life because that emotional box seeks resolution through love.*
  - o *Irritability comes up to be resolved through kindness.*
  - o *Grief burdens the heart, seeking the light of compassion.*
- o *Fear bubbles up to be purged through courage.*
- *If you find any difficulty or entanglement or even an unbearable excitement of emotion, just refer that to Him (God) through prayer at any time or from any place, and it shall go away at once.*'

Key Takeaways

1. Physical pain may have an emotional root, especially in areas of weakness.
2. Trapped emotions can aggravate or prolong physical discomfort.
3. Spiritual practices like cleaning and meditation can release these trapped emotions.
4. Awareness is key – observing when pain correlates with emotional disturbance helps in healing.
5. A balanced approach works best: emotional release + physical strengthening + medical consultation.

'*Unexpressed emotions will never die. They are buried alive and will come forth later in uglier ways.*' – **Sigmund Freud**, neurologist and father of psychoanalysis

'*Every emotion that is left unresolved gets stored in the body and shows up as dis-ease.*' – **Louise Hay, motivational author and founder of Hay House**

'*Stress, anger, and resentment weaken the immune system. Love, forgiveness, and joy strengthen it.*' – Dr. Bernie Siegel, surgeon and author of ***Love, Medicine and Miracles***

'Our biology is influenced by our beliefs and perceptions. Fear and anger shut down growth and healing, while love opens them.'
– Dr. Bruce Lipton, cell biologist and author of *The Biology of Belief*

As seen in the above case, our emotions are powerful forces – often subtle, sometimes overwhelming – that shape not only our inner world but also how we are perceived in the outer world. They colour our thoughts, influence our decisions, and leave footprints in every relationship we hold dear. A single emotion – whether joy, anger, fear, or hope – can alter the course of an entire day, a conversation, or even a life.

This chapter focuses on **Emotional Quotient (EQ)**, a vital dimension of self-awareness and social intelligence. Unlike IQ, which measures cognitive ability, EQ measures the *quality* of our human experience: our ability to recognize emotions, regulate them, and use them wisely. It is the invisible bridge between **self and others**, allowing us to move from reaction to response, and from conflict to connection.

In this chapter, attributes are from 2 categories: **Primary Emotions** (such as joy, sadness, fear, anger, surprise, and disgust) and **Secondary or Complex Emotions** (like jealousy, guilt, pride, envy, shame, admiration, and compassion). The primary emotions are universal – they are hardwired into our biology and can be observed in every culture. The secondary emotions, however, emerge as we grow, shaped by our environment, upbringing, and personal life scripts. Both types together form the emotional vocabulary through which we interpret life.

Through introspection, you will learn to **assess these emotions**:

- Recognize when and how they arise.
- Identify the triggers that set them off.
- Understand the stories and beliefs attached to them.
- Practice new ways of responding rather than reacting.

Cultivating a higher EQ does not mean suppressing emotions or pretending they don't exist. Instead, it means allowing them to be your **teachers**. Anger can teach you about boundaries; sadness can teach you about empathy; joy can remind you to celebrate the present. As you begin to observe emotions rather than be swept away by them, you create the space to choose – responding with balance and wisdom instead of regret or impulse.

The journey of EQ is also deeply relational. The more you understand your own emotions, the more you can **empathize with others**. Emotional awareness softens judgment, reduces misunderstandings, and builds trust. In professional settings, it helps leaders inspire teams; in personal life, it helps families heal; and in friendships, it creates bonds that last through storms.

In this section, you will explore **real-life anecdotes, guided reflections, and scoring frameworks** to examine your emotional landscape. Some stories will remind you of your own experiences; others may challenge your perspective. Each one is designed to help you expand your emotional capacity so that you can live with greater resilience, compassion, and clarity.

Ultimately, *Emotional intelligence is less about what you feel* and more about *how you deal with what you feel.*

By cultivating EQ, you don't eliminate life's challenges – you simply learn to face them with steadier hands and a calmer heart.

1. Fear

Damini was disturbed to see fear grip her friends and colleagues – fuelled by uncertainty in the IT world over AI, trade wars, and geopolitics. Even Sneha, her spirited friend who had recently secured funding for her startup (as we saw in the story on *Adaptability and Flexibility*), was caught in its grip. Damini recalled similar waves of fear during the peak of COVID-19 in 2020–21.

Damini herself was a believer in remaining calm and peaceful within, trusting in the life script written before birth – so fear rarely touched her deeply. Yet, curious to understand it better, she proposed that their usual group take up the subject of *Fear* in their next session.

The group assembled at 2 familiar hubs: Vaibhavi's cosy home in the Bay Area, and Damini's living room in Hyderabad – where Keshav Uncle also joined in person.

Damini opened the discussion by sharing her observations, then posed the big question: **'Why was fear created in the first place?'**

Vaibhavi responded, 'I read that fear was designed as a survival instinct. Without it, humans wouldn't have survived predators in the early stages of creation. When danger appeared, fear sharpened awareness – the adrenaline pumped, reflexes quickened, focus narrowed. It helped to keep us alive. Basically, fear was the original project manager – it made sure you delivered results before the tiger did.'

Damini smiled. 'Back in college, I was always tempted to watch the latest *Step-Up* or *Harry Potter* movies – even just before exams. But it was the fear of exams that pulled me back to my books and motivated me to prepare harder.'

Yash nodded. 'That's the healthy side of fear. Think of how fear of the police stops people from breaking laws – it prevents recklessness, sets boundaries, and enforces discipline. Fear also reminds us we're not invincible. It teaches respect for nature, authority, and the unknown. For example, mountaineers respect nature and avalanches – they climb with caution, not arrogance.

However, at times I also have fear before an important presentation, but I have learned to overcome it through preparation.'

Mudit, Keshav's friend, added: 'Courage has meaning only when fear is present. Fear gives us the chance to practice bravery. In the Armed Forces, I've witnessed it countless times – especially facing the enemy.

In my experience, fear also signals where we need to grow. It highlights our discomfort zones. For example, fear of rejection – when faced – often leads to healthier, more authentic relationships.'

Sneha confessed, 'Uncle, fear is everywhere in our lives. Before my presentations, my hands shake, my heart races... What if I make a mistake?'

Keshav chuckled. '*Beta*, remember David and Goliath? David had every reason to tremble – imagine a giant staring you down! But fear itself wasn't the problem – paralysis was. Courage is not the absence of fear; it's taking action despite it.'

Yash leaned forward. 'So, Uncle, are you saying fear can actually help?'

'Exactly,' Keshav said. 'Fear sharpens awareness. The Israelite soldiers froze because they magnified fear. David reframed it – he trusted his sling more than he feared Goliath's sword.'

'But on the flip side,' Keshav continued, 'when fear takes center stage and floods our mind with worst-case scenarios, our productivity drops instantly. Prolonged fear even harms health.

During the COVID period, I observed a few relatives whose oxygen saturation (SPO_2) dropped up to 10 points whenever they panicked. My doctor friend explained: fear ripples through the body's 50 trillion cells, reducing their performance. The result in such cases during COVID – lower oxygen levels and an immediate risk to life.'

Keshav concluded: 'Fear is natural. But when you let it dictate your script, your life shrinks. Face the giant. Sometimes, one small stone of courage is enough.'

Damini smiled. 'In our office, fear of failure often stops people from trying new things. I guess giants don't always wear armour – sometimes they sit across the table in meetings with a frown! And their weapon of choice is usually a 'follow-up email."

Everyone burst into laughter.

Story of David and Goliath

The Philistine giant Goliath was a sight to behold – armoured like a tank, his booming voice shaking the valley. In a battle when 2 armies were facing each other, it was decided that the outcome of the battle would be decided by each side picking one warrior. The Philistine side picked Goliath, a giant among men. From the Israeli side, nobody came forward to face Goliath.

Day after day, Goliath roared: 'Send me a man to fight!' But soldiers trembled, their courage evaporating. Fear spread like an infection; even the bravest shrank.

Then came David – a shepherd boy, unarmoured, armed only with a sling and 5 stones. Where others saw a giant too dangerous to fight, David saw a target too big to miss. He stepped forward, swung his sling, and felled the giant.

The armies were stunned. Fear had chained hundreds, but one boy's courage changed history.

Key Takeaways

1. Fear was created as a survival tool – it sharpens awareness and prevents recklessness.
2. Courage exists only in the presence of fear. Action despite fear is what counts.
3. Fear, when prolonged, damages health and productivity.
4. Reframing fear, like David did, turns giants into opportunities.
5. Fear signals growth areas – facing it often leads to deeper strength and relationships.

'Courage is resistance to fear, mastery of fear, not absence of fear.'
– **Mark Twain**

'Relationships based on fear require constant attention and energy to maintain.' – **Daaji**

'Courage gives us confidence, and fear allows us to pause and introspect.' – **Daaji**

Scoring Guide

This scale focuses on how fear impacts your thoughts, emotions, behaviours, and overall quality of life. When assessing yourself, consider how often fear prevents you from doing what you want or need to do, how intensely you experience it, and how quickly you can recover from fearful moments.

Score 0: Paralysed by Fear

You are **constantly overwhelmed by fear and anxiety**, making it extremely difficult to function in daily life.

Fear dictates most of your decisions, leading to significant avoidance of new experiences, social situations, or essential responsibilities.

Panic attacks or intense anxiety are frequent occurrences.

Your life feels severely restricted by what you are afraid of, leading to significant distress and stagnation.

Score 1: Frequent and Debilitating Fear

You experience **frequent and intense episodes of fear or anxiety** that often prevent you from pursuing goals or engaging in desired activities.

While not always paralysing, fear significantly limits your comfort zone and keeps you from taking necessary risks.

You spend a lot of time worrying about potential negative outcomes, even for unlikely scenarios.

You might engage in safety behaviours or compulsions to alleviate fear, which in turn reinforces it.

Score 2: Fluctuating Fear, Often Restrictive

You have moments of calm, but **fear frequently arises and can be quite restrictive**, especially in specific situations or concerning certain topics.

You might push through fear sometimes, but it often leaves you feeling drained or highly uncomfortable.

You're aware of how fear impacts you, but you struggle to consistently overcome it or manage its influence effectively.

You often hesitate before trying new things or facing challenges due to apprehension.

Score 3: Growing Resilience to Fear

You are increasingly able to **recognize when fear arises and choose to act despite it.**

While you still feel fear, it's less intense and doesn't paralyse you as often.

You're actively working on understanding the root causes of your fears and developing coping mechanisms.

You're becoming more willing to step outside your comfort zone, even if it feels uncomfortable at first.

Score 4: Consistent Courage and Mastery Over Fear

You consistently **face your fears directly**, understanding that fear is a natural emotion but doesn't have to control your actions.

You can identify fear, acknowledge it, and then proceed with resilience and determination.

You use fear as a signal for growth opportunities rather than a barrier.

Your life choices are driven by your values and goals, not by avoidance of fear.

Score 5: Embodied Fearlessness and Inner Freedom

You embody a profound sense of **inner freedom and fearlessness**, approaching life's challenges with curiosity and an open heart.

Fear, if it arises, is a very fleeting sensation, quickly integrated or transmuted into excitement or wisdom.

You proactively seek growth-oriented experiences, embracing uncertainty and the unknown.

Your life is characterised by bold action, authentic living, and a deep sense of trust in your ability to handle whatever comes your way.

Reflection Prompts

1. How does fear typically manifest in your body, thoughts, and behaviours?
2. Has fear ever prevented you from pursuing something you genuinely desired or needed to do?
3. What is one way you can acknowledge your fear without letting it control your actions?

2. Sadness

'The word 'happiness' would lose its meaning if it were not balanced by sadness.' – **Carl Jung**

'The walls we build around us to keep sadness out also keep out the joy.'
– Jim Roh

'A sad, heavy heart cannot stay open; only a lively heart is open and flowing' – **Daaji**

Scoring Guide

Score 0: Profound or Debilitating Sadness

Sadness is your dominant emotion, and it feels constant and crushing.

You might feel emotionally numb, utterly devoid of joy, or in deep emotional pain.

This level of sadness is severely debilitating, making it very difficult to function in any aspect of your life.

You might have difficulty getting out of bed, taking care of yourself, or interacting with others.

Crying might be continuous, or you might feel too overwhelmed to cry at all.

Score 1: Almost Constant or Intense Sadness

You feel sad nearly all the time, or the sadness is very intense when it occurs.

It's difficult to find relief from these feelings, and they might feel overwhelming.

Your sadness significantly impacts your daily life, including sleep, appetite, social interactions, and work/school.

You might feel a deep sense of despair or hopelessness.

Crying spells can be frequent and prolonged.

Score 2: Frequent or Significant Sadness

You feel sad most days, and these feelings can last for significant portions of the day.

The sadness might feel heavy or pervasive, even when there's no clear trigger.

It can interfere with your enjoyment of activities, concentration, or motivation.

You might find it hard to shake off sad moods.

Crying might be a regular occurrence for you.

Score 3: Occasional or Moderate Sadness

You experience sadness a few times a week, and it might last for a few hours.

These feelings can be triggered by various events, both minor and more significant.

While you can still function, the sadness might affect your mood or energy levels temporarily.

You might feel a noticeable dip in your enthusiasm for activities.

You might cry sometimes, particularly in response to emotional content or personal disappointments.

Score 4: Mild or Fleeting Sadness

You experience brief moments of sadness, perhaps a few times a week.

These feelings are usually tied to specific, minor events, and pass quickly.

You can easily distract yourself or move on from the sadness.

You might feel a little 'down' sometimes, but it doesn't linger or impact your daily functioning.

You might occasionally feel a tear in your eye, but rarely outright cry.

Score 5: Rarely or Never Sad

You almost never experience feelings of sadness.

Even in challenging situations, you tend to feel other emotions like frustration or disappointment, but not typically sadness.

You generally maintain a positive or neutral emotional state.

You rarely, if ever, cry due to sadness.

Reflection Prompts

1. How do you usually cope with feelings of sadness (e.g., withdrawing, seeking comfort, distracting yourself)? Are these methods effective for you?
2. How does expressing (or suppressing) sadness impact your relationships?

3. **Disgust**

'Disgust is a natural reaction, but holding onto it turns into poison.'
– **Buddhist teaching** (paraphrased)

'Our greatest disgusts are usually mirrors of our own hidden flaws.'
– **Carl Jung** (paraphrased)

'Disgust should awaken discernment, not disdain.'
– **Rumi** (interpreted)

Scoring Guide

This scale focuses on how you experience and react to things that evoke feelings of revulsion, strong aversion, or moral offence. When rating yourself, consider how often you feel deeply repulsed, how intensely you react to things you find unpleasant or morally offensive, and how much those feelings impact your choices and interactions.

Score 0: Overly Sensitive and Consumed by Disgust

You feel **frequently and intensely disgusted** by a wide range of things, including common sights, sounds, smells, or human behaviours.

Your feelings of disgust are often overwhelming and can lead to strong physical reactions (e.g., nausea, gagging).

You find it extremely difficult to tolerate anything that triggers your disgust, often avoiding situations or people.

Your life feels restricted by things you find repulsive, impacting your comfort and ability to engage with the world.

Score 1: Easily Triggered and Frequently Repulsed

You are **easily and frequently triggered into a state of disgust** by various things, even those that others might consider minor.

You often feel strong aversion or revulsion, which can lead to immediate avoidance or strong negative vocalisations.

You struggle to manage your initial reactions to things you find unpleasant or morally offensive.

Your strong dislikes often limit your experiences or make social interactions challenging.

Score 2: Fluctuating Disgust, Sometimes Managed

You experience **feelings of disgust regularly**, but you're sometimes able to manage or suppress your reactions, though it often requires effort.

You might still feel significant revulsion, but you can prevent it from completely controlling your behaviour.

You are **aware of your tendencies** towards disgust, but find it challenging to consistently control your initial emotional and physical responses.

Certain specific triggers consistently evoke disgust, while others you can sometimes tolerate.

Score 3: Growing Tolerance and Awareness of Triggers

You are increasingly able to **identify what triggers your disgust** and can often prevent it from escalating into an overwhelming feeling.

While you still feel aversion occasionally, you're better at acknowledging the feeling without letting it consume you.

You're developing strategies to cope with things you find unpleasant, allowing for more adaptability.

You're starting to differentiate between genuine threats and mere discomforts.

Score 4: Consistent Composure and Resilience to Disgust

You consistently **maintain composure and resilience** even when faced with things that might typically evoke disgust in others.

You can acknowledge feelings of aversion without allowing them to significantly impact your mood, actions, or judgment.

You can separate your personal preferences from objective reality, allowing for greater understanding and less reactivity.

Your ability to navigate unpleasantries contributes to a more peaceful and open daily life.

Score 5: Profound Acceptance and Non-Reactive Presence

You embody a profound sense of **acceptance and a non-reactive presence**, rarely experiencing genuine, overwhelming disgust.

You approach things that might be considered unpleasant with a sense of curiosity, understanding, or a neutral observation.

You can process all sensory inputs and moral situations without rigid aversion or judgmental repulsion, leading to deep inner calm.

This deep level of acceptance allows you to engage with the full spectrum of life experiences, maintaining inner peace regardless of external stimuli.

Reflection Prompts

1. Describe something (an action, idea, or physical thing) that recently evoked a feeling of disgust in you.
2. What values or beliefs does this feeling of disgust often point to within you?

3. How does expressing or acting on disgust impact your interactions with others or your openness to new experiences?

4. Irritation

'If you are irritated by every rub, how will your mirror be polished?' – **Rumi**

'Everything that irritates us about others can lead us to an understanding of ourselves.' – **Carl Jung**

'A great way to understand yourself is to seriously reflect on everything you find irritating in others.' – **Kevin Kelly**

Scoring Guide

This scale focuses on how easily and frequently you feel annoyed or bothered by minor inconveniences throughout your day, and how long those feelings tend to linger.

Score 0: Constant State of Annoyance

You feel **frequently, almost constantly, annoyed or bothered** by everyday occurrences, sounds, behaviours of others, or minor inconveniences.

Small things easily trigger a feeling of exasperation or frustration within you.

You often express your irritation through sighs, grumbles, eye rolls, or passive-aggressive behaviour.

You find it very difficult to overlook minor flaws or bothersome habits in others.

Score 1: Easily Triggered and Frequent Irritability

You are **easily and frequently triggered into a state of irritation** by common stressors or others' actions.

Your patience wears thin very quickly, and you find yourself feeling annoyed multiple times a day.

You might internally seethe or outwardly react with sharp words or a terse demeanour.

Minor delays, noises, or slight deviations from your expectations significantly impact your mood.

Score 2: Fluctuating Irritation, Sometimes Managed

You experience **irritation regularly**, but you're sometimes able to manage or dismiss it without significant outward reaction.

You might feel annoyed, but the feeling doesn't always consume you or lead to immediate outbursts.

You are aware of your tendency to get irritated, but find it challenging to consistently control your initial reaction.

Certain specific triggers consistently annoy you, while others you can sometimes overlook.

Score 3: Growing Tolerance and Awareness of Triggers

You are increasingly able to **identify what triggers your irritation** and can often prevent it from escalating.

While you still feel annoyed occasionally, you're better at letting small things go or addressing them calmly.

You're developing strategies to cope with minor inconveniences without allowing them to disrupt your inner peace significantly.

Your default state is less about annoyance and more about general composure.

Score 4: Consistent Composure and Resilience to Annoyance

You consistently **maintain composure and resilience** even when faced with typical everyday annoyances or minor frustrations.

You can acknowledge an irritating situation without allowing it to significantly impact your mood or actions.

You often find yourself shrugging off or humorously observing things that used to bother you.

Your ability to overlook minor irritations contributes to a more peaceful daily life.

Score 5: Profound Equanimity and Unbothered Presence

You embody a profound sense of **equanimity and an unbothered presence**, rarely experiencing genuine irritation.

You approach life's small frictions with acceptance, understanding, or even amusement.

You see minor annoyances as part of the human experience or simply as external noise, and they don't register as personal affronts.

This **deep level of calm allows you to navigate daily life with remarkable ease and grace**, maintaining inner peace regardless of external minor disturbances.

Reflection Prompts

1. How do you typically react when you feel irritated (e.g., sighing, snapping, internal grumbling)?
2. What underlying cause of stress or unmet need might be contributing to your frequent irritation?
3. Have you explored a method by which irritation is rooted out, and you are not irritated 99 per cent of the time?

5. Guilt

Case 1

Arjun and Ravi were close friends who had trained together through their ab initio course in the Air Force. Their bond was built on shared hardships, camaraderie, and the excitement of a career just beginning. When they landed in their first operational unit, both were detailed for training in Missiles (surface-to-air) – not exactly the kind of training where you want to mix up instructions with your gym membership form.

At this point, Arjun realized that Ravi had been nominated for the more coveted role of Guidance Officer – the one who gets to press the missile launch button at enemy fighter aircraft. In childhood, this job description sounds like a video game; in real life, it comes with slightly higher stakes. Without any ill intention, Arjun requested a mutual acquaintance at Air Headquarters to see if he could also be placed in the Guidance Officer training.

What he never foresaw was that their training modules would be completely interchanged – an outcome he had neither asked for nor desired.

Ravi, understandably, was disappointed. Though he never openly confronted Arjun, the incident left a silent scar in their friendship. They continued working in the same unit for 2 years, maintaining professionalism, but something unspoken always lingered in the air – like Wi-Fi signals, invisible yet powerful. Even after their postings separated them, Arjun carried with him a burden of shame and guilt, replaying the incident in his mind over the next 2 decades.

Twenty years later, fate brought them together again in another unit. For Arjun, it was a decisive moment. He gathered courage and, during their first meaningful interaction, confessed the truth to Ravi: the swap of training modules had never been intentional, and he had lived with regret all these years. He offered a heartfelt apology.

To his relief, Ravi smiled warmly. 'Arjun, I had forgotten about that long ago,' he said with disarming grace. 'You shouldn't have carried this weight for so many years. If guilt had air miles, you'd be eligible for free world travel by now.'

At that moment, Arjun felt liberated. The chains of shame and guilt he had carried for twenty years dissolved in Ravi's forgiving words. He realized that sometimes, the prisons we build in our own minds are harsher than any external judgment. The irony being – we're both the jailor and the inmate, and the key was always in our own pocket.

Keshav's Take

'If we are fair in our approach, we can clearly see the hurt caused to others by our actions – whether intentional or unintentional. On the contrary, pride in our defects tends to mask guilt. Arjun, being sensitive and fair, was ashamed of the outcome, though he had not considered its effect on his friend. Ravi, a perfect gentleman with a huge heart, had accepted the outcome and forgiven Arjun. Had he not forgiven Arjun, he would have gathered emotional baggage within himself, which in turn could have caused the formation of *samskaras*. Forgiveness here wasn't just a gift to Arjun – it was also Ravi's way of decluttering his own heart's storage space.'

Case 2

Keshav said, 'When Bhishma lay on his deathbed, he asked the Pandavas to seek Draupadi's forgiveness. Imagine how much shame and guilt such a grand personality must have carried for years. Yet for a man with unparalleled power and responsibility, wouldn't timely action on that fateful day – when Draupadi was being insulted – have been more just?

I sometimes wonder if he felt ashamed while fighting his own great-grandchildren. On the contrary, Arjun's dilemma of fighting his brothers and elders is well documented. It seems even the mightiest warriors sometimes forget that silence can wound deeper than arrows. **It's history's reminder that 'mute' mode works for phones, not for conscience.'**

Keshav further added, 'When Dronacharya decided his time had come, he too asked the Pandavas to seek Draupadi's forgiveness. Like Bhishma, he had to bear his share of shame and guilt. He was never comfortable fighting his own disciples.'

'Similarly, Karna later became aware that Draupadi was the wife of his younger brothers. I often wonder what his reaction must have been when he realized this fact – perhaps even the great giver Karna wished someone could donate him a time machine to undo that day.'

Key Takeaways

1. **Unresolved guilt is a silent burden** – Carrying it for too long can weigh down life's joys.
2. **Self-awareness prevents pride from masking guilt.**
3. **The mind's prison is often harsher than society's judgment.**
4. **Seek closure early** – Resolve not to repeat the mistake; honest conversations, even if uncomfortable, can heal wounds.
5. Even the greatest heroes – Bhishma, Drona, Karna – were not free from **guilt born of inaction or misplaced loyalty**.

'Guilt is perhaps the most painful companion of death.' – **Coco Chanel**

'So whenever you are angry, instead of blaming others, exploding, feeling self-pity, or punishing yourself and feeling guilty, ask yourself, how can I correct myself?'.

Excerpt from the book *Spiritual Anatomy* by **Daaji**

Scoring Guide

When assessing yourself, consider the **frequency, intensity, duration, and impact** of your feelings of guilt.

Score 0: Overwhelming Guilt

Guilt is a constant and consuming force in your life. You are plagued by intense remorse, self-reproach, and potentially self-punishing thoughts or behaviours. This level of guilt can be debilitating, leading to significant emotional distress, anxiety, or depression.

Score 1: Significant Guilt

You frequently experience strong, pervasive feelings of guilt. These feelings can be distressing and may interfere with your daily life, relationships, or overall well-being. You might find it hard to forgive yourself or move past perceived mistakes, even when others have.

Score 2: Moderate Guilt

Guilt is a more frequent and sometimes intense emotion for you. You may ruminate on past actions or feel a persistent sense of responsibility for negative outcomes, even if they weren't entirely your fault. This level of guilt can sometimes affect your mood or decision-making.

Score 3: Occasional Guilt

You feel guilt periodically, particularly when you believe you've genuinely wronged someone or made a significant error. While these feelings are noticeable, they are manageable and don't lead to prolonged distress or self-blame. You often try to make amends.

Score 4: Minimal Guilt

You experience fleeting moments of guilt, usually in response to minor transgressions or inconsiderate actions. These feelings are easily resolved, and they don't significantly impact your mood or behaviour. You can acknowledge your part and move on.

Score 5: No Guilt

You rarely, if ever, feel guilt. You can make decisions and take actions without dwelling on potential negative impacts or feeling remorse for past mistakes. You easily move on from situations.

Reflection Prompts

1. Recall a situation where you felt genuine guilt. What specific action or inaction led to this feeling?
2. What is the difference for you between constructive guilt (leading to amends) and debilitating guilt (leading to self-punishment)?
3. Is there a situation where you might be holding onto guilt unnecessarily, and what would it mean to release it?

6. Shame

'Shame is a soul-eating emotion.' – **Carl Jung**

'Shame is the most powerful, master emotion. It's the fear that we're not good enough.' – **Brené Brown**

Scoring Guide

Score 0: Overwhelming Shame

You are constantly plagued by intense feelings of **shame**. You believe you are fundamentally flawed, worthless, or unlovable. These feelings likely dominate your thoughts, hinder your actions, and severely impact your relationships and self-esteem. You might avoid social situations, hide parts of yourself, or engage in self-sabotaging behaviours due to this deep sense of inadequacy.

Score 1: Significant Shame

You frequently experience strong, pervasive feelings of **shame**. While not always debilitating, these feelings are a significant presence in your life. You often feel inadequate or embarrassed about who you are, what you've done, or aspects of your identity. This can lead to self-criticism, difficulty accepting compliments, and a tendency to withdraw or be overly self-conscious in social interactions.

Score 2: Moderate Shame

You experience feelings of **shame** periodically, often in response to perceived failures, mistakes, or when you feel exposed. These feelings are noticeable and can be uncomfortable, leading to moments of self-doubt or embarrassment. However, you are generally able to process these feelings and move past them without them consuming your entire sense of self. You might still struggle with vulnerability or self-acceptance at times.

Score 3: Occasional Shame

You feel **shame** only occasionally, typically when you've genuinely acted in a way that goes against your values or when you've made a significant error. These feelings are usually tied to specific actions rather than your core identity. You can acknowledge the feeling, learn from the experience, and generally let it go without it deeply impacting your self-worth.

Score 4: Minimal Shame

You rarely experience **shame**. When you do, it's typically a fleeting moment of embarrassment or regret over a specific, minor action. You have a strong sense of self-worth and self-acceptance, allowing you to quickly move past mistakes or perceived flaws without them diminishing your overall sense of value. You are generally comfortable being yourself and are resilient in the face of judgment.

Score 5: No Shame

You do not experience **shame** in a significant way. You have a very healthy self-image and a profound sense of self-acceptance. You understand that mistakes are part of being human, and you can take responsibility for your actions without internalising them as a reflection of your inherent worthlessness. You embrace vulnerability and authenticity, feeling secure in who you are.

Reflection Prompts

1. Think of a time when you felt shame. What was the situation, and what core belief about yourself did it trigger?
2. What is one step you could take to practice self-compassion when feelings of shame arise?
3. Did you take a thought not to repeat the reason that led to the shame?

7. Gratitude

They arrived in the city with nothing more than a battered trunk, 2 little girls clutching their mother's sari, and a heart trembling with fragile hope. In those first months, hunger became their closest companion. Her husband wandered from office to office in search of work, returning each evening with weary eyes and empty pockets, while she carried her daughters from one doorstep to another, asking for odd jobs...washing utensils, sweeping courtyards, chopping vegetables – anything that would fetch a few coins.

There were nights when the kitchen fire never lit, when hunger pressed their stomachs into silence. On some days, Seema managed to buy a single pack of glucose biscuits, dipping them in water to soften before feeding her little girls. She herself went hungry many times, but slept in peace knowing her daughters drifted into dreams with crumbs of sweetness on their tongues.

Slowly, the tide began to shift. Her husband found work as a runner in an office, while Seema became a cook in a few households. With the encouragement of her employers and her own relentless will, she enrolled both daughters in a good school.

Seema never wanted her children to live the life she had endured. Her days blurred into a rhythm of dawns and dusks. She would rise before sunrise, cook in 4 houses, return in the afternoon to wash and clean, and still ensure her daughters' uniforms were pressed crisp enough to pass an army inspection. Then she would sit beside them as they studied under the dim yellow glow of a single bulb.

The girls grew not only with textbooks but with lessons carved out of sacrifice. They watched their mother patch her old saree instead of buying a new one, deny herself even the basics so they could enjoy fruits, and walk miles just to save a rickshaw fare. Every choice of hers whispered one truth: *this struggle is not yours to inherit.*

Years unfolded. They studied hard, secured positions in reputed companies, and pursued higher education. The elder married an army officer after graduation, while the younger earned her MBA. Both built shining careers, spoke fluent English, and stepped confidently into worlds their mother had once only dreamed of. In their homes now, they even had a cook…life's ironic circle, neatly tied with a bow.

Yet Seema continued working. Each time her daughters begged her to move in, she refused firmly but with grace. Pride and dignity anchored her choice…she did not want to lean on the very shoulders she had spent her life strengthening.

But life tests even the strongest. Her husband fell gravely ill, 10 days in the ICU, machines beeping through sleepless nights, bills stacking in her trembling hands. The numbers blurred into a mountain she could never climb.

And then, something remarkable happened. Her daughters stepped in: not with hesitation, not with calculation, but with the full force of love. The bills were cleared as swiftly as Seema had once softened biscuits…with ease. They stood beside her in hospital corridors, arranging doctors, medicines, and care.

One night, as Seema sat on a bench outside the ICU, her elder daughter leaned close and whispered, 'Ma, please listen to us today. All our lives, you gave and gave, without ever asking for anything in return. You patched your sarees while making sure we had new uniforms. You carried hunger so we could carry hope.'

The younger clasped her mother's hands, tears flowing freely. 'Ma, every salary slip we bring home, every degree we earn, every step of confidence we take – it is not ours, it is yours. We are living proof of your sacrifice. What we are today is your reflection.'

The elder added, her voice breaking, 'And today, if we can hold you, protect you, and give you even a fraction of the comfort you deserve, it is not duty – it is gratitude. You are not our responsibility, Ma. You are our blessing, our pride, our reason to stand tall.'

For the first time, Seema felt what it meant to be carried. She no longer saw her daughters as little girls clinging to her sari's edge, but as women who had inherited her strength, multiplied it, and now gave it back to her.

When her husband returned home frail, Seema moved in with her younger daughter. But it was not dependence – it was recognition.

Her presence was honoured, her sacrifices remembered in every gesture: meals served to her first, grandchildren bowing at her feet before school, daughters gazing at her with unspoken reverence.

Sometimes, they would say to her openly, 'Ma, our degrees, our careers, our homes – everything rests on the foundation you built with blistered hands and an unyielding spirit.'

The circle of life had turned. What Seema had given in hunger, they returned in abundance. What she had sown in silence, they repaid in love.

Gratitude needs no words, yet sometimes it overflows. It is not duty that makes children give back – it is Love. For sacrifice is never forgotten; it lives on in the hearts it nurtured and blossoms into love that returns a thousandfold.

Key Takeaways

1. Gratitude is not about repayment – it is about recognition of love and sacrifice.
2. Gratitude is like Wi-Fi – you may not always see it, but it connects you to everything.
3. True dignity is in giving without expectation, and true gratitude is in receiving with devotion.
4. Gratitude shifts focus from what's missing to what's present.

'Gratitude is not only the greatest of virtues, but the parent of all the others.' – **Cicero**

'When it comes to life, the critical thing is whether you take things for granted or take them with gratitude.' – **G.K. Chesterton**

'Gratitude mainly arises when what we have received exceeds our expectations.

How can we remain permanently in a state of gratitude? Have no expectations at all. Then, we experience everything coming to us as a bonus and receive it with thankfulness.' – **Daaji**

Scoring Guide

When assessing yourself, consider how often you feel **grateful**, how intensely you experience it, and how much it impacts your thoughts, feelings, and behaviours.

Score 0: Minimal Gratitude

You rarely, if ever, feel grateful. You might tend to focus on what's lacking or what's gone wrong, **often taking positive things for granted**. Complaining might be a common habit, and you might struggle to see the good in situations or people, even when it's present.

Score 1: Occasional Gratitude

You experience fleeting moments of gratitude, usually in response to significant positive events or when prompted. However, these feelings are not sustained and don't significantly influence your overall outlook. You might acknowledge good things, but don't actively seek them out or deeply appreciate them.

Score 2: Moderate Gratitude

You feel grateful periodically, especially for clear blessings or helpful acts from others. You can identify things you're thankful for when you think about it, and these feelings occasionally brighten your mood. You might express thanks when necessary, but it's not a consistent practice.

Score 3: Consistent Gratitude

You regularly feel grateful for various aspects of your life, both big and small. You make an effort to appreciate the good things and often express your thanks to others. This gratitude positively impacts your mood and helps you maintain a more optimistic perspective, even when facing challenges.

Score 4: Deeply Grateful

You possess a profound sense of gratitude that permeates many areas of your life. You actively seek out reasons to be thankful and consistently acknowledge the positive contributions of others and circumstances. This deep appreciation significantly enhances your well-being, resilience, and connection to the world around you. You might even keep a gratitude journal or regularly reflect on your blessings.

Score 5: Profound Gratitude

Gratitude is a core part of who you are and how you experience life. You consistently feel and **express a deep sense of thankfulness, seeing blessings even in difficult situations**. This level of gratitude brings profound joy, peace, and a strong sense of interconnectedness, influencing your actions, relationships, and overall life philosophy. You embody gratitude as a way of being.

Reflection Prompts

1. How often do you consciously practice gratitude, and what methods do you use (e.g., journaling, verbalising, daily reflection)?
2. How does a mindset of gratitude impact your overall happiness and your relationships?

8. Compassion

Keshav began, 'It was the summer of 2021. In April, COVID spread like wildfire across India. It was one of the most testing times for governments, medical facilities, and ordinary people, especially in the cities. Each day, over 4.5 lakh people were testing positive. It was a nightmare – not only for those infected but even for those untouched by the virus, who lived in constant dread. The air itself seemed to carry both fear and fever.'

'Government hospitals and the Police bore the heaviest load. I happened to be in Kanpur at that time, stuck there due to the lockdown. My friend Navin's parents tested positive, and his condition deteriorated very quickly. Getting a bed in a hospital had become the most difficult job – even for doctors themselves. By what felt like divine grace, Navin's father finally got admission to LLR Hospital of GSVM Medical College, Kanpur.'

'For 21 days, I sat with Navin outside the hospital, 5–6 hours daily, waiting for the doctors' updates. What I observed was a study in contrasts. On one side, patients lay on stretchers with oxygen cylinders, staring at the hospital doors as if waiting for a miracle – that a bed might open up. On the other side, every half an hour, ward boys would emerge carrying body bags. Normally, in India, passersby offer a silent prayer upon seeing a funeral procession. But in those days, such sights perversely rekindled hope for those waiting – because a departed soul meant one bed had become free.'

'The situation was so grim that police were stationed outside every hospital and medical store, not to salute the medical professionals but to defuse confrontations.'

'I observed death and faint hope walking side by side. Those who could afford to stay indoors did so, including many healthcare professionals. Relationships had suddenly lost priority. Even in the death of close relatives, people hesitated to attend funerals or even visit for a few minutes.

I also observed that a few acquaintances were suffering stress, panic attacks, or imagined symptoms of sickness – proof that fear itself was contagious.'

'There were tragic stories everywhere. A 40-year-old man and his 70-year-old father were admitted together; only the father came out alive. A family of 6 was reduced to 2 in just 20 days. There were countless such tales, each a chapter in a collective nightmare.'

'Meanwhile, those fortunate to be healthy lived under the constant shadow of fear. Some even busied themselves hoarding medicines – as if hoarding paracetamol could vaccinate them against destiny.'

'On the positive side, in the emergency reception area of LLR Hospital, young postgraduate students with their seniors attended tirelessly to the flood of incoming patients, armed with nothing more than a flimsy mask and gloves. In their actions, no fear was visible – only duty.'

Siddarth's Story

'It was here that I met a young professor, Shiva, who taught at a local college. He had come to drop off patients for admission. Curious, I asked how he was related to so many of them. His reply startled me: 'They are not my family. I didn't know them a week ago.'

At a time when even close relatives hesitated to help their own, here was a man moving fearlessly for strangers – with only a cotton *angochha* (thin towel used in Uttar Pradesh) covering his face. While I drank water 5 times in 2 hours, Shiva seemed to have no thirst – his focus quenched by service.

He shared his story. Initially, like everyone else, he stayed home with his wife and 3-year-old daughter. But restlessness gnawed at him. He could not watch helplessly. He set up a small 5-bed facility using his savings for mild patients: oxygen cylinders, basic instruments, and a nurse. Soon, neighbours contributed. Donations poured in, volunteers joined, and within days, Shiva managed to hire a 3-story building, medical equipment, and even secured an ambulance from a generous businessman.

Food came from kind households, and Shiva ran this facility for 3 months, until the wave subsided. The most remarkable part – neither Shiva nor his family were ever infected. Later that year, the Vice President of India invited him and honoured his service.'

Keshav paused. The audience sat in awe.

He continued, 'It is easy to give money for charity, but the hardest gift is giving your time. Siddarth gave not just his money but his time and effort at a moment when the risk was greatest. His act was an example of courage, clarity, and above all – compassion. My salute to all the Siddarths who faced COVID like warriors. I also feel deep gratitude to the doctors, nurses, and police who maintained order amid chaos.

And the final note – Compassion is when Vaibhavi shares her fries with me without being asked.'

Key Takeaways

1. **Compassion is action, not just emotion.**
2. In times of crisis, **fear shrinks relationships, but compassion expands them.**
3. True giving is not money alone but **time, courage, and presence.**
4. Compassion transforms ordinary individuals into **heroes of humanity.**

'The purpose of human life is to serve, and to show compassion and the will to help others.' – **Albert Schweitzer**

'Compassion is not religious business, it is human business.'
– **Dalai Lama**

Scoring Guide

When assessing yourself, consider the **frequency, depth, and breadth** of your compassionate feelings and actions. Think about how often you feel empathy, how deeply it moves you, and how widely you extend it to various individuals and groups.

Score 0: Minimal Compassion

You rarely feel or express compassion for others' suffering. You might struggle to empathize with different perspectives, and your focus is primarily on your own needs and concerns. You may react with indifference or even irritation when confronted with someone else's distress.

Score 1: Limited Compassion

You might experience brief moments of pity or concern for others, but these feelings are generally superficial or fleeting. You may acknowledge suffering, but don't feel a strong urge to alleviate it or understand its roots. Your actions are rarely driven by compassionate motives.

Score 2: Moderate Compassion

You can feel empathy and concern for others, especially those you know well or those whose situations you can easily relate to. You might offer help or support when it's convenient, but you may struggle with sustained engagement or extending compassion to those you find challenging or different from yourself.

Score 3: Consistent Compassion

You regularly feel genuine empathy and concern for the suffering of others, even those you don't know personally. You are often moved by others' pain and have a desire to help. You might take steps to offer support, understanding, or kindness when opportunities arise, even if it requires some effort.

Score 4: Deeply Compassionate

You possess a profound capacity for empathy and are consistently moved by the suffering of all beings. You actively seek to understand others' experiences and perspectives, and your actions are often driven by a strong desire to alleviate pain and promote well-being. You might regularly engage in acts of kindness, volunteering, or advocacy.

Score 5: Profound Compassion

Compassion is a fundamental aspect of your character and guides your interactions with the world. You feel a deep, expansive sense of interconnectedness with others and are **consistently motivated to act with kindness**, understanding, and a desire to reduce suffering, even at personal cost. You are **able to extend compassion even to those who may be difficult or challenging**, demonstrating a rare level of altruism and wisdom.

Reflection Prompts

1. In what situations do you find it challenging to feel or express compassion? What might be blocking it?
2. What is one small act of compassion you can extend to someone (or yourself) today?
3. Could you have compassion for a person who harmed you by lying and using unfair means?

9. Happiness

'The happiest man is who is happy under all circumstances.' – **St. Babuji**

Scoring Guide

Remember, happiness is a complex and fluid emotion. Your score can change daily, and that's completely normal! This scale is meant to be a general guide for awareness.

Score 0: Deep Unhappiness

You constantly feel a profound sense of sadness, despair, or emptiness.

You struggle to find happiness in anything, even activities you once enjoyed.

Negative emotions like anxiety, anger, or hopelessness are dominant in your daily life.

You might be experiencing significant challenges that feel overwhelming and insurmountable.

It's difficult for you to connect with others or feel supported.

Score 1: Mostly Unhappy

You generally feel down or discontented for most of the day.

Moments of happiness are rare and fleeting, often overshadowed by negative feelings.

You might feel stuck in a rut, lacking motivation or direction.

Small stressors can easily trigger a negative emotional response.

You may often feel isolated or misunderstood.

Score 2: Neutral/Mixed Feelings

Your mood is often flat or indifferent; you don't feel particularly happy or sad.

You experience some positive moments, but they don't significantly outweigh periods of boredom, stress, or mild discontent.

You're functioning, but you might not feel a strong sense of purpose or excitement.

You might be going through a period of transition or uncertainty that impacts your overall well-being.

You have some connections, but they might not feel deeply fulfilling.

Score 3: Moderately Happy

You generally feel content and experience positive emotions more often than negative ones.

You find enjoyment in daily activities and have things to look forward to.

You can bounce back from challenges relatively well, and problems don't typically consume you.

You have a sense of purpose and feel generally stable in your life.

You have supportive relationships and feel connected to others.

Score 4: Very Happy

You frequently experience happiness, contentment, and enthusiasm.

You have a strong sense of well-being and optimism about the future.

You feel resilient and capable of handling life's ups and downs effectively.

You feel fulfilled in your work, relationships, and personal pursuits.

You are grateful for what you have and often feel a sense of appreciation.

Score 5: Extremely Happy/Radiant

You consistently feel an abundance of happiness, love, and inner peace.

You are thriving in multiple areas of your life and feel a deep sense of purpose.

Challenges are seen as opportunities for growth, and you approach them with a positive mindset.

You have strong, meaningful connections and feel deeply supported and loved.

You feel energised, inspired, and often share your positive outlook with others. You might even feel like you're 'glowing.'

Reflection Prompts

1. Do you tend to seek happiness externally, or can you cultivate it from within?
2. Make a list of 10 instances when you felt happy and also categorise it into its reason, such as shopping, playing games, helping others, spending time with grandparents, relatives, comparing your possessions with others (and finding yourself better), gossiping etc. In this list, observe which one has a higher frequency?

10. Joy

'A happy man is he who is happy under all circumstances.
Joy is unconditional.
It flowers when we place no demands that certain conditions must be fulfilled.
To remain joyful, expect NOT.'

– St. Babu ji.

Scoring Guide

When assessing yourself, consider the **frequency, intensity, and pervasiveness** of your feelings of joy. How often you truly feel happy, how deeply those feelings resonate, and whether joy is a constant undercurrent in your life or merely an occasional visitor.

Score 0: Minimal Joy

You rarely experience feelings of joy. Life might often feel dull, difficult, or overwhelming, with little to no moments of genuine happiness or delight. You may struggle to find pleasure in activities or connections, and a sense of flatness or negativity might be your prevailing emotional state.

Score 1: Occasional Glimmers of Joy

You experience fleeting moments of joy, but they are rare and often quickly overshadowed by other emotions or concerns. You might notice small pleasures but struggle to savour them or maintain a positive outlook for long. Your default emotional state is generally neutral or slightly negative.

Score 2: Moderate Joy

You experience moments of joy and happiness periodically, often in response to specific positive events or achievements. You can appreciate good things when they happen, and these feelings provide temporary uplift. However, joy might not be a consistent presence in your daily life, and you might still find yourself easily brought down by challenges.

Score 3: Consistent Joy

You regularly feel joy and contentment in your life, even amidst everyday challenges. You have a good capacity to appreciate simple pleasures, positive interactions, and the beauty around you. While you experience other emotions, joy is a frequent and noticeable part of your emotional landscape, contributing to a generally positive outlook.

Score 4: Deeply Joyful

You possess a profound capacity for joy that often arises spontaneously from within, beyond just external circumstances. You frequently experience feelings of delight, contentment, and gratitude. You have a strong ability to find positive meaning in experiences, to celebrate life's moments, and to bounce back from setbacks with a sense of underlying optimism.

Score 5: Profound Joy

Joy is a core, abiding state of being for you, transcending temporary circumstances. You experience an expansive sense of inner lightness, appreciation, and delight in existence itself. Even in the face of adversity, you maintain an underlying sense of peace and optimism. Your joy is often infectious, inspiring others and contributing to a radiant presence.

Reflection Prompts

1. Recall a moment of pure, unadulterated joy. What was happening, and what did it feel like in your body and mind?

2. How is joy different from happiness for you? Is it more fleeting, or more profound?
3. How often do you allow yourself to fully experience and express joy?

11. Empathy

August 1996. Bareilly – nestled in the Terai plains – was sweltering under the sticky 'break-monsoon' heat. Ravi and Umesh felt sidelined while the 'Snow Tigers,' a premier IAF helicopter unit, were off on glamorous operational detachments. One lonely helicopter remained at Bareilly for SAR (Search and Rescue) cover of fighter operations, and Ravi and Umesh were picked to man it – also because they had to take the Part 'B' promotion exam that would qualify them for the next rank.

Umesh, the junior-most Pilot Officer, partnered with Ravi, a Flying Officer. For Ravi, this exam was the last throw of the dice before his next rank – Flight Lieutenant – due in a couple of months.

Still, both were peeved at missing the action. 'Why us?' Umesh fumed, pacing a lawn decorated with more cigarette butts than grass.

'*Saheb, itna cigarette mat piyo*,' pleaded Balakram, the unit cook and unofficial self-appointed wellness officer – he'd watched pilots grow into Air Marshals on a steady diet of chai and courage.

'*Do chai aur lao*,' Umesh waved him off, grumbling, 'We aren't even supposed to fly together,' citing the ops instruction that required at least a Flight Lieutenant for missions beyond the local circuit.

Ravi grinned. 'Exactly why we're here – why waste a precious Flight Lieutenant for base SAR during a big exercise?'

Umesh bristled. 'Think of the nap-of-earth runs along Bikaner and Jaisalmer, we're missing!'

'And the moon-lit dune parties,' Ravi winked – clearly enjoying Umesh working himself into a righteous rage.

Command Headquarters permitted, on request, a Pilot Officer and a Flying Officer to man SAR coverage at Bareilly for 3 days owing to manning constraints – **strictly** SAR for base fighter ops and nothing more.

Mid-sip of their nth cup of chai, the ops phone barked in the Flight Commander's office.

Ravi picked up.

'This is Gp Capt Naik – are you up for a casualty evacuation from Fatehgarh to Command Hospital, Lucknow?' boomed the Chief Ops Officer.

Ravi hesitated. 'Sir, I'm paired with a Pilot Officer, and our mandate is SAR for base fighter ops only.'

'I know, son. I also know you have your Air Force Law exam this afternoon – I even suspended fighter flying for 3 hours for it – and it's your last attempt before promotion.'

Then the brief: a training accident at the Sikh Regimental Centre, Fatehgarh. During grenade practice, a recruit froze after pulling the pin; the blast shredded his hand and head, and a Subedar beside him suffered devastating chest injuries. Command Ops wanted to know if *we* could evacuate – Gorakhpur's helicopter would take over an hour; Bareilly could be there in forty minutes.

'You have 5 minutes to decide,' he boomed. 'If you miss the exam, I can't guarantee your rank.' *Click.*

Umesh, who'd heard every word on speaker, looked unsure. '*Bhaiji, soch lo* – you may not be able to put on your rank,' he said, worried about the seniority hit.

'What's there to think?' Ravi pointed to the wall motto blazing in paint: **'HELICOPTERS, ABOVE ALL, SAVE LIVES.'**

As Ravi dialled the Chief Ops Officer, Umesh was already sprinting to the hangar to get a second stretcher fitted. 5 minutes later, checks complete.

Ravi started up; Umesh traced Bareilly-to-Fatehgarh on his shiny laminated 1:1,000,000 map – trusty nav aid when paired with Human Thumb Mk-II.

They launched urgently. The last fighter turned short finals – fighter flying had been suspended because the only SAR bird was now a CASEVAC bird.

Butterflies. This was Ravi's first pilot-in-command casualty evacuation – every military pilot's coming-of-age. He prayed to

Bajrangbali: 'keep them alive till we land; help us get them to Lucknow in time.'

The leg to Fatehgarh flashed by with Ravi holding Vne (never exceed speed) and Umesh the apocalypse-navigator – no bend, Y-fork, nullah, or crack went unnoticed.

They landed and switched off at Fatehgarh Cantt helipad. The air felt heavy – like the entire regimental centre had gathered to pre-mourn 2 of its own.

The Regimental Centre Dr arrived to accompany the casualties to Command Hospital, Lucknow.

As the ambulance drew alongside, the sight stunned them: the Subedar's chest was held together by blood-soaked bandages; he groaned despite heavy sedation – the blast had opened his chest as he stood next to the recruit he was training.

The second patient arrived: a bandaged stump where the right arm had been; the skull held gingerly by layers of bloody gauze, a medical attendant balancing a petri dish to keep grey matter from spilling. For Ravi and Umesh, it felt like Bajrangbali's grace that both were still alive.

The real test began: Ravi and Umesh couldn't just watch. The army team and the doctor weren't trained to load helicopter stretchers. It was delicate, slow, and brutal – 2 stretchers stacked, blood, bandages, and careful angles. Nausea rose often; prayer steadied their hands.

The hop to Lucknow Cantt felt instantaneous. As they came in to land, only one question burned: *Are they still alive?*

With the rotors winding down, Ravi heard the Subedar groan. The doctor checked the recruit – still breathing.

There was no space for elation – only a quiet, sobering philosophical pondering of how fragile and transient physical existence really is.

A couple of cigarettes later, they lifted from Lucknow. The flight back to Bareilly was wordless – no energy, no space, no words.

Back at Bareilly, smiling Balakram awaited them with tea and biscuits. His only question: '*Saheb, woh bach gaye na*?'

That evening, during the briefing call, the Flight Commander – away at Bikaner – was furious.

'Do you realize what you've done? I left you to take Part 'B'. Why go when Chief Ops Officer offered you the option to sit the exam? What difference would twenty minutes have made? Now face the consequences (of missing the rank)!'

Ravi had no energy left to explain the patients' condition – or what had driven his decision.

The next day, Umesh called Command Hospital, Lucknow. The recruit with the head injury had passed in the night. The Subedar was still fighting – hard – but his fate was uncertain.

P.S. The next week, with everyone back from detachments, an in-person dressing-down awaited them – especially Ravi, the senior of the two and, on paper, the one who'd 'lost' the most.

Two weeks later, the Commandant of the Sikh Regimental Centre, Fatehgarh, called the AOC, AF Station Bareilly, and the CO to thank the unit for the prompt airlift – crediting it with saving the Subedar's life.

Ravi put on his next rank on time, thanks to the CO and AOC Bareilly securing authorisation for a special Part 'B' exam the following month – just for him.

His name now features on the Snow Tigers' honour roll, following a commendation from the AOC-in-C for the casualty evacuation.

Keshav: 'Ravi, why choose the mission when you had the option not to?'

Ravi: 'Sir, when I heard a Jawan's head and a Subedar's chest were shattered, one thought came – if it were my own brother, would I still be thinking about my last attempt at the promotion exam?'

Keshav: 'I was speechless – an act of empathy and selflessness.'

Key Takeaways

1. **Empathy before self-interest:** In real crises, human life outranks exams, rules, and career calculus.
2. **Character is a choice:** Decisions under pressure reveal our inner script.

3. **Compassion = empathy in motion:** Feeling moved is not enough; action completes the virtue.
4. **Leadership lesson:** Institutions remember courage and humanity longer than test scores.
5. **Witnessing suffering matures us:** Proximity to pain deepens humility and perspective.

'Empathy is a precursor to compassion. Compassion is empathy in action.' – **Daaji**

'Could a greater miracle take place than for us to look through each other's eyes for an instant?' – **Henry David Thoreau**

'The highest form of knowledge is empathy.' – **Bill Bullard**

Scoring Guide

When assessing yourself, consider the **frequency, depth, and breadth** of your empathetic experiences. Think about how often you truly understand what others are feeling, how deeply those emotions resonate with you, and how widely you extend this understanding to various individuals and situations.

Score 0: Minimal or Absent Empathy

You rarely, if ever, consider or accurately understand the feelings, thoughts, or perspectives of others. You might struggle to connect with people on an emotional level and often find yourself focused solely on your own needs and experiences, making it difficult to respond sensitively to others.

Score 1: Limited Empathy

You occasionally recognize the emotions of others, but it's often superficial or only in very obvious situations. You might intellectually grasp what someone is feeling, but struggle to genuinely feel *with* them or understand their situation from their point of view. Your responses might sometimes seem insensitive or detached.

Score 2: Moderate, Situational Empathy

You can experience empathy periodically, especially with people you know well or in situations that are clearly relatable. You might be able to put yourself in others' shoes sometimes, but your empathy can be inconsistent, and you may struggle to connect with those whose experiences are very different from your own.

Score 3: Consistent Empathety

You regularly demonstrate the ability to understand and share the feelings of others. You often consider different perspectives and can accurately perceive emotional states. This empathy guides your interactions, helping you respond thoughtfully and provide support when needed, even if you don't always fully *feel* their emotions.

Score 4: Deeply Empathic

You possess a strong and pervasive capacity for deep empathy. You **frequently sense and understand the underlying emotions and perspectives of others**, often without them needing to explicitly state them. This **allows you to connect genuinely**, offer profound support, and tailor your responses with great sensitivity and compassion.

Score 5: Profound Empathy/Highly Attuned

Empathy is a core and consistently active part of your being. You possess an exceptional ability to deeply understand, feel, and resonate with the emotional states and experiences of others, often sensing nuances that others miss. You are highly attuned to human emotion, which profoundly influences your interactions and allows you to connect with a wide range of people on a very deep level.

Reflection Prompts

1. Recall a recent situation where you felt you truly experienced empathy for another person. What was the context, and what allowed you to connect with their feelings?
2. How does your ability to experience empathy impact your relationships, your communication, and your capacity to offer support to others?
3. In what situations or with what types of people do you find it most challenging to experience empathy? What might be blocking it?

12. Jealousy

Kavya and Sunaina were cousins, born just months apart – double-bonded, for their mothers were sisters and their fathers brothers. Yet their childhoods unfolded in 2 very different worlds. Kavya was strikingly beautiful: green eyes like glass marbles, porcelain skin that made people turn twice. Sunaina, too, was beautiful, but her true distinction lay not in looks but in the world she inhabited.

Sunaina's father held a senior position in the Central Government, and they lived in a sprawling Delhi bungalow. Servants bustled in crisp uniforms, cars lined the porch, and dinner parties glimmered with ministers, artists, and intellectuals. Theirs was a home where laughter was abundant and generosity flowed like wine at the dining table. Her mother managed it all with effortless elegance; life for her was steeped in comfort, not chores.

Kavya, meanwhile, lived in a smaller city. Her father, too, held a respectable government post, but a miserly streak kept the family to a bare minimum – not for lack of money, but by choice. Their house had no servants, no luxuries. Her mother cooked, scrubbed, and cleaned with her own hands, often with Kavya beside her. She grew up hearing her mother's bangles clink against buckets of water, while knowing that her aunt, just hours away in Delhi, hosted tea parties with silver spoons. In short, while one household polished silver, the other polished steel utensils – both shining, but with very different budgets.

Every summer, Kavya's family spent a month at Sunaina's house. To outsiders, the visits looked like warm reunions. But in Kavya's heart, a silent fire smouldered – the contrast pricked her like a thorn. Those weeks felt like standing before a mirror that only reflected her lacks. She would sit on the polished marble floor, sipping juice poured by a maid, while her thoughts drifted to the struggles back home. Her beauty – those green eyes, that porcelain skin – felt worthless when weighed against the effortless grace of Sunaina's life.

Jealousy revealed itself in small, sharp ways. It crept into their innocent childhood games. At 7, Kavya once proposed they wash their faces to see who was fairer. She already knew her pale skin would 'win,' yet she pushed Sunaina to try again and again, mocking each attempt – 'Nah, it's still me. Try again!'

Every child loves a game, but some games come with invisible scoreboards that stay long after the toys are put away.

Another time, on a family holiday in Haridwar, when they were 9, Sunaina leaned too close to the river's edge. Kavya gave a shove. Sunaina tumbled into the rushing Ganga. Panic spread, adults screamed, and both father and uncle dived in to rescue her. Kavya stood by nervously, insisting it was just play. But even she knew there was more to it. Such moments piled up silently, like invisible bricks building a wall between them. Sunaina, gentle by nature, never fought back. But as a child, she could never understand why her cousin treated her like a rival.

Years passed, and the cousins' lives branched further apart. Sunaina blossomed in the world of art and literature that her parents had nurtured. Kavya, craving her own wings, became an air hostess – flying high, yet still carrying an invisible weight inside.

As Sunaina grew older, her perspective softened her heart. She saw that Kavya's sharpness was not born of cruelty, but of an ache. The root of Kavya's behaviour was not malice, but circumstance. Sunaina had grown up in a privilege she had never earned, while Kavya lived with restraint, her pride constantly bruised by comparison. So Sunaina chose never to hold grudges. She let go of childhood wounds, though an unspoken distance remained between them.

Eventually, still carrying her old wounds, Kavya made a choice that shocked everyone. She married a man eighteen years older – a prominent industrialist whose name graced glossy magazines. For a moment, Kavya seemed to have everything she once envied. To outsiders, it looked like a fairy-tale match. For a short while, her name filled newspapers, her face adorned society pages. But behind the closed doors of his mansion, the marriage lacked love. Within a year, it collapsed, leaving Kavya lonelier than before.

Sometimes, what we chase to fill the void ends up giving us front-row seats to emptiness – but in designer clothes.

The cousins drifted apart, meeting only at family functions. Their bond stayed cordial but distant, like guests in each other's lives. Until one winter, when life tilted. Kavya fell seriously ill, and illness stripped away all her masks. When Sunaina visited her in the hospital, time dissolved. 2 cousins, now women in their forties, sat staring at each other with eyes heavy with memories. Kavya's voice, once sharp with pride, broke into a whisper: 'I'm glad you came.' Perhaps it was the intimacy of that moment that cracked open years of silence.

Kavya spoke hesitantly.

'Do you remember Haridwar? Do you remember that silly game about who's fairer?'

Sunaina smiled softly. 'Of course I do.'

Kavya's eyes welled. 'I don't know why I did those things. The child in me just wanted to win at something.'

She reached for Sunaina's hand.

'You know, visiting you every summer was the hardest thing. I'd see your home, your effortless comfort… and then return to mine. I felt small. So I acted out. Not because I hated you, but because I hated what life denied me. I'm sorry.'

Sunaina's own eyes brimmed. 'Kavya… I understood long ago. It was never you against me – it was you against circumstance. I never resented you. I just didn't know how to reach you. That's why we stayed distant.'

Kavya blinked, surprised. 'You… understood?'

'Yes,' Sunaina whispered. 'And I only wish I had told you sooner.'

Tears brimmed, not of shame but of release. For the first time, the unspoken was spoken. They laughed through their tears, remembering silly games – even the near-drowning in the Ganga. Years of silence collapsed, leaving only 2 women who finally saw each other clearly.

As they laughed, Sunaina joked, 'Well, at least you didn't try to push me into corporate politics next time!' and they both burst out laughing, healing years of unsaid words in one shared chuckle.

Sunaina and Kavya proved that even the heaviest baggage of childhood can, at last, be unpacked – together. And so, they healed. The lesson remained: jealousy is not always born of malice. Often it is born of circumstance, too heavy for a child to carry or comprehend. But when met with empathy, even decades of distance can dissolve into forgiveness.

Keshav's Take

Envy and jealousy may look alike, but they are not the same. Envy is when we see something good in others, admire it with a clean heart, and perhaps wish to have it too. Jealousy, however, arises when we see something good in others and, unable to have it, start breeding negative thoughts. We may make nasty comments, speak ill behind their back, or highlight their shortcomings just to dim their light.

At its root, jealousy comes from our own desires – for wealth, power, status, or possessions – constantly compared with what others have. These negative thoughts disturb our inner energy centres (Chakras), and when repeated, they harden into *samskaras*.

Envy is when your neighbour buys a new car; jealousy is when you secretly hope it breaks down. Or worse, when you start calculating his EMI with suspiciously divine accuracy.

Remember: everyone has their own life script. Success and failure arrive according to that script. Just as you cannot walk another person's path, you need not compare your possessions or capabilities with theirs. The best way forward is to appreciate what others have and if possible, learn from them.

Duryodhana's jealousy

Suyodhana's (Duryodhan) jealousy toward the Pandavas is legendary. It was partly fuelled by his father, partly by his uncle Shakuni, but mostly ignited by himself. Despite repeated counsel from elders – even from Lord Krishna himself – he stuck to it. That jealousy eventually consumed everything: his kingdom, his brothers, his elders, his army, and finally his own life.

Jealousy, when left unchecked, can destroy not only relationships but entire legacies.

Key Takeaways

1. **Jealousy is not proof of hate – it often hides unhealed pain.**
2. **Envy admires, jealousy resents.** Envy can inspire us, jealousy corrodes us.
3. **Privilege is invisible from the inside.** Sunaina couldn't see her own comfort until she understood Kavya's pain.
4. **Life scripts are unique.** No comparison is valid, because no 2 journeys are the same.
5. **Forgiveness is freedom.** It releases both the one who hurt and the one who was hurt.

'Some filters like prejudice, jealousy, envy, greed, and anger are so effective that they function like an underground nuclear bunker – they do not allow anything to penetrate.
They prevent the beam of love from working it's magic.' – **Daaji**
'Envy can make us aspire; jealousy only makes us conspire.'
'Jealousy is the root of all evil, and a most difficult thing to conquer.'
– **Swami Vivekananda**

Scoring Guide

Score 0: Overwhelming, Debilitating Jealousy

Jealousy is a constant and consuming force in your life. You are plagued by intense, often irrational, jealousy that interferes with your daily functioning, destroys trust in relationships, and causes extreme emotional turmoil. These feelings lead to highly possessive, controlling, or even aggressive behaviours, and severely impact your mental well-being and ability to form healthy connections.

Score 1: Significant, Distressing Jealousy

You frequently experience strong, pervasive feelings of jealousy that cause significant distress. These feelings might lead to obsessive thoughts, suspicion, insecurity, and potentially controlling or irrational behaviours in relationships or other areas. It significantly impacts your peace of mind and can strain your connections with others.

Score 2: Frequent, Impactful Jealousy

Jealousy is a more frequent and sometimes intense emotion for you. It might arise in various areas of your life (e.g., relationships, career, social circles). These feelings can lead to noticeable discomfort, self-doubt, or even some minor behavioural changes (e.g., checking up on someone, feeling competitive). While you try to control it, it can sometimes influence your mood or interactions.

Score 3: Moderate, Manageable Jealousy

You experience jealousy periodically, perhaps in certain types of situations or relationships (e.g., romantic, professional). These feelings are noticeable and can cause mild discomfort, but you are generally able to manage them, communicate your feelings constructively if needed, and prevent them from escalating or negatively impacting your actions.

Score 4: Occasional, Fleeting Jealousy

You might experience brief, mild pangs of jealousy on rare occasions, usually in very specific or unusual circumstances. These feelings are fleeting, easily dismissed, and don't lead to significant distress or impact your behaviour. You can quickly recognize and rationalise them away.

Score 5: Minimal or No Jealousy

You rarely, if ever, experience feelings of jealousy. You feel secure in your relationships and self-worth, and you genuinely celebrate the successes and good fortune of others without feeling threatened or resentful. You trust easily and don't often compare yourself to others in a negative light.

Reflection Prompts

1. What underlying insecurities or fears does jealousy typically reveal for you?
2. How does jealousy manifest in your thoughts or behaviours (e.g., comparison, possessiveness, resentment)?
3. What is one positive action you could take when jealousy arises, instead of succumbing to its negative aspects?

13. **Pride**

'It was pride that changed angels into devils; it is humility that makes men as angels.' – **Saint Augustine**

'He that is proud eats up himself: pride is his own glass, his own trumpet, his own chronicle.' – **William Shakespeare**

Scoring Guide

It's important to clarify that 'pride' can have both positive and negative connotations. This **scale leans towards assessing the *negative* aspects**

of excessive pride, moving towards a healthier, more balanced sense of self at the higher scores.

When assessing yourself, consider the **impact** of your pride on your learning, relationships, and ability to accept reality. Think about whether it empowers you positively or creates barriers to growth and connection.

Score 0: Overwhelming, Detrimental Pride

Your sense of self-importance is pervasive and often leads to arrogance, stubbornness, and an inability to admit fault. You might struggle to learn from mistakes, dismiss feedback, and believe you are consistently superior to others. This level of pride severely hinders personal growth, meaningful relationships, and objective self-assessment (awareness). Humility is almost absent.

Score 1: Significant, Impeding Pride

You frequently exhibit strong pride that makes it difficult to acknowledge your weaknesses, accept criticism, or truly appreciate others' contributions. You might be highly sensitive to perceived slights or challenges to your authority/competence. This level of pride often creates friction in relationships and can prevent you from seeking help or collaborating effectively.

Score 2: Noticeable, Occasional Pride

You experience moments where pride influences your thoughts and behaviours, making it harder to admit mistakes or genuinely listen to opposing viewpoints. While you might eventually come around, your **initial reaction is often defensive or self-protective**. You might sometimes struggle with feeling superior or needing to be right.

Score 3: Balanced, Healthy Pride (with occasional slips)

You generally possess a healthy sense of self-worth and take appropriate pride in your achievements. However, there are still times when pride can get in the way, making it slightly difficult to accept criticism or genuinely apologize. You are mostly able to distinguish between healthy self-esteem and excessive self-focus.

Score 4: Healthy Self-Esteem with Humility

You have a strong and secure sense of your own value and capabilities, allowing you to take satisfaction in your accomplishments. Crucially, this is balanced with a genuine sense of humility; you can acknowledge your limitations, learn from others, admit mistakes readily, and appreciate the contributions of everyone around you.

Score 5: Secure Humility and Self-Acceptance

Your sense of self is deeply rooted in genuine self-acceptance and a profound understanding of your place in the larger scheme of things. You experience joy in your achievements without needing external validation or superiority. You are highly open to learning, genuinely value others, and are free from the need to prove yourself. True humility and self-awareness are defining characteristics.

Reflection Prompts

1. Recall a time when excessive pride or ego created a barrier in a relationship or led to a negative outcome.
2. What is the distinction for you between healthy self-esteem and unproductive pride?
3. Do you take pride in the achievements of your children while having a feeling of superiority?

14. Embarrassment

'The first and best victory is to conquer self; to be conquered by self is, of all things, the most shameful and vile.' – **Plato**

'Anyone who isn't embarrassed of who they were last year probably isn't learning enough'. – **Alain de Botton**

Scoring Guide

Here 0 represents **maximum (frequent/intense) embarrassment** and 5 represents **minimum (rare/mild) embarrassment**.

When assessing yourself, consider the **frequency, intensity, and duration** of your feelings of embarrassment. Think about how often you feel it, how strongly it affects you, and how long it takes you to recover from an embarrassing moment.

Score 0: Overwhelming, Debilitating Embarrassment

You are constantly plagued by intense feelings of embarrassment, even in minor social interactions or for imagined flaws. These feelings are highly distressing and lead to severe social anxiety, avoidance of new experiences, and difficulty functioning in public. You frequently dwell on perceived mistakes or awkward moments, even long after they've passed.

Score 1: Significant, Frequent Embarrassment

You frequently experience strong feelings of embarrassment that can be highly uncomfortable and noticeable. You might be overly concerned with how others perceive you, leading to self-consciousness, hesitation in speaking up, or a tendency to blush/fidget often. These feelings can significantly limit your social comfort and willingness to take risks.

Score 2: Moderate, Occasional Embarrassment

You experience feelings of embarrassment periodically, especially in situations where you make a noticeable mistake or feel exposed. While uncomfortable, these feelings are typically manageable and don't lead to long-term distress or severe social avoidance. You might feel a flush of heat or awkwardness, but you can usually recover fairly quickly.

Score 3: Mild, Infrequent Embarrassment

You experience mild feelings of embarrassment only occasionally, usually in response to genuine blunders or truly awkward social situations. These feelings are fleeting, and you can quickly brush them off or laugh at yourself. You are generally comfortable in social settings and don't dwell on minor missteps.

Score 4: Rare, Minimal Embarrassment

You very rarely experience feelings of embarrassment. When you do, they are extremely mild and short-lived, more akin to a slight awkwardness than true distress. You possess a high degree of self-acceptance and are not easily flustered by social mishaps or the opinions of others.

Score 5: Virtually No Embarrassment

You are highly resilient to feelings of embarrassment. You possess a strong sense of self-acceptance and humour, allowing you to navigate social blunders or awkward moments with ease. You don't take yourself too seriously, and your focus is more on genuine connection and authenticity than on how you are perceived by others.

Reflection Prompts

1. How do you typically react when you feel embarrassed (e.g., blushing, wanting to disappear, laughing it off)?
2. Could you identify the root cause of one of your embarrassing moments and take a thought not to repeat the same action (which led to shame) in future?

15. Anxiety

Once I was sitting with a spiritual trainer, Pathak ji, when Raj – a 28-year-old professional – came to meet him. Raj explained that he had been struggling with stomach issues for a few months and that his doctor had suggested he learn meditation.

Pathak ji smiled and said, 'I am not a doctor; perhaps you should consult one.'

Raj replied, 'As I said, my doctor is the one who advised me to try meditation.'

Pathak ji asked Raj to narrate the whole story.

Raj said, '2 months ago, I began having frequent stomach upsets, so I visited a premier government hospital. After a month, my problem had reduced by about 50 per cent. But I grew anxious and switched hospitals – this time to one of India's top 3 private hospitals.

After more than a month of treatment there, my condition improved further, but it wasn't fully cured. During my last visit, I asked the doctor, *'When will I be completely healthy?'* He replied, *'Keep taking the medication, but you also need to learn meditation for full recovery.'* So, here I am.'

Pathak ji then asked Raj to share about his life.

Raj explained that he came from a farming family and that his father had passed away a year ago. He was working in Hyderabad in the private sector, while his mother and younger sister lived in his ancestral village. His *patidars* (cousins and uncles) were using every trick to try and snatch his farmland.

Raj had developed a fear – unfounded but very real to him – that they might even attempt on his life. He worried constantly, *'What will happen to my mother and sister if I am murdered?'*

This concern spiralled into a loop of negative thoughts, where he kept making plans for imagined scenarios. After a few months, health problems surfaced. He had already visited 2 hospitals. 'Even at work, my performance has slipped,' Raj admitted. 'I'm falling behind schedule, and my boss isn't happy with me. I am also facing a dilemma whether I should leave my job and shift to my village or leave everything at the village and shift my family here with me. But I know that my mother shall feel uprooted and would never be happy with this decision.'

Pathak ji explained, 'In certain cases, the root cause of your stomach issues may not be food or infection – it may be fear.' He suggested Raj read 2 books: *The Biology of Belief* and *You Can Heal Your Life* to understand the root cause of his disease.

Raj reminded him, 'But I'd still like to learn meditation, to get rid of this problem.'

Pathak ji replied, 'You must continue your medication. Meditation is not a treatment in itself – it is something deeper. But if you wish to learn and observe its effect on your health, you're most welcome. Remember, meditation is a way of life, not the 'PCM phenomenon' – where you pop a pill for fever and forget about it later.'

He chuckled and added, 'You can't outsource peace of mind to a pharmacy yet – not even in the age of AI.'

On Raj's insistence, Pathak ji agreed to introduce him to meditation. The process required 3 sessions on consecutive days.

- After the **first session**, Raj said he felt better, as if 50 per cent of his problems had dissolved.
- After the **second session**, he claimed 90 per cent relief.
- After the **third session**, he said, 'I feel cured.'

Pathak ji also taught him the Meditation and Cleaning technique, which was to be practised daily.

I was keen to know the effect on Raj after these sessions. Within 15 days, his gut health had returned to a normal state, and Raj said he was sleeping very well. Seeing the progress, his doctor – the same one who had recommended meditation – also stopped his medicines.

Raj even joked, 'Doctor *saab* cured my stomach, but Pathak ji cured the reason I had it in knots.'

One day, while sitting with Pathak ji, the topic of Raj came up again. Pathak ji explained:

'Raj had begun accumulating unwanted energy from his initial concerns. Later, this pattern intensified, since he didn't know how to handle his stress. That stress then upgraded into anxiety, and during this time, his health began to deteriorate. Had he delayed further, it could have probably escalated into panic attacks.

During the first few sessions, these accumulated energies were cleaned. That's why he felt instant relief, and since then, he has continued his own daily meditation and cleaning.'

With a smile, he added, '**See the effect of this ancient technique! And the beauty is – it's free of charge.**'

He shared further his experiences – cases of young students and professionals burdened with stress, and even a middle-aged lady struggling with panic attacks – all of whom found relief through meditation and Cleaning.

Then Pathak ji asked my views. I replied, 'I understand that the first filter of fear began obstructing Raj's vision. Then, more filters of emotions were added. This led to confusion and helplessness, and eventually to anxiety and his health issues. Dr Bruce H. Lipton also says the same thing.

I continued, 'From what I've observed, real healing and correction in our approach usually happen at 3 levels:

1. **Energetic level** – First, by meeting a spiritual trainer and receiving help in cleaning the subtle residues that cling to us. Think of it as spring-cleaning the unseen corners of our system.
2. **Daily discipline** – Then, by learning to clean ourselves every day, so that new unwanted impressions don't pile up like dust.
3. **Understanding the mind** – Finally, by studying and reflecting through books or teachings that explain how the noise of the mind impacts our health, peace, and productivity.

When these 3 work together, the storm of anxiety begins to lose its power, and what remains is a lighter, clearer state of being.'

Key Takeaways

1. **Fear is the Seed** – What begins as concern can, if unchecked, grow into stress, anxiety, panic attacks, and even physical illness.
2. **Loop of Thoughts** – Anxiety thrives on 'what if' scenarios. The mind can invent battles long before reality arrives.

3. **Medicine and Meditation** – Medicine addresses the body, meditation addresses the mind. Healing works best when both are balanced.
4. **Cleaning Matters** – Removing accumulated unwanted energies prevents fear from snowballing into anxiety or panic attacks.
5. **Filters of Perception** – Fear, emotions, and confusion act like filters over our vision, blocking clarity and peace. Running from one external solution to another without addressing these inner filters rarely brings lasting relief.
6. **Wisdom Doesn't Always Come with a Bill** – As Pathak ji reminded, sometimes the most profound ancient cures are free of charge – like meditation.

'Try to accept the changing seasons of your heart, even if they cause anxiety. Who knows what new spring is waiting to be born?' – **Rumi**

'Our anxiety does not come from thinking about the future, but from wanting to control it.' – **Kahlil Gibran**

'Anxiety does not empty tomorrow of its sorrows, but only empties today of its strength.' – **Charles Spurgeon**

Scoring Guide

Here, 0 represents **maximum (severe/debilitating) anxiety** and 5 represents **minimum (healthy/absent) anxiety**.

Score 0: Overwhelming, Debilitating Anxiety

You are constantly plagued by severe, pervasive anxiety that significantly interferes with nearly every aspect of your life. You experience **frequent panic attacks, intense worry that is difficult to control,** and physical symptoms of anxiety (e.g., racing heart, shortness of breath, trembling) nearly daily. This level of anxiety makes it extremely difficult to work, maintain relationships, or engage in daily activities.

Score 1: Significant, Frequent Anxiety

You experience strong, persistent feelings of anxiety much of the time. While you might not have constant panic attacks, you often feel a deep sense of worry, dread, or apprehension about various aspects of your life. Physical symptoms are common, and your anxiety frequently impacts your decisions, sleep, concentration, and social interactions.

Score 2: Moderate, Disruptive Anxiety

You experience noticeable anxiety frequently, perhaps several times a week or in specific recurring situations. While you can generally function, your anxiety causes significant discomfort, restlessness, and can sometimes disrupt your focus, sleep, or ability to enjoy activities. **You often find yourself worrying excessively**.

Score 3: Mild, Occasional Anxiety

You experience **mild feelings of anxiety from time to time**, typically in response to specific stressors (e.g., public speaking, deadlines, major life changes). These feelings are manageable, don't last long, and you can usually calm yourself down or find ways to cope. While you may have moments of worry, it doesn't significantly impact your daily life.

Score 4: Rare, Brief Anxiety (Adaptive)

You very **rarely experience anxiety**. When you do, it's a brief, mild, and often adaptive response to a genuine threat or challenge, which helps you focus and perform better. You quickly return to a calm state once the situation passes. You have a strong sense of inner peace and resilience.

Score 5: Virtually No Anxiety (High Calm/Resilience)

You rarely **experience anxiety**. You approach life with a profound sense of calm, confidence, and equanimity. You are highly resilient to stress, adaptable to change, and maintain a steady, positive outlook even in challenging circumstances. Worry is not a part of your typical emotional landscape.

Reflection Prompts

1. What are the most common situations or thoughts that trigger anxiety for you?
2. How does anxiety manifest physically, mentally, and emotionally in your body?
3. What coping mechanisms do you typically employ when feeling anxious? Are they effective long-term?

16. Loneliness

It was a breezy Saturday evening. Vaibhavi and Yash were walking towards Keshav Uncle's house, balancing a box of *samosas* and a bowl of mint *chutney*. The neighbourhood already knew the drill: whenever Keshav Uncle was around, deep conversations, oranges from his tree, and snacks went hand in hand.

This time, however, the garden felt quieter. Keshav was seated alone on the veranda, staring at the fading orange horizon. His usual spark was dimmer.

'Uncle, are you okay?' Vaibhavi asked, placing the snacks on the table.

Keshav smiled faintly. 'Yes, beta. Just… a little thoughtful today. You know, despite all the people we meet in life, loneliness is one companion that somehow sneaks in uninvited.'

Yash plopped onto a chair. 'Loneliness? But you're never alone, Uncle. You have friends, family, grandchildren chasing you with water guns… the works!'

Keshav chuckled. 'True, Yash. I was remembering an amazing friend who faced loneliness after taking a divorce and had to endure its adverse effects. The loneliness isn't about *how many* people are around you – it's about *how connected* you feel. You can be in a crowd and still feel unseen, unheard, or misunderstood. It's like being added to ten WhatsApp groups and still feeling nobody really gets your good morning GIFs.'

Vaibhavi nodded softly. 'I've felt that too. Like when your mind is buzzing with worries and no one seems to get it.'

'Exactly,' Keshav said. 'Loneliness does tricky things. Mentally, it breeds negative loops – our own thoughts keep replaying old worries like a broken cassette. Emotionally, it reduces self-worth – you start believing maybe you don't deserve a connection. Some even slip into anxiety or depression. And in that hollow, people turn to escapes – binge shows, food, or worse.

Yash whistled. 'That explains my 3 tubs of ice cream last week.'

They all laughed, but Keshav continued with seriousness. 'Relationships also take a hit. Some get clingy, desperate for attention. Others withdraw completely, afraid of rejection. Either way, loneliness distorts perceptions – you start reading harmless gestures as personal slights.

When my friend was in the grip of loneliness, he used to have difficulty in finding his bearings. At times, we need confirmation for a decision or mystical experience from someone whom we trust and who is also capable. At times, even one may start doubting themselves. Then desperation is not very far.'

He paused, sipping his tea. 'And the body suffers too. Did you know chronic loneliness weakens immunity as much as smoking 15 cigarettes a day? Sleep suffers, blood pressure rises, even the heart weakens.'

Vaibhavi's brows furrowed. 'That's scary. And spiritually?'

Keshav leaned back, his voice softer. 'Spiritually, loneliness shrinks awareness. You get so entangled in self-centred thoughts that you forget the bigger picture. Life begins to feel hollow, meaningless. Inner peace becomes a distant guest.'

The trio sat in reflective silence. Even the squirrels seemed unusually quiet, as if they too were absorbing the weight of his words.

Yash finally asked, 'So what do we do, Uncle? How do we deal with it?'

Keshav smiled gently. 'First, by acknowledging it – loneliness thrives in shadows. Second, by balancing solitude and connection. Solitude heals, but only when you're at peace with yourself. Loneliness hurts when you're at war within. And third, by reaching out – whether through family, friends, or spiritual practice. Connection with others begins with connection inside.'

Vaibhavi placed her hand on his. 'Uncle, thank you. You turned a *samosa* evening into a therapy session again.'

Keshav laughed heartily.

Key Takeaways

1. Loneliness is not about being alone, but about feeling disconnected.
2. It **harms the mind** (negative loops, anxiety, depression), **relationships** (clinginess or withdrawal), **body** (weakened immunity, poor sleep, chronic illness), and **spirit** (loss of meaning, shrinking awareness).
3. **Loneliness thrives in silence** – naming and sharing it is the first step to healing.
4. **True antidote**: balancing solitude with meaningful connection, and cultivating peace within.

'The eternal quest of the individual human being is to shatter his loneliness.' – **Norman Cousins**

'Loneliness and the feeling of being unwanted is the most terrible poverty.' – **Dalai Lama**

'Loneliness narrows the mind, weakens the body, and burdens the spirit. But the flip side is also true: ***connection, community, and meaningful relationships*** *act like medicine at all three levels.'* – **Anonymous**

Scoring Guide

Here, 0 represents **maximum (severe/debilitating) loneliness** and 5 represents **minimum (healthy connection/contentment) loneliness.**

Score 0: Profound, Debilitating Loneliness

You experience a constant, deep, and overwhelming sense of isolation and disconnection, even when surrounded by others. This feeling is severely distressing and permeates almost every aspect of your life, making it difficult to find joy, engage in activities, or believe in the possibility of meaningful connection. You feel **fundamentally alone and misunderstood**.

Score 1: Severe, Frequent Loneliness

You experience intense feelings of loneliness much of the time. While you might have some interactions, they often feel superficial or unfulfilling, leaving you with a persistent ache for deeper connection. This loneliness significantly impacts your mood, energy levels, and motivation to engage with the world. You might struggle to initiate or maintain close relationships.

Score 2: Moderate, Noticeable Loneliness

You experience feelings of loneliness periodically, perhaps several times a week or during specific periods (e.g., evenings, weekends). While you have some social connections, they might not fully meet your needs for intimacy or belonging. This loneliness causes discomfort and can sometimes lead to feelings of sadness or a yearning for more meaningful social interaction.

Score 3: Mild, Occasional Loneliness

You experience mild feelings of loneliness from time to time, usually in specific situations or when reflecting on a particular lack (e.g., wishing for a romantic partner, missing a distant friend). These feelings are fleeting, manageable, and don't significantly impact your overall well-being. You generally feel connected to a supportive network.

Score 4: Rare, Brief Loneliness (Healthy Solitude)

You very rarely experience loneliness. When you do, it's a brief, mild feeling that quickly passes, perhaps when a loved one is away or during a transition. You generally enjoy your own company and can distinguish between healthy solitude (time alone that recharges you) and genuine loneliness.

Score 5: Securely Connected and Content

You almost never experience loneliness. You feel deeply connected to yourself and a strong network of friends, family, or community, and your relationships are fulfilling and supportive. You are content with your social life, enjoy both time with others and healthy solitude, and possess a strong sense of belonging and inner peace.

Reflection Prompts

1. When do you most often experience feelings of loneliness, even if you are surrounded by people?
2. What needs do you believe are unmet when you feel lonely?
3. How does loneliness impact your energy, motivation, or willingness to connect with others?

17. Confidence

'Courage gives us confidence, and fear allows us to pause and introspect.' – **Daaji**

'Confidence comes not from always being right but from not fearing to be wrong.' – **Peter T. Mcintyre**

'You gain strength, courage, and confidence by every experience in which you really stop to look fear in the face.' – **Eleanor Roosevelt**

Scoring Guide

When assessing yourself, consider the **consistency, breadth, and resilience** of your confidence. Think about how often you feel confident, in what types of situations, and how well you recover when faced with doubt or setbacks.

Score 0: Minimal Confidence

You constantly doubt your abilities, decisions, and worth. You frequently hesitate, avoid challenges, and seek external validation. You might feel inadequate in most situations, struggle to voice your opinions, and fear failure or judgment to a debilitating degree. Your self-esteem is very low.

Score 1: Limited Confidence

You often lack belief in yourself and your capabilities. You might feel nervous or uncertain in new situations, tend to second-guess yourself, and be easily swayed by others' opinions. You might avoid taking risks or pursuing opportunities due to fear of not being good enough.

Score 2: Moderate Confidence (Situational)

You have some confidence in familiar or specific areas where you have proven competence, but it often wavers in new or challenging situations. You might feel confident in some roles (e.g., at work) but lack it in others (e.g., social settings). You can be assertive sometimes, but might struggle with self-doubt.

Score 3: Consistent Confidence

You generally feel confident in your abilities and decisions across various aspects of your life. You're willing to take on new challenges, express your opinions, and recover relatively quickly from setbacks.

While you might have occasional moments of self-doubt, they don't typically deter you.

Score 4: Strong Confidence

You possess a robust and stable belief in yourself and your capacity to handle most situations. You approach challenges with a positive attitude, readily express your ideas, and are resilient in the face of obstacles. You trust your judgment and inspire confidence in others.

Score 5: Profound Confidence

Your confidence is deep-seated, resilient, and unshakeable. You exude a calm self-assurance that comes from a strong understanding of your strengths and an acceptance of your limitations. You embrace challenges as opportunities, are highly adaptable, and can lead and inspire others without needing external validation. You navigate life with a strong sense of self-efficacy and purpose.

Reflection Prompts

1. Recall a time when your confidence wavered. What thoughts, fears, or external circumstances contributed to that lack of confidence?
2. How does your level of confidence impact your willingness to take risks, express your opinions, pursue opportunities, and form connections with others?
3. What specific actions, achievements, or internal shifts help you build and sustain your sense of confidence?

18. Hope – The Last Journey

It was mid-October 1998. Snow had smothered the Siachen Base Camp in a white silence, signalling the arrival of what was expected to be a brutal winter. On this crisp morning, the air buzzed with anticipation – the *Raksha Mantri* (Defence Minister) was to visit the troops stationed on the glacier, his **third visit in just 6 months**. For Manish and the 3 other helicopter pilots of the famed *Siachen Pioneers* detachment, it promised to be a busy and high-stakes day. Their task was to ferry the RM to 2 critical posts: Chandan in the Central Glacier, and later, the Northern Glacier battalion headquarters at Kumar. Normally, the Unit Commanding Officer would have undertaken such a mission, but the Khardung La Pass had been blocked for 2 days by a western disturbance. This meant the CO and Flight Commander could not make it from Leh to Base Camp – leaving Manish and his crew to shoulder the responsibility.

The mission brief was clear. Manish, the senior-most 'Glacier Captain' on detachment, would pilot the RM's helicopter. His co-pilot was to be Sushant – an experienced aviator, though relatively new to glacier flying. The second helicopter would ferry the Partapur Brigade Commander. Their first destination was Chandan, with a scheduled departure of 0830 hours from Base Camp.

The plan allowed **no margin for error**. The RM and Brigade Commander were to be dropped on twin helipads at Chandan, then picked up exactly 30 minutes later. The RM was neither acclimatized nor young enough for the punishing altitude of over 16,000 feet. The helicopters could not shut down on the icy helipad, since a restart at –20°C was uncertain. Nor could they loiter with engines running – the Pakistani post across the ridge would instantly detect the sound resonance and likely open fire on Chandan. The safety of the nation's RM depended on flawless execution.

The day began with a meticulous briefing at the Operations hut – attended personally by the RM. Every detail was synchronised to the clock. Given the enemy's hair-trigger reactions and the heavy exchanges of the past 8 months, timing was non-negotiable.

The flight plan was by the book: a sharp zoom climb through the Zulu Valley, crossing the Zulu–Chandan ledge at 18,000 feet, followed by a steep descent into the Chandan Valley floor – the most vulnerable stretch, fully exposed to enemy eyes and fire. From there, the helicopters would make a terrain-masked, nap-of-the-earth dash across the valley, execute a reversal, and land. Each helicopter had a window of **no more**

than 30 seconds to offload its passengers and depart, minimising the 'bowl resonance' of rotor noise that could trigger Pakistani fire.

Manish had privately instructed the crew that the return leg from Chandan would be at maximum speed, hugging the terrain nap-of-the-earth, followed by a sharp zoom climb across the Chandan–Zulu ledge, and then a swift dive into the Zulu Valley. Back at Base Camp, they were to land, disengage rotors, and hold with engines running. Exactly 12 minutes before pickup, they would lift off again to pick the RM.

This manoeuvre – nicknamed *Hell's Elevator* – was efficient, precise, and rehearsed countless times during Central Glacier operations. Yet Manish carried a quiet unease. After all, he was flying perhaps the oldest and least acclimatised human being ever across such forbidding altitudes and terrain. The previous evening, he had spoken to his co-pilot, Sushant. They had agreed that Sushant would closely monitor the RM throughout the flight, gently checking on his condition. At the first sign of distress, the mission would be aborted.

That morning, however, the RM seemed spirited. When Sushant repeated his queries one too many times, the veteran politician snapped with a mix of irritation and humour: *'Don't worry about me, son. I'll be happier if you look ahead and fly!'*

Everything unfolded smoothly. As they hovered over the Chandan helipad, Manish felt a wave of relief. In the past 6 months, Siachen had offered him hardly a dull or uneventful moment. *'Jai Bajrangbali,'* he whispered, as the skids touched down.

The RM was whisked away by the waiting party. Just then, the radio crackled with an unexpected message: 'Request from Brigade Commander – please evacuate some dead bodies back to Base Camp on your return trip.'

Manish stiffened. This was not part of the briefing. Any delay on the helipad could invite enemy fire, putting the RM's safety at risk. Even as he weighed the risks, he caught sight of 2 frozen forms being heaved into his helicopter, one from each door. Their bodies were cocooned in glacier sleeping bags, grotesque in stillness.

He glanced at Sushant. 'I guess the quickest way out is to shut up and get out of here.'

Sushant gave a grim nod.

The next 10 minutes were among the most unsettling of Manish's life. Thc 2 fallen soldiers, frozen stiff, sat upright in their glacier bags. One, seated directly behind him, had a rigid right arm jutting forward in a grotesque 'Heil mein Führer' pose – its stiff hand jabbing Manish's shoulder with every vibration of the rotor.

5 years earlier, the sight might have terrified him. But now, it stirred something different – an aching tenderness. It was as though these soldiers were silently pleading to be taken home, to their families. Yet Manish knew their destiny. After routine documentation at the Base Adjutant's office, they would be cremated at the Base Camp grounds, perhaps by nightfall. No farewells from loved ones. No homecoming.

As the helicopter plunged through the Zulu Valley, a thought began to crystallise. A new possibility.

'Sir,' Manish turned to Sushant, 'I have something on my mind. I'll share it once we land and disengage rotors at Base Camp.'

Sushant nodded. 'Sure.' He had no idea what Manish was thinking.

As the rotors wound down at Base Camp, Manish felt the seconds slipping away. He hurried to the loadmaster, gesturing firmly.

'*Saheb,* Don't move them from the helipad unless you get an order from the Base Commander.'

The loadmaster, seasoned and unflappable, nodded. 'Understood Sir.'

Without losing a moment, Manish sprinted to the Ops hut and asked the exchange operator to urgently connect him to the Base Commander. He was confident – the 2 shared a strong rapport.

'Sir, Jai Hind. This is Manish. We've just dropped the RM at Chandan, but we were surprised by the Brigade Commander's request to bring back bodies from Chandan.'

The Base Commander explained: the evening patrol at Chandan had discovered 7 bodies – soldiers of a Jat Regiment patrol, lost 7 years earlier in an avalanche. Recent crevasse movement had thrown them up, and they'd been recovered early that morning. Sensitive to 'wasting' scarce air effort, the Brigade Commander had requested that 5 of the bodies be brought back on the returning helicopters.

Manish pressed on. 'Sir, I must take off again in 5 minutes. But may I request – please keep the bodies at the helipad until we return with the RM. I have something in mind which, if we can convince the RM about, could change forever how our dead are treated.'

A pause, then the Base Commander's calm reply: 'Manish, I don't know what you're planning. But I've known you long enough to trust your judgment. Consider it done.'

Climbing out of Base Camp toward the Zulu entrance, Manish finally revealed his plan to Sushant.

'Sir, when we land back, we must catch the RM before anyone else does. Since you'll be on the left side and opening the door for him, please engage him immediately – before the reception party arrives. I'll circle around, join you, and block others from stepping in. We must speak to him privately.'

Manish then outlined his idea – the request he had already made to the Base Commander to keep the bodies at the helipad until their return.

The return leg unfolded like a textbook operation. Every move was executed with clockwork precision. The RM showed surprising air sense – quiet, observant, and focused until they cleared the Chandan–Zulu ledge.

As they descended into the Zulu Valley, his voice crackled over the intercom, buoyant with emotion: '*Gentlemen, thank you for carrying me safely through one of the most remarkable experiences of my life. I truly appreciate now what soldiers like you endure for India. I hope to return and tell your story to the nation, from my own firsthand experience.*'

Manish seized the opportunity – earlier than expected. '*Sir, we equally appreciate your spirit. I'm certain you are the first RM to visit soldiers on a high-altitude post in Siachen. To be honest, we, as your crew, were deeply concerned about your lack of acclimatization. Now we look forward to flying you to Kumar after a short break – and we pray it goes just as smoothly.*'

The RM's laughter rang through the mask. '*Yes, I am looking forward to that trip. And I feel fine – literally on top of the world!*'

Manish refused to let the moment slip. *'Sir, if you don't mind, may we request just 5 minutes of your time after landing at Base Camp? We wish to raise an issue of deep emotional importance for every soldier serving here in Siachen.'*

The RM smiled warmly. *'Of course, young man. I am here to help in any way possible.'*

The rest of the descent blurred past. At the helipad, Sushant disembarked swiftly while Manish joined him at once. They saluted smartly and helped the RM out of the helicopter. Before the reception party could converge, the 2 pilots gently steered him toward the row of fallen soldiers' bodies – laid neatly in glacier bags beside the helipad.

Manish spoke plainly, his voice steady. He told the RM how these 5 Bravehearts of the Jat Regiment had been lost in an avalanche 7 years earlier and recovered only that morning. Their bodies had been ferried down after the RM's drop at Chandan.

He continued, pointing gently toward the glacier bags. 'Sir, these men will be cremated here at Base Camp, just south of the helipad, before the day ends – without their families present, without a final farewell. The rules allow no provision for their remains to be flown back to their towns and villages for the last rites.'

The RM's expression grew solemn. By now, the Brigade Commander, Base Commander, and senior officers had gathered, curious to overhear this quiet but charged exchange.

The RM's face hardened, his voice low but firm. *'I am shocked and deeply disappointed by what you have just shared. I apologize on behalf of the Nation. I promise to do everything in my power to change this. You shall hear from me very soon.'* His tone carried both gravity and sincerity.

The Brigade Commander and Base Commander exchanged uneasy glances. They had only caught fragments of the conversation and were unsure of its full scope.

Later, Manish quietly briefed the Base Commander on what had transpired. The commander gave a curt nod. *'Good job.'*

Later that day, as the RM boarded the helicopter for his onward trip to Kumar – the Northern Glacier Battalion HQ – he made a quiet request: he wished to see the Base Camp cremation ground.

Obliging, Manish banked the helicopter into a slow orbit over the site, just south of the helipad. By chance, a funeral pyre was burning at that very moment, its smoke drifting southward with the glacier's wind. The RM watched silently, his gaze fixed, his expression pensive. Manish could not tell if the flames belonged to one of the Jat Bravehearts, but the timing felt almost fated.

Quartered In Snow
Silent To Remain
When The Bugle Calls
They Shall Rise And March Again

P.S.: Within a month, in November 1998, the Ministry of Defence issued authorisation for the airlift of deceased battle casualties to the nearest airport, and thereafter by surface transport to their native towns and villages for last rites. With this, the long-standing hope of families – who yearned to see their loved ones one final time – was fulfilled.

Later, the Kargil War of 1999 became the first conflict where **every fallen soldier** was transported home through this system: airlift to the nearest airport, followed by onward surface transport. Whether the November 1998 order was directly applied or served as a template for a new one remains uncertain.

Note: The author recognizes that MoD clearances are often long-drawn. The order may already have been under process. In no way does he seek personal credit for the outcome, though he believes this incident may have contributed to expediting it.

This narration is a tribute to a veteran politician, George Fernandes, who, at nearly 70, dared to risk his life for the morale of the troops; and to his integrity, for keeping his promise to the soldiers of Siachen – not only in this matter, but in many others beyond the scope of this story.

Key Takeaways

1. **Hope can move institutions.** What began as one pilot's heartfelt idea became a policy change that touched thousands of families of fallen soldiers. A single spark of hope, when acted upon, can ripple far beyond its origin.
2. **Hope is born in moments of compassion.** Manish's determination to give dignity to the fallen came not from strategy manuals, but from an inner voice that said: '*They deserve to go home.*' True hope often arises when empathy meets action.
3. **Hope inspires courage.** It takes courage to speak truth to authority, especially in high-stakes situations. Hope gives that courage its purpose and strength.
4. **Hope restores dignity.** For families who had lost loved ones, the new policy meant closure, rituals, and respect. Hope does not erase pain – but it restores meaning and dignity in the face of loss.
5. **Hope is a shared legacy.** The RM's fulfilment of the promise shows that leadership rooted in hope can outlast individuals, wars, and even generations.

'Hope is being able to see that there is light despite all of the darkness.'
– Desmond Tutu

'We must accept finite disappointment, but never lose infinite hope.'
– Martin Luther King Jr.

'Hope is important because it can make the present moment less difficult to bear. If we believe that tomorrow will be better, we can bear a hardship today.' – **Thich Nhat Hanh**

Scoring Guide

When assessing yourself, consider the **frequency, strength, and pervasiveness** of your sense of hope. Think about how often you feel optimistic about the future, how resilient that feeling is in the face of adversity, and whether it's an active force in your life.

Score 0: Minimal Hope

You consistently feel a profound sense of despair, pessimism, or hopelessness. You struggle to envision a positive future, believe things will get better, or see a way forward, even in minor challenges. You might feel stuck, resigned, or convinced that efforts are futile.

Score 1: Limited Hope

You rarely experience hope. When you do, it's typically a fleeting thought quickly overshadowed by negativity or doubt. You might find it hard to believe in positive outcomes, often focusing on potential failures or insurmountable obstacles. A sense of resignation is frequently present.

Score 2: Occasional Hope

You experience glimmers of hope occasionally, usually in response to significant external positive events or when things are going particularly well. However, this hope can be fragile and easily diminished by setbacks or difficulties. You might struggle to maintain a hopeful outlook during challenging times.

Score 3: Consistent Hope

You generally maintain a hopeful outlook, believing that things can improve and that you can work towards positive outcomes. You can identify goals and pathways, even when facing challenges. While you experience moments of doubt, hope is a noticeable and often present part of your mindset.

Score 4: Deeply Hopeful

You possess a strong and resilient sense of hope that allows you to face adversity with optimism and determination. You can envision multiple pathways to your goals and believe in your capacity to adapt and grow, even when circumstances are difficult. This hope is a powerful internal resource.

Score 5: Profound Hope

Hope is a core, unwavering aspect of your being. You consistently maintain an optimistic and proactive outlook, even in the most challenging or uncertain situations. You deeply believe in the possibility of positive change, your own agency, and the inherent goodness or potential in life. This profound hope fuels your resilience, motivation, and ability to inspire others.

Reflection Prompts

1. Describe a time when you felt a significant lack of hope. How did that impact your thoughts, feelings, and actions?
2. What practices or beliefs help you cultivate and sustain hope, especially during difficult periods?

19. Excitement

'The excitement of learning separates youth from old age. As long as you're learning, you're not old.' – **Rosalyn Sussman Yalow**

'Stop being afraid of what could go wrong, and start being excited about what could go right.' – **Tony Robbins**

'Excitement is a state of being in which our cells of body, mind, and heart are engaged by the orchestration of our spirit.' – **Linda Chandler**

Scoring Guide

When assessing yourself, consider the **frequency, intensity, and duration** of your feelings of excitement. Think about how often you truly feel thrilled or eager, how deeply those feelings resonate, and whether excitement is an active and recurring part of your emotional experience.

Score 0: Minimal Excitement

You rarely, if ever, feel excited about anything. Life might often feel flat, dull, or monotonous. You may struggle to find enthusiasm for new experiences, opportunities, or even daily activities. A general sense of apathy or disinterest is common.

Score 1: Occasional Glimmers of Excitement

You experience fleeting moments of excitement, typically only in response to very significant or rare positive events. These feelings are brief and don't significantly influence your overall mood or engagement with life. You might acknowledge something as 'good' but lack genuine enthusiasm.

Score 2: Moderate, Situational Excitement

You experience excitement periodically, often tied to specific, planned events (e.g., a trip, a party, a new purchase). While you can feel genuinely thrilled in these moments, the feeling isn't sustained or easily generated in everyday life. Your excitement might be somewhat reserved or contained.

Score 3: Consistent Excitement

You regularly feel excited about various aspects of your life, both big and small. You find enthusiasm in planning, learning new things, engaging in hobbies, or anticipating future events. This excitement contributes positively to your energy levels and overall zest for life, even if it's not always outwardly effusive.

Score 4: Deeply Enthusiastic

You possess a strong capacity for excitement and often approach new experiences, ideas, and challenges with genuine eagerness and anticipation. You frequently feel a vibrant sense of joy and keen interest in what life has to offer, and this enthusiasm is often contagious to those around you.

Score 5: Profound Excitement/Vibrancy

Excitement is a core and frequently felt emotion for you. **You consistently experience a deep sense of wonder**, eagerness, and delight in life, finding excitement in everyday moments, new possibilities, and your interactions with the world. You are highly animated, proactive, and inspire a sense of vibrancy in others. Life feels like a continuous adventure.

Reflection Prompts

1. In what ways does excitement contribute positively to your experiences, relationships, or pursuit of goals?
2. Have you ever felt a sense of wonder towards any of nature's creations?

20. Admiration

Some people enter our lives quietly – strangers at first, seemingly insignificant, not meant to leave a mark. Yet, they somehow change the script of our destiny. Perhaps this is life's charm: our ignorance of what awaits us keeps the journey exciting, full of surprises, and at times, profound lessons.

In January 2013, after taking early retirement from the IAF, I moved to Delhi. I carried a dream close to my heart: to pursue oil painting. Of course, I was also practical – I knew my pension alone would not fully support the family. So, I rented a modest office space that doubled as my business desk and painting studio. Life was unfolding as per plan… until Nature introduced a twist. Around that time, a young man, Ved – walked quietly into the script of my life.

Ved entered my life through his elder brother, who worked with me. 'Sir, my younger brother loves drawing,' he said. 'Would you guide him?' I agreed casually, without expecting much. When Ved first stood before me – simple, shy, almost invisible – I assumed he would be like others who start with enthusiasm but fade away.

I tested him with a simple sketch of a sculpture at home. His work was ordinary. My first thought? *'Not much potential here.'* Still, not wanting to discourage him, I invited him to the studio. Secretly, I was sure he would disappear in a week.

But Ved was made of sterner stuff. He came every single day, rain or shine, sitting quietly for 5–6 hours, practising charcoal and pencil sketches. He expected only 1 thing from me: a little time, a little guidance. While I often got pulled away by business commitments, his discipline never wavered. Slowly, my indifference melted into admiration.

Behind his quiet presence was an extraordinary story. The youngest of ten siblings, orphaned early, Ved grew up in a poor UP village. In Delhi, he survived working as a labourer by sterilising OT instruments at AIIMS, working 9–10 hour shifts, sometimes at night, so he could paint by day. His 1-hour DTC bus ride became his 'sleeping compartment.' He lived on little but dreamt big.

Family pressures mounted – 'When will you earn properly? When will you marry?' His brother, though caring, often echoed these. Once, Ved even left home impulsively, renting a cramped space with no privacy. I intervened, convinced him to return, and his brother, too, assured me of support. In today's world, such sibling solidarity is rare.

When Ved shifted to oil painting, his ambition grew: admission to a premier art college. He failed the first attempt – not due to lack of talent but gaps in theory. Disheartened, he almost gave up, ready to surrender to societal norms. But I urged him, *'Give it one more year. Try again.'* He agreed reluctantly. That extra year of relentless work bore fruit: he secured admission to Delhi's prestigious Lalit Kala Mahavidyalaya.

Just when things were finally looking up, COVID struck. Classes froze, opportunities vanished. For the first time since we met, Ved called me in distress. We met at Mandi House, where he spoke with rare heaviness about fading hopes and financial exhaustion.

Sensing his struggle, I offered financial support. He surprised me with a firm 'No.' Then, with quiet dignity, he said, *'I want to be your strength, not your weakness. If I succeed, it will be because of you. But if I fail, again, you will be the reason.'*

In that moment, I realized: Ved was far richer in spirit than many who are wealthy in material terms.

Ved finally graduated in 2022. Today, he works as a freelance artist, teaches schoolchildren, and spends long days in the studio. Financial stability still eludes him, and he remains unmarried at 37. Yet, his brush carries more strength now than ever before.

This story is my tribute to Ved. Over a decade of knowing him, I have not found a single crack in his dedication or character. He personifies hope, perseverance, tolerance, and patience. I once thought I was his teacher – but in truth, he became mine. Through him, I learned the meaning of hope, patience, resilience, dignity, and humanity.

His biography is still unfolding. I continue to watch, curious and grateful, for what his journey will reveal next.

Keshav's Take

This story is not only about Ved's perseverance but also about the quiet strength of his mentor, who stood by him. Dreams need wings, but they also need someone to hold the ladder steady. Both deserve admiration – one for his relentless pursuit, and the other for his unwavering support. May life continue to bless them both, for in their bond we see how teacher and student become reflections of each other.

Key Takeaways

1. True admiration is earned not by talent alone, but by **discipline, humility, and consistency**.
2. We often begin by underestimating people, only to later discover that one of them is going to be the greatest source of inspiration.
3. Sometimes, those we think we are mentoring turn out to be the ones **teaching us life's deeper lessons**.

'Blessed is he who has learned to admire but not envy, to follow but not imitate, to praise but not flatter, and to lead but not manipulate.' **– William Arthur Ward**

'The true measure of a man is how he treats someone who can do him absolutely no good.' **– Samuel Johnson**

'Admiration is a kind of love that does not ask for possession.' **– George Sand**

Scoring Guide

When assessing yourself, consider the **frequency, depth, and breadth** of your feelings of admiration. Think about how often you truly look up to someone, how deeply those feelings resonate, and how widely you extend this appreciation to various individuals and their qualities.

Score 0: Minimal or Absent Admiration

You rarely, if ever, feel genuine admiration for others. You might find it difficult to acknowledge or appreciate the exceptional qualities, achievements, or virtues of people around you. You may tend to be critical, dismissive, or focused on flaws, making it hard to look up to anyone.

Score 1: Occasional, Superficial Admiration

You experience brief, mild moments of admiration, typically for very public figures or widely recognized accomplishments. These feelings are often fleeting and don't involve a deep appreciation or understanding of the admired person's qualities or efforts. You might acknowledge success without truly feeling inspired by it.

Score 2: Moderate, Situational Admiration

You feel admiration periodically, often for specific skills, talents, or achievements that are directly relevant to your interests or profession.

You can **appreciate excellence when you see it, but it might be limited to certain domains or individuals**. This admiration may not often translate into a deeper respect for the person's character.

Score 3: Consistent, Genuine Admiration

You regularly feel genuine admiration for the positive qualities, talents, or accomplishments of various individuals in your life, including friends, colleagues, and public figures. You can articulate *why* you admire someone, and these feelings often inspire you or foster a sense of respect.

Score 4: Deeply Appreciative Admiration

You possess a strong capacity for deep and authentic admiration. You are **quick to notice and appreciate the virtues, wisdom, courage, or unique contributions of others**. This admiration goes beyond surface-level achievements, focusing on character and effort. It often fuels your own personal growth and fosters rich connections.

Score 5: Profound Admiration/Awe

Admiration is a frequently felt and profound emotion for you. You are consistently attuned to and deeply moved by the extraordinary qualities, grace, or profound impact of others. This often borders on awe and inspires you deeply, enhancing your perception of human potential and fostering a rich inner life. You **actively seek out and appreciate the best in people**.

Reflection Prompts

1. Who is someone you genuinely admire, and what specific qualities or actions do you admire in them?
2. How does feeling admiration for others impact your own aspirations or sense of possibility?

3. How can you draw inspiration from those you admire without falling into comparison or envy?

21. Satisfaction

The Yamuna flowed quietly under the golden morning sun, carrying with it both ritual flowers and centuries of whispered prayers. In the bustling lanes of Mathura, life moved to its own unique rhythm. The fragrance of freshly made *peda* (sweet) drifted from sweet shops, mingling with the thick smoke of incense rising from Krishna's temples. Cows meandered lazily through the narrow alleys, bells clinking softly, while children darted past pilgrims chanting hymns in sing-song voices. Amid this blend of devotion and chaos worked Hari, a poor rickshaw puller.

Carl, Keshav's friend from Austria, had come to India with his father, Anton. Anton was a successful architect back home – wealthy, well-travelled, accustomed to fine hotels and polished dinners. Yet beneath the glitter of success lingered a quiet emptiness. He longed to see the soul of India – its temple towns and heritage cities – hoping to find something no blueprint or banquet could ever give him.

In Mathura, they hired Hari to take them around for their 3-day stay. Hari was wiry and sunburnt, his clothes faded from years of wear. Sweat streamed down his back in the heavy sun, soaking his cotton shirt until it clung to his skin. On his feet were oversized rubber slippers – clearly someone else's discard – that slapped the dust with every pull. His rickshaw creaked at each turn, the wooden frame groaning like an old companion. And yet, his smile never wavered – wide and easy across his weathered face, as though no burden in the world could dim his laughter.

On the second day, Anton and Carl got down at a crowded *chauraha* (crossroad), from where they wanted to walk to the inner temples that stood hidden in narrow lanes. Anton pressed a few notes into Hari's hand and said kindly, 'Go have some lunch while we finish here.'

When they came out after an hour, Anton stopped in his tracks. His eyes locked on a scene so ordinary, yet strangely unforgettable.

There, on a weathered, splintered wooden bench outside a cramped, bustling *thela* (street vendor's cart), sat Hari.

A steel plate piled with *poori* and *sabzi* rested precariously on his knees. Beside him sat another man, an absolute stranger. The 2 of them were deep in conversation, heads bent forward one moment, throwing their arms up in mock debate the next. And then, suddenly, they both burst into laughter. 'This wasn't polite dinner-table laughter. It was raw, joyous, shoulder-shaking laughter that carried no weight of yesterday and no worry of tomorrow. This was raw, unrestrained, joyous laughter that shook their thin shoulders and made their eyes glisten with tears.

For a moment, Anton felt the street around him blur. He stood frozen, watching. That image etched itself into his heart... 2 poor men on a broken bench, sharing a humble meal, laughing as though they had the world in their pocket.

Days later, when Anton and Carl were back in Hyderabad with Keshav, the memory returned with the same sharpness. One evening, over tea on Keshav's veranda, Anton leaned back, staring into the fading sky, and spoke softly.

'You know, Keshav. I've designed skyscrapers, travelled to almost every continent, and built a house that could be mistaken for a palace. I have a wife I adore, a son I'm so proud of. And yet...' he paused, his voice breaking into wonder, 'I cannot recall the last time I laughed as hard, as purely, as Hari did on that broken bench.' Keshav said nothing, his eyes steady, inviting Anton to continue.

'I asked him later, about his life,' Anton said slowly, almost reverently. Anton's voice dropped. 'Hari owns no house. He has 3 sets of clothes. At night, he spreads a sheet on his rickshaw and sleeps under the stars. No savings, no family nearby. And yet when I asked if he was happy, he smiled and said, *Babuji, what is there not to be happy about? I eat, I work, I laugh, I live. Isn't that enough?*'

Anton's voice dropped to a whisper. 'I was stunned. Here I am, with everything I could wish for, and still I wrestle with restlessness. And there he was, with almost nothing, yet filled with satisfaction so deep it shone through his laughter.'

Keshav reached across the table, resting a hand on Anton's. His voice was gentle, but firm, like truth itself… 'Perhaps satisfaction has little to do with what fills our homes, and everything to do with what fills our hearts.' Anton nodded slowly, his eyes moist. 'Yes… I travelled all the way to Mathura to see the temples. But perhaps the greatest *darshan* I received was not of stone idols or sacred rituals. It was of a man who owned nothing, yet lived as if he had everything.'

That night, Anton sat reflecting on his life's journey. Again and again, the image returned – Hari laughing on a broken bench, eating *poori* with a stranger. With it came a revelation: wealth was never a guarantee of joy.

For the first time in years, Anton felt humbled – perhaps even liberated – by a truth so simple it sounded like a prayer:

Satisfaction is not measured by possessions. It is the freedom of needing little, the art of living fully, and the ability to laugh without reason – like a rickshaw puller in Mathura, eating poori on a broken bench.

A poor man may own little yet walk as a king, while a rich man may own kingdoms yet remain a prisoner of desire.

Key Takeaways

1. **Satisfaction is not linked to possessions** but to simplicity and acceptance.
2. Joy often resides in ordinary places – on a splintered bench with a shared meal.
3. Wealth without peace feels empty; scarcity with laughter can feel abundant.
4. True satisfaction comes from **needing little and living fully**.

'He is richest who is content with the least, for content is the wealth of nature.' – **Socrates**

'When you are content to be simply yourself and don't compare or compete, everybody will respect you.' – **Lao Tzu**

'He who is not satisfied with a little, is satisfied with nothing.' – **Epicurus**

Scoring Guide

When assessing yourself, consider the **frequency, intensity, and breadth** of your feelings of satisfaction. Think about how often you truly feel content, how deeply those feelings resonate, and how widely this satisfaction extends across different areas of your life.

Score 0: Minimal or Absent Satisfaction

You rarely, if ever, feel a sense of satisfaction or fulfilment. Life often feels frustrating, unrewarding, or disappointing. You might constantly focus on what's missing or what's wrong, struggling to find pleasure or appreciation in your daily experiences, achievements, or circumstances.

Score 1: Occasional, Fleeting Satisfaction

You experience brief, mild moments of satisfaction, usually after completing a specific task or achieving a minor goal. However, these feelings are short-lived and don't contribute to an overall sense of well-being. You might quickly move on to the next task without savouring the accomplishment.

Score 2: Moderate, Situational Satisfaction

You feel satisfaction periodically, often tied to specific positive events, successful outcomes, or personal accomplishments. You can appreciate when things go well, but this satisfaction might not extend beyond those particular moments. You might still feel a general lack of contentment in other areas of your life.

Score 3: Consistent Satisfaction

You regularly feel a sense of satisfaction and mild fulfilment in various aspects of your life. You can appreciate your efforts and progress, and find satisfaction in your work, relationships, or personal pursuits.

While you still encounter challenges, you generally maintain a positive outlook and find reasons to feel content.

Score 4: Deeply Satisfied

You possess a strong and consistent sense of satisfaction with your life, your choices, and your accomplishments. You often feel fulfilled and content, taking genuine pleasure in both major successes and everyday moments. This deep satisfaction contributes significantly to your overall happiness and well-being.

Score 5: Profound Satisfaction/Contentment

Satisfaction is a core and abiding state of being for you. You experience a deep, pervasive sense of fulfilment, peace, and contentment with your life as a whole. You find profound meaning and joy in your experiences, efforts, and connections, often feeling a strong sense of purpose and gratitude for where you are.

Reflection Prompts

1. Recall a recent moment or an achievement that brought you a genuine sense of satisfaction. What made that experience so fulfilling?
2. What is the difference for you between temporary pleasure and lasting satisfaction?
3. Are there times when you struggle to feel satisfied, even after achieving something significant? What might contribute to that feeling?

22. Contentment

Satisfaction vs. Contentment

Aspect	Satisfaction	Contentment
Nature	Temporary feeling	Lasting state of mind
Trigger	Achieving a goal, fulfilling a desire, external success	Inner acceptance, peace with what is

Dependency	Depends on circumstances and outcomes	Independent of circumstances
Examples	Scoring well in an exam, finishing a project, enjoying a delicious meal	Feeling at peace with life even when desires are unmet
Duration	Short-lived; fades once desire is met or replaced by new desires	Long-lasting; not easily shaken by ups and downs
Emotional Tone	Relief, happiness, pride in achievement	Calmness, serenity, deep joy
Focus	'I got what I wanted.'	'I am grateful for what I have.'
Philosophical Lens	Satisfaction = event-based success	Contentment = life-based acceptance
Risk	Can lead to endless chasing of new wants	Can drift into complacency if misunderstood
Ideal Balance	Achieve goals (satisfaction) without losing inner peace (contentment)	Stay content while still striving meaningfully

'He who is not contented with what he has, would not be contented with what he would like to have.' – **Socrates**

'Health is the greatest gift, contentment the greatest wealth, faithfulness the best relationship.' – **Buddha**

'Satisfaction is the dessert after a good meal, but contentment is the health that lets you enjoy every meal.' – Anonymous

Scoring Guide

Here, 0 represents **minimum (rare/absent) contentment** and 5 represents **maximum (frequent/deep) contentment**. When assessing yourself, consider the **frequency, depth, and resilience** of your feelings of contentment. Think about how often you truly feel at peace, how deeply that feeling resonates, and how well it sustains itself even when facing difficulties.

Score 0: Minimal or Absent Contentment

You rarely, if ever, feel a sense of peace, ease, or contentment with your current state. You might constantly feel restless, agitated, or focused on what's lacking or what needs to be different. A pervasive sense of dissatisfaction or unease is common.

Score 1: Occasional, Fleeting Contentment

You experience brief, mild moments of contentment, usually when something specific goes exactly as desired. These feelings are short-lived and don't contribute to an overall sense of inner peace. You might find yourself quickly moving on to the next desire or worry.

Score 2: Moderate, Situational Contentment

You feel contentment periodically, often in specific, ideal circumstances (e.g., on vacation, after a major achievement). You can find satisfaction when things are going well, but it might not extend to your everyday life or when facing challenges. Your sense of inner peace is often dependent on external factors.

Score 3: Consistent Contentment

You regularly feel a sense of inner peace and contentment with your life as it is. You can appreciate the present moment and find comfort in routine, your relationships, and your daily activities. While you still experience challenges, you generally maintain a calm and settled outlook.

Score 4: Deeply Content

You possess a strong and consistent sense of inner contentment that allows you to be at ease with life's flow, regardless of external circumstances. You often feel a quiet joy and appreciation for the present, and you are not easily swayed by minor discomforts or unfulfilled desires. This deep contentment contributes significantly to your well-being.

Score 5: Profound Contentment/Inner Peace

Contentment is a fundamental and abiding state of being for you. You experience a deep, pervasive sense of peace, acceptance, and fulfilment with life as a whole. You are able to embrace both the good and the challenging with equanimity, finding contentment within yourself independent of external factors. This profound inner peace guides your actions and outlook.

Reflection Prompts

1. What prevents you from experiencing contentment more often (e.g., constant striving, external comparisons)?
2. What is one small shift in perspective or practice that could help you cultivate greater contentment?

23. Despair

Draupadi, the queen of Indraprastha, was aghast at King Yudhisthir for putting his brothers at stake in the game of dice, and later, herself. She thought, 'What the hell is he doing – and for what – a mere game of gambling? Shouldn't a man known as *Dharmaraja* (the one best known for following Dharma) also know the balance between a game for entertainment and the pull of ego, and know when to stop?'

It's the ancient version of 'I told you not to gamble on a Sunday,' except this one ended up in history books.

However, as a loyal wife, she remained silent, and then Yudhisthir lost her also to the Kauravas. During the whole process, neither Draupadi nor the Pandavas felt the need to bring in their proven consultant, Krishna, for advice or to play the game of dice on their behalf. It's what today's corporate world would call 'not looping in the stakeholder before making a catastrophic decision.'

This was one of the very few occasions when Duryodhana did better than the Pandavas, knowing both his own capacity and his uncle Shakuni's mastery in gambling. Shakuni had been blessed that the dice would obey him and produce results as per his wish.

The Pandavas already knew that their cousin Krishna had the unique gift of always being right, and he was always a winner. Looking back, we can say that had they deputed Krishna to play on their behalf, Shakuni would have gone bonkers. Imagine Shakuni trying to cheat against Krishna – it would've been the first and last case of 'loaded dice experiencing karma in real time.'

This was later displayed by Krishna after the 17th day of the great Mahabharata war, when He invited Shakuni for a game of dice with bets. But that is another story for another day.

And then, in what seemed like slow motion, Draupadi saw Duryodhana ask his brother to bring her to the main hall by pulling her hair. Duryodhana commanded his brother to disrobe Draupadi in the royal court in front of everyone. Draupadi was in an extreme state of despair and prayed to a few characters who still stand in the top 10 list of the greatest Indian *Yoddhas* (warriors) ever born.

Among these characters, the foremost was Bhishma – the most powerful person born after Lord Rama, who also knew *Dharma* and followed it in most of his dealings. Had he stood up and roared, the whole assembly would have trembled like dry leaves. Bhishma had the capacity to single-handedly defeat everyone present there, and everyone knew it. But blinded by his own vow, he remained silent, as if a Yogi merely observing an act in *Sakshi Bhava* (witness-consciousness).

Another great character was the warrior Dronacharya – the teacher of the Kauravas and Pandavas since they were children. His skills in war were next only to Bhishma. In front of him, the wife of his favourite students was being disrobed, yet he decided to remain silent, as he had tied himself to the benefits granted to him by King Dhritarashtra and did not want to lose them for his son Asvathama's sake.

Karna was another great warrior, ranked at par with Arjuna. Karna, the son of the Sun God and a great giver, also remained silent during the heinous act out of his loyalty to Duryodhana.

The remaining 2 great warriors, Arjuna and Bhima, also decided not to act despite fuming inside – out of allegiance to their elder brother and King Yudhisthir. It was probably the world's first recorded case of emotional paralysis caused by family hierarchy.

Draupadi, undergoing the pain of humiliation, prayed to each of the above characters and to a few more, but it was Duryodhana's day. She had **reached the most extreme state of shock – despair – and only then did she think of Krishna and pray to Him**. We know the rest of the story: how Lord Krishna saved her dignity by a miracle, while Dushashana and Duryodhana went mad – even though Krishna was not physically present there.

Keshav paused.

Damini asked, **'What's wrong with remembering someone in a moment of despair?'**

Keshav replied, 'It's perfectly fine. However, a Divine person or an elder is not a cobbler whom you remember only when a torn shoe starts to cause discomfort. **If you have the attention of a Divine entity, doesn't it make sense to carry him in your heart and thoughts at all times, irrespective of what you are doing?'**

'After all,' he smiled, 'Divinity offers a 24x7 helpline; if subscribers are regular and always connected.'

Damini responded, 'Yes, it makes sense.'

Keshav said, **'When you remain connected to your chosen divinity residing in your heart, then all of your acts and relationships can rise to a far better level than your own natural performance**. You may consider taking this as a hypothesis and experiment with it.'

'In the above case, had the Pandavas invoked Lord Krishna not only in bad times but also at the moment of starting the game of dice – imagine what the outcome might have been on that day, which remains one of the most disgraceful days in Indian history.'

Damini was nodding her head.

Damini nodded her head.

Keshav further added, 'Let's give the benefit of doubt to the Pandavas on 2 counts:

They were not aware that Krishna was the Avatar, and the technique of keeping divinity in one's heart and remaining connected to him was not known to the Pandavas.'

'By then, most of the Upanishads had already been written, and there are 49 mentions that **'Divinity resides in the Heart'** and 42 mentions that **'Meditate on the divinity in the Heart.' Unfortunately, the Pandavas were not taught this as part of their education. Had they known this amazing tool of performance enhancement, the story might have been a little different.'**

Damini asked, 'Uncle, why so much bloodshed – and that too in the presence of an Avatar?'

Keshav replied, 'Divinity wishes all of its children well. However, when we refuse to live in harmony and society is affected by the actions of the high and mighty, then divinity intervenes. Krishna tried every option, including diplomacy and the offer of peace. But humans must sometimes be taught in the one language they will always listen to – and of course, the last teaching technique or resort is war.'

Damini said, 'I agree. Uncle, tell me more about this **performance enhancement tool (being aware and connected to divinity in the heart)** you mentioned a little earlier.'

Keshav laughed, 'That's for another day.'

'Good,' said Damini. 'That gives me time to prepare my homework – on not gambling with my destiny before consulting my inner Krishna.'

Key Takeaways

1. **Despair narrows vision** – only when Draupadi exhausted every human option did she remember divinity – Krishna.
2. **The silence of the powerful** can be more destructive than the actions of the wicked.
3. **Divinity is not an emergency service**; to carry it in the heart consistently transforms all actions.

4. **Performance enhancement through spiritual connection** – invoking divinity early prevents downfall.
5. Mahabharata remains a timeless **case study in leadership, loyalty, relationships and the consequences of choices.**

'When you are in the deepest valley of despair, remember you may be closest to the peak of grace.' – **Anonymous**

'Faith is the bird that feels the light when the dawn is still dark.' – **Rabindranath Tagore**

Scoring Guide

When assessing yourself, consider the **frequency, intensity, duration, and pervasiveness** of your feelings of despair. Think about **how often you feel this way, how deeply it affects your emotions and thoughts**, and whether it impacts various areas of your life or is limited to specific, very challenging situations.

Score 0: Overwhelming, Debilitating Despair

You are constantly consumed by a profound sense of utter hopelessness and the complete absence of any positive feeling or possibility. Life feels meaningless, future prospects are non-existent, and you see no way out of your suffering. This level of despair is overwhelming and often leads to severe functional impairment, apathy, and a complete lack of motivation to live.

Score 1: Severe, Frequent Despair

You frequently experience intense periods of despair, where the weight of your circumstances feels crushing and insurmountable. You struggle to find any joy, purpose, or reason to continue. While not constant, these feelings are a regular and significant part of your emotional landscape, making it very difficult to engage with life or see any light at the end of the tunnel.

Score 2: Moderate, Noticeable Despair

You experience feelings of despair periodically, especially when faced with major setbacks, losses, or prolonged difficulties. These feelings are deep and painful, causing significant emotional distress and potentially affecting your ability to cope. While you may have moments of respite, despair is a recurring and impactful emotion.

Score 3: Mild, Occasional Despair

You experience mild, fleeting moments of despair from time to time, usually in response to significant disappointments or when grappling with existential questions. These feelings are manageable, don't last long, and you are generally able to process them and find your way back to a more hopeful or stable emotional state.

Score 4: Rare, Brief Despair

You very rarely experience despair. When you do, it's a brief, mild, and quickly resolved feeling, often in response to a truly profound loss or a genuinely dire situation. You possess strong emotional resilience and are able to find meaning and positive outlooks even in difficult circumstances.

Score 5: Minimal or Absent Despair

You rarely experience despair. You maintain a fundamental sense of purpose, meaning, and resilience in life. **Even when facing profound challenges or losses, you are able to find acceptance,** a path forward, or an underlying sense of peace. You possess an enduring spirit and belief in life's inherent value.

Reflection Prompts

1. What impact has a sense of despair had on your ability to see solutions, take action, or connect with sources of support?

2. In moments of despair, what small act of self-compassion or connection could you initiate to alleviate the intensity of the feeling, even slightly?

24. Frustration

'Our fatigue is often caused not by work, but by worry, frustration, and resentment.' – **Dale Carnegie**

'Don't let your frustration consume you. Turn it into fascination.' – **Albert Einstein (attributed)**

'Patience is the cure for frustration. Every problem carries the seed of its solution.' – **Anonymous**

Scoring Guide

When assessing yourself, consider the **frequency, intensity, duration, and pervasiveness** of your feelings of frustration. Think about how often you feel blocked or annoyed, how strongly it affects your emotions and thoughts, and whether it impacts various areas of your life or is limited to specific situations.

Score 0: Overwhelming, Debilitating Frustration

You are constantly consumed by intense frustration that makes it **nearly impossible to focus, problem-solve, or function effectively.** Even minor obstacles can trigger explosive anger, deep resentment, or complete shutdown. You **frequently feel blocked, defeated, and overwhelmed by situations** that don't go exactly as planned.

Score 1: Severe, Frequent Frustration

You frequently experience strong, persistent feelings of frustration that significantly interfere with your daily life. You **often feel easily annoyed, irritated, or impatient when faced with delays,**

difficulties, or perceived incompetence. This can lead to frequent outbursts, passive-aggressive behaviour, or withdrawal when things don't go your way.

Score 2: Moderate, Noticeable Frustration

You experience feelings of frustration periodically, especially when encountering significant obstacles, unexpected changes, or prolonged difficulties. These feelings are noticeable and can cause discomfort, affecting your mood and making it harder to stay calm or patient. You might vent or express your irritation more often than you'd like.

Score 3: Mild, Occasional Frustration

You experience mild, fleeting moments of frustration from time to time, usually in response to minor inconveniences or temporary setbacks. These feelings are manageable, don't last long, and you are generally able to process them and find constructive ways to cope or adapt.

Score 4: Rare, Brief Frustration

You very rarely experience significant frustration. When you do, it's a brief, mild, and quickly resolved feeling, often acknowledging a momentary obstacle without internalizing lasting irritation. You possess strong patience and a generally resilient attitude when faced with challenges.

Score 5: Minimal or Absent Frustration

You almost never experience frustration. You approach challenges with remarkable patience, adaptability, and an unshakeable sense of calm. You see obstacles as opportunities to learn or find alternative paths, and you rarely allow external circumstances to disturb your inner peace.

Reflection Prompts

1. What specific obstacles, people, or situations consistently lead to frustration for you?
2. How do you typically express or deal with your frustration? Are these methods effective or counterproductive?
3. What underlying expectation or desire might be fuelling your frustration in a particular recurring scenario?

25. Resentment

Keshav walked with his steady stride, though his face carried none of the calm smile it usually did. In his hand swung a cloth bag, warm from the sun and heavy with the morning's purchases. He had just returned from the street vendors outside the old park in his hometown of Hyderabad. The stalls were alive with their usual chorus, vendors calling out with rehearsed enthusiasm, bargaining voices rising and falling like tidal waves, the smell of ripe melons mixing with the earthy scent of damp burlap sacks.

In his bag, oranges blazed like pocket-sized suns, bananas arched like weary half-moons, and 2 pomegranates lingered in silence, their tough shells guarding oceans of red within. At the very bottom, a melon rested quietly… round, cool, and heavy like a solitary planet adrift among smaller stars.

Yet, despite the vibrancy he carried, Keshav's usual smile was missing. His brow sat heavier than the bag in his hand. It wasn't the fruit that weighed him down, but something deeper, lodged within.

From a distance, Ravi spotted him. The two had been childhood friends, once inseparable in the streets of Hyderabad, though time had turned them into infrequent callers. Still, the warmth remained, and Ravi could read Keshav's posture like an old book. Usually, Keshav's presence carried the freshness of morning itself – brisk, kind, with a warm greeting. But today, his shoulders drooped and his eyes lingered too long on the gravel beneath his feet.

When they finally walked side by side, Ravi glanced at the fruits, then at Keshav's drawn face. 'You look heavy, Keshav. Not your usual self,' he said gently. Keshav let out a sigh, the kind that carried not minutes but years. He didn't stop walking. With each step, the bag brushed softly against his leg.

'These fruits,' he murmured, shaking the bag slightly, 'remind me of people. Sweet on the outside, sometimes sour inside. Some ripen perfectly, others never ripen at all, leaving only a bitter aftertaste. And sometimes, Ravi, we hold on to them longer than we should, until they rot in our hands.'

Somewhere, a fruit-seller sneezed – probably allergic to metaphors.

Ravi frowned, sensing a wound beneath the words. 'What's troubling you?' he asked.

Keshav gave a sad smile. 'Not troubling… haunting.'

He slowed, his eyes drifting far beyond the trees and the chatter of passersby.

'Ravi… today marks 20 years since my elder brother left this world. His 19th *barsi* (death anniversary). Perhaps that is why the air feels heavier to me. On days like this, regret speaks louder than memory. It reminds me of the time I lost to pride. If I could trade anything to sit beside him once more, I would. But all I can do now is pray and remind others not to make the same mistake.'

Ravi felt his chest tighten. The word *barsi* struck him with a stillness, as though the city's sounds had momentarily dimmed. He suddenly understood why Keshav's bag of fruits looked so heavy, why his eyes seemed so far away. It wasn't just memory he carried, but mourning wrapped in regret.

Keshav placed a hand on his old friend's shoulder. 'Do you know, Ravi,' he said softly, 'resentment is like carrying a burning coal. You think you're saving it to throw at someone, but in the end, it burns you alone.'

He paused, then began unfolding the story. 'Many years ago, my elder brother and I had a quarrel over our ancestral land… silly, petty, meaningless in the long run. But in that moment, it felt like everything. Words were exchanged, doors were closed shut, and silence replaced affection. Festivals came and went. Holi, Diwali, weddings, and though we lived in the same city, we stood at opposite ends, pretending the other didn't exist. If avoidance were an Olympic sport, we would've brought home gold.

The saddest part? Our children learned from us. They copied our silence, inherited our distance, and 2 families were torn apart not by fate, but by our stubbornness. My pride told me I was right. His pride probably told him the same. And so, the years rolled on like sand slipping through clenched fists.'

His lips trembled. 'One day, I got a phone call that Bhaiya had collapsed. By the time I reached the hospital, it was too late. He was gone. Just like that. And do you know what haunted me most? The last words we had exchanged were bitter ones, spoken years ago'.

'Imagine... a lifetime of shared childhood memories: flying kites, mangoes stolen from neighbours' trees, all our shared secrets growing up....erased by silence. All poisoned by pride. And why? Because I carried resentment, if only I hadn't resisted the pull to reach out... the urge came many times, but I buried it beneath pride. If only I had not fought against that small voice urging me to call him... but I resisted, and that resistance became my greatest regret.'

He drew a trembling breath. 'That day I realized resentment punishes only the one who carries it. It's like drinking poison and waiting for the other to suffer. Pride is the most expensive thing a man can own; it costs relationships, years, and love itself. And bitterness? Bitterness builds walls so tall that even love can't climb them. And yet, somehow, gossip still manages to find a way over.'

They both fell silent, watching children chasing kites in the open field, their laughter spilling like sunlight over the grass.

Finally, Keshav whispered, almost like a prayer: 'Ravi, **no argument, no ego, no 'I am right' is worth more than a relationship**. Pride leaves you empty, resentment leaves you bitter... and sometimes, it leaves you alone with no chance to fix what's broken.'

Ravi swallowed, his voice low. 'Keshav... I think I need to call my younger sister today. We've barely spoken in years... some silly fight. I can't even recall how it began.'

Keshav's lips curved into the faintest smile. 'Do it, Ravi. Don't let resentment outlive love. Life is too short to carry stones in your heart. Besides, stones are bad for both knees and relationships.'

As they walked, Ravi pulled out his phone. His hand trembled over his sister's name, the screen staring back like a challenge. Keshav noticed.

'Go on,' he said gently. 'Sometimes the heaviest step is pressing that green button.'

Ravi took a breath, pressed call, and lifted the phone to his ear.

For a moment, only the ringtone filled the air. Then a 'Hello?' A familiar voice answered. His lips curved into a trembling smile. 'It's me... It's been too long.'

There was silence, then a soft smile emerged on his face...awkward but warm, like a door creaking open after years.

Keshav's eyes softened as he watched his old friend's face light up. He whispered, almost to himself, but loud enough for Ravi to hear. 'See? Sweetness returns the moment bitterness is swept away. **Resentment is just a stone in your shoe...the longer you carry it, the harder it becomes to walk.**'

The 2 friends continued walking down the familiar lane.

As Ravi's laughter rippled through the phone, he seemed to drift into another world, lost in the mending of an old bond. Keshav watched for a moment, then turned towards home. The bag of fruits still swung at his side, but for the first time that morning, it felt a little lighter.... lightened not by the fruit he carried, but by the weight he had finally shared. Sometimes the best detox isn't green juice – it's forgiveness.

Key Takeaways

1. **Resentment burns the one who carries it.** Like coal or poison, it harms you before anyone else.
2. **Bitterness builds walls.** Silence and distance echo across generations.
3. **Regret is the child of resentment.** By the time we wish to repair, the chance may be gone.

4. **Healing begins with humility** – one call, one step, one gesture can dissolve years of bitterness.
5. Life is too short to carry unnecessary stones in the heart.

'Resentment is like taking poison and waiting for the other person to die.' – **Nelson Mandela**

'Holding onto resentment is letting someone you dislike live rent-free in your head.' – **Anonymous**

'Resentment is the burden we choose to carry when we refuse to let go.' – **Anonymous**

Scoring Guide

When assessing yourself, consider the **frequency, intensity, duration, and pervasiveness** of your feelings of resentment. Think about how often you feel this way, how strongly it affects your emotions and thoughts, and whether it impacts various areas of your life or is limited to specific, quickly resolved situations.

Score 0: Overwhelming, Debilitating Resentment

You are constantly consumed by intense, deep-seated resentment towards individuals, groups, or life circumstances. This feeling is pervasive, making it nearly impossible to experience joy, trust others, or move forward in a positive way. You frequently dwell on perceived wrongs, feel unforgiving, and might actively wish ill upon those you resent.

Score 1: Severe, Frequent Resentment

You frequently experience strong, persistent feelings of **resentment, often stemming from unresolved past hurts, betrayals, or injustices**. These feelings regularly colour your perception, lead to cynicism, and significantly strain your relationships. You find it very difficult to forgive or let go of grievances.

Score 2: Moderate, Noticeable Resentment

You experience feelings of resentment periodically, usually when reminded of specific past events, people, or situations that caused you pain or unfairness. While you might try to move past it, these feelings can still surface, causing discomfort, bitterness, or difficulty trusting. You might find yourself occasionally holding grudges.

Score 3: Mild, Occasional Resentment

You experience mild, fleeting moments of resentment from time to time, typically in response to a fresh disappointment, a perceived slight, or an unfair situation. These feelings are manageable, don't last long, and you are generally able to process them and find constructive ways to cope or let go without dwelling.

Score 4: Rare, Brief Resentment

You very rarely experience significant resentment. When you do, it's a brief, mild, and quickly resolved feeling, often acknowledging an injustice without internalizing lasting ill-will. You possess a strong capacity for forgiveness and a generally understanding and compassionate outlook towards others.

Score 5: Minimal or Absent Resentment

You almost never experience resentment. You have a profound ability to process past hurts, forgive (yourself and others), and maintain a positive, accepting, and open perspective on life and people. You are free from lingering grudges and approach situations with equanimity and a genuine desire for understanding.

Reflection Prompts

1. How does holding onto resentment manifest in your thoughts, words, or actions towards that person or situation (e.g., bitterness, passive-aggressiveness, avoiding them)?

2. What impact does this resentment have on your inner peace, your relationships, and your ability to move forward?

26. Regret

Key Takeaways

1. Regret is the echo of choices unmade and words unsaid.
2. Pride delayed today becomes sorrow tomorrow.
3. Regret cannot change the past, but it can shape wiser choices in the future.
4. Often, what we regret most are the silences, not the arguments.
5. Healing regret requires action in the present – reaching out before it's too late.

'In the end, we only regret the chances we didn't take.' – **Lewis Carroll**

'Of all the words of tongue and pen, the saddest are these: it might have been.' – **John Greenleaf Whittier**

'Regret is an appalling waste of energy; you can't build on it, it's only good for wallowing.' – **Katherine Mansfield**

Scoring Guide

Here, 0 represents **maximum (severe/pervasive) regret** and 5 represents **minimum (rare/absent) regret**. When assessing yourself, consider the **frequency, intensity, duration, and pervasiveness** of your feelings of regret. Think about how often you feel it, how strongly it affects your emotions and thoughts, and whether it impacts various areas of your life or is limited to specific situations.

Score 0: Overwhelming, Debilitating Regret

You are constantly consumed by deep, painful regret over past decisions, actions, or inactions. These feelings are pervasive, make it nearly impossible to move forward, and significantly interfere with your daily life, peace of mind, and ability to make new choices. You often ruminate on what 'could have been' or 'should have been repeatedly.'

Score 1: Severe, Frequent Regret

You frequently experience strong, persistent feelings of regret. You often dwell on past mistakes, missed opportunities, or hurtful actions, and these feelings can be distressing and difficult to shake. While not always debilitating, this level of regret significantly impacts your mood, self-esteem, and willingness to take risks.

Score 2: Moderate, Noticeable Regret

You experience feelings of regret periodically, usually when reminded of specific past events or decisions that didn't turn out as hoped. While uncomfortable, these feelings are typically tied to particular situations and don't completely overshadow your general outlook. You might reflect on past choices but are generally able to process and learn from them.

Score 3: Mild, Occasional Regret

You experience mild, fleeting moments of regret from time to time, typically in response to minor missteps or less-than-ideal outcomes. These feelings are manageable, don't last long, and you are generally able to acknowledge them, learn from the experience, and move on without dwelling.

Score 4: Rare, Brief Regret

You very rarely experience significant regret. When you do, it's a brief, mild, and quickly resolved feeling, often acknowledging an opportunity missed or a better path that could have been taken, but without self-reproach or lingering distress. You possess strong resilience and acceptance of past events.

Score 5: Minimal or Absent Regret

You almost never experience regret. You have a profound ability to accept your past choices and their consequences, focusing instead on learning, growth, and the present moment. You understand that every decision, good or bad, has led you to where you are, and you are able to let go of 'what ifs' with ease.

Reflection Prompts

1. How does dwelling on past regret impact your present mood and future choices?
2. What steps, if any, can you take to make amends, learn, or release the burden of this regret?

27. Bitterness

Key Takeaways

1. Bitterness is the residue of wounds left unhealed.
2. It builds walls so high that even love finds it difficult to climb them.
3. Bitterness starves the heart – it feeds on anger but yields no nourishment.
4. Releasing bitterness frees not just others, but yourself.
5. A bitter heart cannot hold gratitude and joy at the same time.

'Bitterness imprisons life; love releases it.' – **Harry Emerson Fosdick**
'Bitterness is like cancer. It eats upon the host.' – **Maya Angelou**
'The cure for bitterness is gratitude.' – **Steve Maraboli**

Scoring Guide

Here, 0 represents **maximum (severe/pervasive) bitterness** and 5 represents **minimum (rare/absent) bitterness**. When assessing yourself, consider the **frequency, intensity, duration, and pervasiveness** of your feelings of bitterness. Think about how often you feel bitterness, how deeply it affects your emotions and thoughts, and whether it colours your overall outlook on life.

Score 0: Overwhelming, Debilitating Bitterness

You are constantly consumed by deep-seated resentment, anger, and cynicism, **often directed at past wrongs, people, or life in general.** This bitterness permeates nearly all your thoughts and interactions, making it impossible to feel joy, forgive, or move forward. You **frequently dwell on grievances and might project negativity onto others.**

Score 1: Severe, Frequent Bitterness

You frequently experience strong feelings of bitterness and resentment, often stemming from unresolved past hurts or perceived injustices. These feelings regularly colour your perception, lead to cynical outlooks, and can strain your relationships. You find it very difficult to forgive or let go of grievances.

Score 2: Moderate, Noticeable Bitterness

You experience bitterness periodically, usually when reminded of specific past events, people, or situations that caused you pain. While you might try to move past it, these feelings can still surface and cause discomfort, leading to moments of resentment or difficulty trusting.

Score 3: Mild, Occasional Bitterness

You experience mild, fleeting moments of bitterness from time to time, typically in response to a fresh disappointment or an unfair situation. These feelings are manageable, don't last long, and you are generally able to process them and move on without dwelling.

Score 4: Rare, Brief Bitterness

You very rarely experience bitterness. When you do, it's a brief, mild, and quickly resolved feeling, often acknowledging an injustice without internalizing lasting resentment. You possess a strong capacity for forgiveness and a generally positive outlook.

Score 5: Minimal or Absent Bitterness

You almost never experience bitterness. You are **able to process past hurts, forgive (yourself and others), and maintain a positive, accepting, and open perspective on life and people**. You are free from lingering resentment and approach situations with equanimity and optimism.

Reflection Prompts

1. How does bitterness manifest in your thoughts, words, or actions (e.g., cynicism, resentment, dwelling on past wrongs)?
2. What impact does holding onto bitterness have on your inner peace, your relationships, and your ability to move forward?

28. Curiosity (Positive)

'Be less curious about people and more curious about ideas.'
– Marie Curie
'The man who asks a question is a fool for a minute,
the man who does not ask is a fool for life.' **– Confucius**
'I have no special talent. I am only passionately curious.'
– Albert Einstein
'Curiosity is the beginning of wisdom.' **– Socrates**

Scoring Guide

When assessing yourself, consider the **frequency, depth, and breadth** of your curiosity. Think about how often you feel compelled to learn or explore, how deeply you delve into subjects, and how widely your interests span across different areas of life.

Score 0: Minimal or Absent Curiosity

You rarely, if ever, feel curious about anything. You tend to be disengaged from new information, different perspectives, or unexplored ideas. You might prefer routine and predictability, showing little interest in learning, exploring, or asking 'why.'

Score 1: Limited Curiosity

You experience fleeting moments of curiosity, usually only when directly presented with something novel or highly stimulating. These feelings are brief and don't typically lead to further investigation or sustained interest. You might be content with surface-level understanding.

Score 2: Moderate, Situational Curiosity

You feel curious periodically, often in specific areas of interest (e.g., your job, a particular hobby). You can be engaged by new information in these domains, but your curiosity might not extend broadly to other subjects, people, or experiences. You might ask questions, but not always delve deeply.

Score 3: Consistent Curiosity

You **regularly feel curious about various aspects of the world** around you. You enjoy learning new things, asking questions, and seeking out different perspectives. You are open to new experiences and ideas, and your curiosity often prompts you to explore and investigate.

Score 4: Deeply Curious

You possess a strong and pervasive sense of curiosity that drives you to continuously learn, explore, and understand. You actively seek out new knowledge, diverse viewpoints, and novel experiences. You are **often asking 'why' and 'how,'** and your intellectual and experiential hunger is a significant part of your personality.

Score 5: Profound Curiosity/Inquisitiveness

Curiosity is a fundamental and insatiable drive for you. You **approach life with an insatiable desire to discover, understand, and experience everything possible. You are a lifelong learner,** an avid explorer of ideas and phenomena, and your profound inquisitiveness consistently leads to new insights, connections, and personal growth. You thrive on the unknown.

Reflection Prompts

1. What topics, ideas, or people genuinely spark your curiosity?
2. How often do you allow your curiosity to lead you to new knowledge or experiences?
3. How does being curious (or lacking curiosity) impact your learning, problem-solving, and relationships?

29. Victim Thoughts

The ceiling fan groaned above, wobbling as if debating early retirement. After years of loyal service, it now seemed to sigh, '*One more summer and I'm filing for pension.*' Keshav was long used to its orchestra of creaks, which by now felt less like a complaint and more like background music specially composed for his evenings.

Keshav hunched over his study table, scribbling into a thick, weathered notebook, when an old friend walked in after many years. So absorbed was Keshav that he didn't even notice.

His friend cleared his throat and grinned. 'Keshav, what are you writing so intently? A secret love letter at this age?'

Keshav looked up over his glasses, smirked, and tapped the diary.

'Love letter? *Arre*, at this age, the only thing I write with passion is my medical history for the doctor.' Both burst into laughter. Then Keshav tapped the diary again with fondness. 'This is no ordinary diary, my friend. Some collect stamps, others coins – but I collect characters. People with strange habits and stranger stories. Every page is a tale.'

His friend shook his head, amused. 'Characters? Don't tell me you've started writing gossip columns now.'

Keshav wagged a finger. 'Gossip is temporary, my friend. Today I was penning down the story of Meera.'

Leaning slowly with narrowed eyes, he looked ready to narrate an epic saga.

'A woman who turned victimhood into a full-time profession. If it were a sport, she'd have taken home the gold.'

Keshav allowed a sly smile to creep in, memories flickering through his mind like quick flashes. Then, with a sigh as though introducing a tragic heroine from an old play, he began, 'Meera… she was a frail-looking woman who seemed to carry the world's burden on her shoulders. The first time I met her, I thought life had been cruel to her, as if fate had beaten her black and blue. I felt deep sympathy.' He shook his head slowly, almost in disbelief.

'She was that convincing.' He continued. 'The woman who could make even a sunny day sound like a funeral'

'But here's the thing,' Keshav said, settling deeper in his chair like a judge about to deliver a verdict. 'After years of watching her, I realized her life wasn't half as cruel as she made it sound. She had simply mastered the art of victimhood. She was both the writer of the script and the lead actress on stage.' Keshav chuckled, shaking his head. 'To her, every conversation was a stage rehearsal, and the only role she ever played was that of the wronged heroine.'

He tapped the diary with his pen unconsciously as if recollecting episodes.

'And the pattern, oh, it never ended. Parents? Villains... In-laws? Cruel masterminds... Boss? A ruthless tyrant... Colleagues? Jealous conspirators. You name the relationship, she had turned it into a courtroom where she was always the plaintiff and the rest of the world guilty.'

'It wasn't that people hated her. Many began with sympathy, just as I did. But gradually they realized the truth – Meera didn't want solutions, only validation. Advice irritated her, but pity... Ah, pity was her oxygen. The moment you said, *'Poor you, that's so unfair!'* her eyes sparkled like a student who had just scored full marks. If victimhood had a loyalty program, she'd have been platinum tier with lifetime benefits.'

A weary smile crossed his lips.

'By the end, her life looked less like a tragedy and more like a daily soap on repeat – same script, different characters, always with her in the starring role.'

Keshav closed the diary softly, as if shutting the chapter on Meera once and for all.

'You know, my friend,' he said thoughtfully, 'sympathy is like sugar; in small doses, it sweetens life. However, taken every day in excess, it can make you sick. Meera never understood that. She built her world on sympathy, but in the process, she lost the very thing she was craving – genuine connections.'

He leaned back with a half-smile.

'Eventually, people stopped clapping for her performance. And when the applause fades, the actress finds herself alone on stage, lights dimmed, wondering where everyone went.'

His friend sat quietly, letting the words sink in.

Keshav poured them both a glass of water, raised his own as though in a toast, and said with a wry smile, 'That's where people like Meera go wrong. The moment you believe the whole world is conspiring against you, chances are – you're the common factor. It's not a conspiracy, it's a pattern. And patterns don't lie.'

The ceiling fan groaned overhead, as if nodding in agreement. Keshav smiled at the timing, then called toward the kitchen,

'*Arre*, 2 cups of tea, please! And make it *kadak* (strong) – because unlike sympathy, tea only gets better the stronger you make it,' he added with a wink.

His friend laughed aloud, raising his glass of water in salute.

Key Takeaways

1. **Victimhood thrives on sympathy, not solutions.**
2. **Sympathy is like sugar – healthy in small doses, harmful in excess.**
3. **Patterns don't lie.** If every story casts you as the victim, check your role.
4. **Genuine connections need responsibility.** Overplaying the victim role isolates you.

'Playing the victim is a sure way to remain powerless.' – **Anonymous**
'You can't start the next chapter of your life if you keep re-reading the last one.' – **Michael McMillian** (an American actor and writer).

Scoring Guide

Score 0: Overwhelming, Debilitating Victim Thoughts

You are almost constantly consumed by a profound and overwhelming sense of victimhood. You believe you are perpetually at the mercy of external forces, that **everything bad that happens is someone else's fault or an unavoidable fate, and that you have no control over your life**. This thinking is debilitating, making it impossible to take action, grow, find solutions, or form healthy relationships, often leading to deep resentment, passivity, and chronic unhappiness.

Score 1: Significant, Pervasive Victim Thoughts

You frequently experience strong, pervasive victim thoughts that significantly colour your perception of many aspects of your life. You **often feel helpless, targeted, or constantly wronged by**

circumstances or others, even in minor events. This leads to a strong tendency to blame, avoid responsibility, and feel that life is unfairly stacked against you, impacting your motivation, relationships, and overall well-being.

Score 2: Consistent Victim Thoughts (Mild to Moderate)

You regularly fall into patterns of victim thinking. You might frequently feel that external factors, other people, or bad luck are primarily responsible for your challenges, unhappiness, or lack of progress. This can lead to a **tendency to blame, frequent complaining, or a sense of helplessness**, though you may still occasionally try to overcome obstacles.

Score 3: Moderate, Situational Victim Thoughts

You periodically find yourself experiencing victim thoughts, especially in specific challenging situations or relationships where you feel wronged or let down. While these thoughts are noticeable and can cause temporary frustration or self-pity, you are **generally able to move past them, perhaps after some venting or reflection, and regain a sense of personal power**.

Score 4: Occasional, Fleeting Victim Thoughts

You might experience brief, mild moments where you feel unfairly treated, unlucky, or powerless, usually in response to significant setbacks or unexpected negative events. However, these thoughts are quickly recognized, challenged, and you actively shift your perspective towards problem-solving, acceptance, or personal accountability. They do not linger or dictate your actions.

Score 5: Minimal or Absent Victim Thoughts

You rarely, if ever, perceive yourself as a victim of circumstances, others, or external forces. You consistently take personal responsibility for your responses, choices, and current situation, even when faced with genuine adversity. You focus on what you can control and how to move forward, feeling empowered and agentic in your life.

Reflection Prompts

1. How does adopting a victim mindset impact your ability to take action or find solutions?
2. What would it mean to take full responsibility for your response in a situation where you typically feel like a victim?
3. What is one small step you can take to shift from a 'why me?' mindset to a 'what now?' mindset?

30. Boredom

'Boredom is the feeling that everything is a waste of time; serenity, that nothing is.' – **Thomas Szasz**

'Boredom is the root of all evil – the despairing refusal to be oneself.' – **Søren Kierkegaard**

'In order to live free and happily, you must sacrifice boredom. It is not always an easy sacrifice.' – **Richard Bach**

Scoring Guide

When assessing yourself, consider the **frequency, intensity, and pervasiveness** of your feelings of boredom. Think about how often you feel unengaged, restless due to a lack of stimulation, or find activities tedious.

Score 0: Overwhelming, Debilitating Boredom

You are almost constantly consumed by a profound sense of boredom, apathy, and restlessness. Life feels utterly meaningless, monotonous, and devoid of interest. You struggle to find engagement in any activity, feel chronically under-stimulated, and often find yourself craving novelty without being able to find or pursue it effectively.

Score 1: Severe, Frequent Boredom

You frequently experience strong, persistent feelings of boredom. You often feel a lack of stimulation or purpose in your daily life, and many activities feel dull or unfulfilling. This boredom significantly impacts your motivation, energy levels, and overall enjoyment, often leading to a desire for escape or distraction.

Score 2: Moderate, Noticeable Boredom

You experience feelings of boredom periodically, especially during routine tasks, downtime, or when lacking specific plans. While you can find engagement sometimes, boredom is a recurring and noticeable part of your emotional landscape, causing discomfort and a desire for more stimulation or meaning.

Score 3: Mild, Occasional Boredom

You experience mild, fleeting moments of boredom from time to time, usually in response to very specific, unengaging situations (e.g., waiting in line, a repetitive task). These feelings are manageable, don't last long, and you can usually find ways to occupy your mind or shift your focus.

Score 4: Rare, Brief Boredom

You very rarely experience significant boredom. When you do, it's a brief, mild, and quickly resolved feeling, perhaps acknowledging a temporary lull in activity without internalizing a sense of listlessness. You are generally adept at finding things to engage your mind or body.

Score 5: Minimal or Absent Boredom

You almost never experience boredom. You approach life with a profound sense of curiosity, engagement, and purpose. You are adept at finding interest in diverse activities, learning new things, and connecting with the world around you. Your mind is often stimulated, and you feel generally content and fulfilled, even in quiet moments.

Reflection Prompts

1. What do you typically do when you feel bored? Do you seek stimulation, passively endure it, or feel restless?
2. How does boredom impact your motivation, creativity, or willingness to engage in new activities or with others?
3. Can boredom ever be a useful signal, perhaps pointing to a need for change, new challenges, or deeper engagement?

3

TENDENCIES

Beyond our core attributes and emotions lie the **Tendencies** – those quiet yet persistent forces that nudge us toward certain ways of thinking, feeling, or behaving. They are not always loud enough to catch our immediate attention, but like background music in a room, they shape the mood and direction of our lives.

Some tendencies are **innate**, perhaps linked to our temperament or early conditioning. Others are **learned patterns**, accumulated over years of repeated choices and reinforced by environment, upbringing, and experiences. Together, they form an invisible compass that often guides our actions more than we realize.

Think of them as the *default settings* of the mind:

- Some people tend to **worry** before opportunities.
- Others tend to **procrastinate** despite having the ability.
- Some lean naturally toward **generosity**, while others gravitate to **self-protection**.

These tendencies are not inherently good or bad. What matters is how aware we are of them – and whether we allow them to control us or consciously refine them.

By engaging in **introspection**, you begin to notice these recurring patterns. Perhaps you find that in stressful meetings, you tend to grow defensive. Or that when faced with change, your first instinct is resistance rather than curiosity. Such discoveries are not reasons for self-criticism; they are opportunities for **self-understanding.**

Recognizing tendencies is the **first step towards freedom**. Once named, they lose much of their hidden power. You can then choose whether to strengthen a helpful tendency – like patience, persistence, or curiosity – or to recalibrate an unhelpful one, like fault-finding, complaining, or avoidance.

This chapter encourages you to:

- Map your personal tendencies across situations (home, work, relationships).
- Reflect on how they influence outcomes – positively or negatively.
- Explore anecdotes that bring these patterns to life in relatable ways.
- Use scoring guidelines to assess the strength of each tendency in your own life.

Tendencies are subtle teachers. Left unchecked, they can bind you in repetitive cycles; but observed and refined, they can become stepping stones for growth. Over time, you will see how even a small shift in a tendency – say, from impulsiveness to considered action – creates ripples of transformation in relationships and self-development.

Ultimately, to work with tendencies is to walk a middle path: neither denying them nor surrendering to them. It is about **seeing clearly, choosing wisely, and living consciously**.

1. Harbouring Hurt

Karna was among the top 5 warriors of the Mahabharata era. Equally famous for his unmatched generosity, he could give away almost anything – sometimes to the point of reckless charity. He knew in advance that before the great war, the Mahabharata, Lord Indra would arrive disguised as a Brahmin to ask for his divine *kavach* (shield) and *kundal* (earrings), a ploy to ensure Arjuna – Indra's son – could one day defeat him. Yet Karna, bound to his Dharma of giving, resolved that if someone asked, he would part with it – even if it cost him his life.

Born to the Sun God, Karna was blessed with extraordinary abilities. Yet, in a cruel twist of fate, his mother Kunti had to abandon him at birth. Raised by a charioteer's family, he grew up being taunted as *Sarathi-putra* (charioteer's son) – a label that stung him more than an arrow.

Karna's brilliance took him to the feet of the great Parashurama, also the guru of Bhishma and Dronacharya. Under his tutelage, Karna honed his warrior skills to near perfection. But the world was not ready to see beyond his parentage. When he stepped forward to display his archery skills, Prince Bhima sneered, 'Go back to your chariot, *Sarathi-putra!*' That single insult pierced Karna deeper than any arrow, planting the more seeds of hurt.

The hurt of rejection and insult drove Karna straight into Duryodhana's embrace – the one man who gave him dignity and declared him King of Anga when the world mocked him. In gratitude and in resentment, Karna's loyalty to Duryodhana became unshakable, his rivalry with Arjuna unquenchable.

On one side, the taunts of *Sarathi-putra* weighed on him; on the other, his brilliance cried out for recognition. This hurt festered into a burning obsession: to prove himself the greatest archer of his time. His rival was clear – Arjuna, who was considered to be the greatest Archer among his generation. And if defeating Arjuna meant killing him, so be it. Little did Karna know, Arjuna was his own brother.

His wounds deepened at Draupadi's *swayamvar* (for the selection of a groom). The *swayamvar* was a grand archery contest arranged by Draupadi's father, King Drupada. The challenge was formidable: competitors had to string an enormous, unyielding bow and shoot the eye of a golden fish spinning on a wheel – relying only on its reflection in a pool of oil below. One after another, kings and princes tried and failed. Then Karna rose. His reputation as a master archer was so legendary that even the disguised Pandavas and the expectant crowd believed he could achieve the impossible. With effortless strength, he strung the bow and steadied himself to take aim.

But Draupadi's voice rang out: 'I will not marry a *Sarathi-putra!*' Before all the gathered kings, Karna was publicly humiliated. He laughed bitterly, dropped the bow, and returned to his seat – his pride shredded. This insult etched itself deep, fuelling his hostility toward the Pandavas and his chilling silence during Draupadi's disrobing.

On the eve of war, Kunti (mother of Pandavas) revealed the truth – Karna was her firstborn, elder to the Pandavas, rightful heir to the throne. She begged him to return. But Karna, harbouring his old wounds like a knife pressed to his chest, could not let go. He promised not to harm his brothers – except Arjuna. Proving himself better than Arjuna had become his life's mission, more important than reconciliation, even more important than survival.

And thus, burdened by hurt and blinded by rivalry, Karna met his end on the battlefield – brave, but broken from within.

Keshav's Take

Karna was a victim of a system in which a profession was chosen for a boy based on the caste in which he was born. Of course, there were bound to be exceptions to this rule.

Suyodhana helped Karna after knowing his potential. Karna, after gaining the confidence of Suyodhana-didn't make any effort to change the system (the one because of which Karna was feeling hurt), where capable ones should have been given equal opportunity to learn irrespective of the cast in which they were born. He chose to establish only himself while carrying the hurt, bitterness, resentment, pride, and his ego.

In life, if every word and slight becomes a wound we carry, we remain stuck in Karna's dilemma. The reasons for our hurt may be genuine, but how we handle them – that's the real test. We can either polish our scars into wisdom or weaponise them into bitterness.

Clutching hurt is like carrying a cactus – it only pricks you.

The practice of cleaning and meditation helps us let go of accumulated hurts – before they become our life's curse and drag us down.

Key Takeaways

1. **Harbouring hurt corrodes from within** – it harms us more than those who insult us.

2. Recognition from others cannot replace self-acceptance.
3. A single insult can shape destiny – unless consciously released.
4. Loyalty built on hurt can blind us to truth and reconciliation.
5. **Regular self-reflection, cleaning, and meditation** are tools to release stored bitterness and hurt.

'Bitterness is like cancer. It eats upon the host.' – **Maya Angelou**

'The weak can never forgive. Forgiveness is the attribute of the strong.' – **Mahatma Gandhi**

Scoring Guide

When scoring yourself, consider the **frequency, intensity, and duration** of negative feelings (like hurt, resentment, bitterness, or anger) you carry from past events or interactions. Think about how easily you can truly let go and move on from perceived wrongs.

The higher score indicates a greater ability to let go of past hurts, resentment, and bitterness, leading to more inner peace.

Score 0: Overwhelming, Debilitating Harbouring of Hurt

You almost constantly hold onto past hurts, grudges, and resentment. Even minor slights from years ago can still trigger intense negative emotions. This pervasive unforgiveness consumes your thoughts, poisons your relationships, and significantly interferes with your ability to find peace, joy, and new connections.

Score 1: Severe, Frequent Harbouring of Hurt

You frequently find yourself dwelling on past hurts or perceived wrongs, often replaying scenarios and feeling bitterness or anger. While you might try to let go, these feelings resurface often, impacting your mood, energy, and relationships. You find it very difficult to truly forgive or move on from significant past hurts.

Score 2: Moderate, Noticeable Harbouring of Hurt

You periodically hold onto hurts, especially when reminded of past negative experiences or when dealing with specific individuals who have wronged you. You might find yourself occasionally ruminating on these issues, and while they don't consume your every thought, they can noticeably affect your emotional state and create lingering tension.

Score 3: Mild, Occasional Harbouring of Hurt

You experience mild, fleeting moments where you might hold onto a hurt, usually in response to a fresh slight or a particularly challenging situation. These feelings are manageable, don't last long, and you are generally able to process them, forgive, or release them without significant effort or long-term impact.

Score 4: Rare, Brief Lingering of Hurt

You very rarely harbour hurt. When a negative experience occurs, you process it quickly and effectively. You might feel a brief sting, but you actively choose to let go, learn from the experience, and move forward without holding a grudge or letting it fester.

Score 5: Minimal or Absent Harbouring of Hurt

You almost never harbour hurt or resentment. You possess a remarkable ability to process negative experiences, practice forgiveness (for yourself and others), and release emotional burdens. You live with a profound sense of inner peace, emotional freedom, and an open heart, rarely allowing past events to dictate your present emotional state.

Reflection Prompts

1. How does harbouring a hurt manifest in your thoughts, emotions, or even physically (e.g., bitterness, anger, withdrawal, tension)?

2. What **impact does holding onto this hurt have on your current relationships**, your inner peace, and your ability to fully engage with life?
3. What do you believe would happen if you were to genuinely let go of this specific hurt? What fears or resistance come up around that idea?

2. Complaining

The railway platform throbbed with its usual chaos. The iron roof trembled with the shrill cry of a departing train on a nearby track, sending pigeons flapping in noisy protest like irritated tenants. Coolies in red shirts sprinted around – some locked in eternal bargaining battles with stubborn passengers, others balancing luggage stacks that looked more like Himalayan peaks on 2 skinny shoulders.

Vendors floated through the crowd with kettles of steaming tea, chanting their chorus of '*Chai garam, chai garam*!' In the middle of it all, a skinny boy with a tray of *samosas* zigzagged past luggage piles stacked like pyramids… balancing his tray of samosas at angles that made every samosa seem poised for jailbreak.

A train screeched into another platform, drowning the chatter for a moment, while the loudspeakers crackled to life, half swallowed by static: '…Bhopal Express… arriving shortly on platform number 6…'

Through the crowd, Keshav checked his watch and quickened his pace, adjusting his bag and spectacles. His bag thumped against his side as he scanned the sea of bobbing heads.

'KE-SHAV!' He turned to see Aman lumbering forward, dragging a suitcase with a wheel that squeaked like a dying bird.

'This wretched bag!' Aman puffed. 'I swear it has its own moods – rolls only when it feels like it.'

Keshav chuckled.

Just then, the Bhopal Express screeched in. Amid the rush of elbows, cries of 'Side, side!' from coolies, and families herding children like goats. After elbow-duelling, they joined the tide of passengers climbing aboard the train, squeezing through the aisle past families already spreading tiffin. They sank into their seats by the window, the train's whistle announcing its departure. As the platform blurred and fields began to unfurl outside, silence finally settled for a brief moment.

Aman stretched his legs, catching his breath. 'Hard to believe we're on our way to Piyush's daughter's wedding. Feels like yesterday we were stealing mangoes and dodging the gardener. How time flies.'

Keshav chuckled, eyes softening. 'Yes, and uff! And remember his golden era of complaints? No matter what we did, Piyush had a comment ready.'

Aman laughed knowingly. 'True! If you hit a 6, he'd say your stance was wrong. If you aced an exam, he'd remind you of your bad handwriting.'

Both burst into laughter so loud that the man on the upper berth adjusted his blanket with theatrical irritation.

But Keshav's laughter softened into thought. 'Thick as thieves we were,' Keshav said, his voice lowering, 'but his habit of complaining clung to him like a second skin. The funny thing is, Piyush never saw it that way. He thought he was being observant. But slowly, without meaning to, it made people pull away....even me.'

Aman nodded, leaning closer.

'True. Sadly, we always have such people around us. They call it being attentive to details, but really, it's a constant urge to point out flaws. And often, without even realizing it, they start to push joy right out of the room.'

The train rattled on, fields flying past, the rhythm of steel on track echoing their memories.

Keshav's laugh carried both amusement and a hint of nostalgia. 'Oh, we had one at home too – My cousin Aarti, legendary in her own right. She could fold more complaints into the laundry than clothes. Nothing escaped her radar. Though elders complain of the government and Gen Z complain of Wi-Fi speed, she was capable of complaining not only about Wi-Fi speed but also about the absence of TikTok for Indians and holding the government responsible for not making an equivalent Indian version.'

Aman perked up, eyes twinkling. 'Oh? So you have a legendary family critic?'

Keshav chuckled. 'Legendary indeed.'

Aman leaned forward, amused. 'Go on... she sounds like a character I'd like to know about. What did she do, file inspection reports?'

'Almost,' Keshav said, eyes crinkling. 'She'd bicker about the tiniest things. If her husband, Raj, left his shirt on a chair instead of the basket, she'd check instantly, 'Is this a chair or your personal wardrobe?' If his socks weren't paired, she'd sigh, 'Maybe I should run a matchmaking service for your footwear?"

He shook his head with mock sympathy. 'Even her daughter Meera wasn't spared. If she left a bite on her plate, Aarti would declare, 'There are children starving in the world, and you choose to waste food?"

Aman burst out laughing. 'Poor Raj. Poor Meera. Living under constant cross-examination!'

Keshav smiled, then his tone softened. 'Yes... But here's the thing. She thought she was being observant, too. What she didn't see was how quietly it was sucking the joy out of her home. Raj stopped humming Kishore Kumar while making tea. Meera, once a chatterbox, locked herself in her room with headphones on. Constant complaining doesn't just drain others – it drains the complainer too. It builds walls where there should be warmth.'

The train rattled on. Aman's smile faded as he listened.

'One evening,' Keshav said softly, 'I was there for dinner. I stayed with them for a few days while attending a workshop in the city, so I saw these things up close. That night, Raj forgot to put a coaster under his glass of water. Aarti snapped, 'How many times do I have to tell you, these rings will ruin the wood!' Raj didn't argue... he just lowered his eyes and kept eating. And Meera muttered under her breath, 'Everything's a problem for you, Maa. You're suffocating."

The words seemed to echo even in the noisy compartment.

'Later that night,' Keshav continued, 'Meera and I sat on the terrace with cups of tea. She was holding an old family photograph – Raj with his arm around Aarti, little Meera beaming in the middle. She stared at it for the longest time and whispered, 'When was the last time we looked like this?"

Keshav sat silently, recalling how her words carried both pain and a strange self-awareness.

Days later, Aarti overheard Meera telling a friend, 'My mom never appreciates anything. Even if I score 95, she asks about the missing 5. I don't even feel like trying anymore.' Those words cut deeper than any knife – and that was her turning point.

That evening, Meera found Keshav reading on the terrace. She hesitated before sitting beside him, hugging her knees. After a long silence, she finally spoke.

'You know, Uncle,' she sighed, 'I've started sounding like Maa myself. I snap at her, I snap at Papa... even my friends say I'm too sharp sometimes. Maybe I picked it up without realizing. Maa's constant complaints, my friends' sarcasm, and all those shows where teenagers slam doors and roll their eyes – I thought it was normal. But if I keep going this way, I'll only be proving her right. I don't want to become the same kind of mirror I complain about.'

Keshav closed his book and looked at her gently, his eyes soft with understanding.

'It takes wisdom to notice the habits we inherit, Meera. Most people just repeat them blindly, thinking that's the only way. But you – **you've already begun to see the pattern. That's rare**. Don't be your mother's echo...be her evolution. You've caught yourself at the crossroads early. Now you get to decide whether your words drain light from a room, or fill it.'

Meera sat very still, the weight of his words settling into her like rain sinking into thirsty soil. For the first time, she didn't feel defensive, only seen. She nodded slowly, a resolve silently stirring in her chest. 'Then I want to choose light,' she whispered, almost to herself, as though making a promise she knew she had to keep.

Aman exhaled slowly, his eyes softening. Keshav nodded. 'But a sea change came into Aarti's life... the next time Raj left his bag on the wrong chair, the old complaint rose in her throat... but she stopped. Instead, she touched his arm and said, 'You must be tired. Come, I'll make you tea.' Raj looked at her like she'd spoken another language. And when Meera showed her a drawing, instead of pointing out smudges, Aarti said, 'Your imagination is beautiful.' The way Meera's face lit up like sunlight after rain was when Aarti finally realized something profound. It wasn't her family that was imperfect. It was her lens that needed cleaning.'

Keshav's voice lingered, almost like a lesson carried by the train's wheels. 'Complaints are easy, Aman. They slip off the tongue like habit. But appreciation... that takes awareness, and courage. Aarti learned that too late, but not too late to change. And when she did, her home didn't just grow quieter – it grew warmer.'

The train roared into the night, carrying both men deeper into memory and reflection.

Keshav's words lingered like the steady rhythm of wheels on steel.

'There is a fine line between the constant urge to correct those we love and the gentle art of reminding them toward betterment. Complaints build walls. Appreciation builds homes. In the end, only those who master this balance can hold their relationships together without losing their warmth.'

'People 'complain' for many reasons, and it's rarely about the surface issue alone. Here are some lenses to see it through: non-acceptance, unmet expectations, seeking validation, emotional venting, a habitual lens (instead of asking, 'What can I do?', the default is, 'Why is this happening to me?'). We also tend to avoid responsibility by pointing fingers elsewhere – and yes, sometimes it's even about social bonding, especially for the Mantharas and Suparnakhas among us.'

And as their conversation settled into silence, the train rolled steadily ahead on its journey – like theirs, still unfolding with every passing mile.

Key Takeaways

1. Complaining often disguises itself as observation but drains joy from relationships.
2. Chronic complaining slowly pushes people away – family, friends, colleagues – without the complainer realizing it.

3. Children absorb these habits unconsciously.
4. Replacing complaints with appreciation doesn't just change the atmosphere – it rebuilds trust and warmth.
5. **Awareness allows us to break inherited cycles of tendency and evolve.**

'Complaining is draining. Complaining only makes you miserable.' – **Catherine Pulsifer**

'Instead of complaining that the rosebush is full of thorns, be happy that the thorn bush has roses.' – **Proverb**

'Any fool can criticize, condemn, and complain – and most fools do.' – **Dale Carnegie**

Scoring Guide

When scoring yourself, consider the **frequency, intensity, and pervasive impact** of your complaining on your emotional state, your relationships, and your overall outlook on life.

Score 0: Overwhelming, Debilitating Complaining

You are almost constantly complaining about nearly everything – situations, people, life circumstances, the weather, etc. Your **conversations are dominated by negativity, grievances, and expressions of dissatisfaction. This pervasive complaining significantly impacts your mood, relationships**, and prevents you from finding contentment or focusing on solutions.

Score 1: Severe, Frequent Complaining

You frequently find yourself cribbing or complaining about various aspects of your life. While you might occasionally have positive moments, your tendency to focus on what's wrong is a prominent part of your daily interactions. This often leads to feelings of frustration and can wear down those around you.

Score 2: Moderate, Noticeable Complaining

You periodically engage in complaining, especially when you are stressed, tired, or faced with inconveniences. While you might sometimes catch yourself, it's a noticeable pattern. You express dissatisfaction more often than you'd like, and it can sometimes overshadow more positive discussions.

Score 3: Mild, Occasional Complaining

You experience mild, fleeting moments where you might complain, typically in response to significant frustrations or legitimate inconveniences. These instances are rare, usually brief, and you generally process the frustration and move on without dwelling on it or letting it define your interactions.

Score 4: Rare, Brief Complaining

You very rarely complain. If you do, it's an isolated and brief expression of dissatisfaction, perhaps when facing a truly unfair or difficult situation. You quickly shift to problem-solving or acceptance, maintaining a generally positive and constructive outlook.

Score 5: Minimal or Absent Complaining

You almost never complain. You consistently approach situations with a positive, grateful, or solution-oriented mindset. You accept what you cannot change, focus on what you can control, and express dissatisfaction constructively if at all. You embody a high degree of resilience and optimism.

Reflection Prompts

1. How does complaining typically manifest in your words, tone, or overall demeanour? Do you find yourself dwelling on issues without seeking solutions?

2. What impact does your complaining have on your own mood, your energy levels, and the **atmosphere in your relationships or work environment**?
3. What underlying need or belief might be driving your tendency to complain (e.g., a desire for control, feeling unheard, avoiding responsibility)?

3. Tendency to Find Fault

In traditional Indian weddings, ***Fufas*** (husbands of the father's sister) and ***Jijas*** (husbands of one's sister) often get a bad reputation. In my humble experience, I have found this reputation a bit disproportionate. After all, they're not always the villains people make them out to be – sometimes, they're just innocent bystanders who happened to arrive in a Sherwani.

But then there are the true legends – those who, like the infamous **Manthara** of Ramayana, arrive in every wedding disguised as the 'concerned relative.' In my circle, one such character was **Manthara *Mausi*** (occasionally doubling as *Nanad* or *chacheri bua*, depending on the family tree).

Sometimes, Manthara didn't come alone. She summoned her *all-star squad*: Suparnakha and Shakuni. Together, they were like the Avengers of annoyance – except no one invited them.

Suparnakha would quietly descend upon the unsuspecting ***chachi*** (father's younger brother's wife) or the ever-patient ***bua*** (father's sister), slicing through their peace with her sharp tongue. Meanwhile, Shakuni – master of strategies gone wrong – would cast his mischievous net over the poor ***mama*** (mother's brother) or the long-suffering ***fufa***. By the end, everyone had a story to complain about, even if they hadn't planned on it.

Now, marriages in India are not just weddings – they're full-scale festivals where relatives, friends, neighbours, and even the neighbourhood grocer's second cousin gather. It's a few days of food, fun, gossip, laughter, minor politics, and the occasional stage collapse. It's also the perfect playground for professional fault-finders. And in this league, Manthara *Mausi* was Sachin Tendulkar – consistently scoring centuries.

Her qualities were remarkable: she was a keen observer, a sweet talker, and a listener with the patience of a monk. She portrayed herself as nothing less than the **Goddess of Empathy**. People confided in her, thinking she was their emotional anchor. But *Mausi's* listening sessions were less about empathy and more about data collection. She could have given Google a run for its money – except her search engine only filtered out faults.

Once her 'data gathering' was done, she would swoop down on the unsuspecting. Imagine this scene:

'Bhaiya! It's already 7 a.m. and no tea has been served. There are small children here, too. What kind of arrangement is this?'

Delivered in a tone that could guilt-trip even the most stone-hearted host. Then, without waiting for a reply, she would repeat the same dialogue to another group. Within minutes, irritation would spread faster than the aroma of ginger tea. And once tempers started flaring and confrontations brewed, *Mausi* would quietly retreat, looking as innocent as if she had just prevented a nuclear war.

In another marriage, she applied her judgment as though she were ISO-certifying the event: stage design, flower placement, queue length at the buffet counter, efficiency of the waiters, quality of the *rasgulla* – all had to pass her invisible checklist. Spoiler alert: nothing ever did.

By then, I had become fascinated by her. Was she genuinely concerned, or was she just addicted to fault-finding? My curiosity peaked when her own daughter's wedding was announced. 'Finally!' I thought, 'Now the Goddess of Empathy must descend on her own battlefield. Will she criticize her own arrangements?'

I kept watch like a soldier on the border – 2 nights, no sleep, sharper eyes than even the wedding photographer's zoom lens. And what was the grand discovery after such relentless surveillance? To my shock, Manthara Mausi didn't find a single fault. Not one! She didn't even mutter about the *samosas*, which were admittedly softer than an overripe banana.

The cherry on top? Her usual partners-in-crime – Suparnakha and Shakuni – hadn't made it to the guest list. Perhaps the wedding planners had finally cracked the code: *banish the trio, and peace shall prevail.*

That day, I realized: some people are born to find faults in others but go blind when it comes to their own. Manthara *Mausi* had proven the ancient principle: *self-criticism is the hardest ritual of all.*

Keshav's Take

An aware person shall welcome the legendary trio to find the fault – as mirrors for growth. However, most of us prefer the gentler version: *constructive feedback.*

Key Takeaways

1. **Fault-finding is easy; contribution is rare.** Anyone can point fingers, but not everyone can lend a hand.
2. **The fault-finder's empathy is often a disguise.** Behind the sweet talk lies the thrill of stirring conflict.
3. **Double standards exist.** Many who scrutinize others' actions fail to apply the same scrutiny to themselves.
4. **Awareness matters.** Recognizing this tendency in ourselves helps us shift from complaining to contributing.

'Any fool can criticize, condemn and complain – and most fools do.'
– Dale Carnegie

'Don't find fault, find a remedy.' – **Henry Ford**

'The ability to observe without evaluating is the highest form of intelligence.' – **Jiddu Krishnamurti**

Scoring Guide

When scoring yourself, consider the **frequency, intensity, and impact** of your tendency to identify and highlight flaws or mistakes in others, situations, or even in your own performance. Think about whether this habit leads to improved outcomes or simply fosters negativity.

Score 0: Overwhelming, Debilitating Fault Finding

You are almost constantly looking for and pointing out flaws, mistakes, and imperfections in others, situations, and even yourself. Your default mode is critical, and you struggle to see positive aspects. This **pervasive fault-finding poisons your relationships**, creates an adversarial environment, and severely limits your ability to appreciate or find joy.

Score 1: Severe, Frequent Fault Finding

You frequently identify and vocalize faults, errors, or weaknesses in others or circumstances. While you might sometimes acknowledge positives, your **tendency to focus on what's wrong is a dominant part of your interactions and observations**. This behaviour often leads to others feeling judged, inadequate, or defensive, and **can create tension in your relationships**.

Score 2: Moderate, Noticeable Fault Finding

You periodically find yourself pinpointing faults, especially when stressed, irritated, or when something doesn't meet your expectations. You might sometimes offer unsolicited critiques or highlight imperfections. While you can also be appreciative, your **inclination to find flaws is noticeable and can sometimes overshadow positive interactions**.

Score 3: Mild, Occasional Fault Finding

You experience mild, fleeting moments where you might notice or even point out a fault, typically when it's a clear error or a significant issue. These instances are rare, usually brief, and you generally offer constructive feedback or move on quickly without dwelling on the negative aspect.

Score 4: Rare, Brief Identification of Faults

You very rarely focus on finding faults. If you do notice a flaw, it's typically in a situation that genuinely warrants attention for improvement, and your approach is usually constructive and compassionate rather than critical. You easily overlook minor imperfections and focus on the bigger picture or positive attributes.

Score 5: Minimal or Absent Fault Finding

You almost never engage in fault-finding. Your **default perspective is one of acceptance, appreciation, and seeking the good in people and situations**. You are highly tolerant of imperfections, offer grace readily, and when issues arise, you approach them with a problem-solving, constructive, or empathetic mindset rather than a critical one. You see the best in others and yourself.

Reflection Prompts

1. What thoughts or feelings accompany your tendency to find fault (e.g., frustration, judgment, a need for perfection, insecurity)?
2. How does this **tendency impact your relationships**, your ability to appreciate positive aspects, or your overall sense of contentment?

4. The Need For and Sense of Belonging

'A deep sense of love and belonging is an irreducible need of all people. We are biologically, cognitively, physically, and spiritually wired to love, to be loved, and to belong. When those needs are not met, we don't function as we were meant to.' – **Brené Brown**

'Giving connects 2 people, the giver and the receiver, and this connection gives birth to a new sense of belonging.' – **Deepak Chopra**
'The sense of belonging creates the urgency to care, to protect, to nurture, to nourish, and, most important of all, to love.' – **Daaji**

Scoring Guide

When assessing yourself, consider the **frequency, depth, and breadth** of your felt sense of belonging. Think about how often you feel truly connected and accepted, how deeply those feelings resonate, and how widely this sense extends across different areas of your life. Also, reflect on whether your inherent need for belonging feels adequately met.

Score 0: Minimal or Absent Sense of Belonging

You rarely, if ever, feel a sense of connection, acceptance, or belonging within any group, community, or relationship. You might feel fundamentally isolated, misunderstood, or like an outsider everywhere you go. The *need* for belonging may be deeply unfulfilled, leading to profound loneliness and detachment.

Score 1: Limited Sense of Belonging

You experience only fleeting or superficial moments of belonging. While you might interact with others, these connections often feel shallow, leaving you with a persistent underlying feeling of not truly fitting in or being fully accepted. Your need for belonging might be present but largely unmet, causing regular feelings of social isolation.

Score 2: Moderate, Situational Sense of Belonging

You feel a sense of belonging periodically, often within specific contexts (e.g., your family, a small group of friends) or when performing a particular role. However, this feeling might not extend broadly to other areas of your life, and you may still experience moments of feeling like an outsider or wishing for a deeper connection in other settings. Your need for belonging is met in some areas, but not others.

Score 3: Consistent Sense of Belonging

You regularly feel a strong sense of connection, acceptance, and belonging within your various social circles or communities. You feel valued and understood by others. While you might occasionally experience moments of slight detachment, your need for belonging is generally well-met, contributing positively to your emotional well-being.

Score 4: Deeply Connected and Integrated

You possess a strong and pervasive sense of belonging across multiple aspects of your life (e.g., family, friends, work, community). You feel deeply integrated, understood, and accepted for who you are. This strong sense of connection is a significant source of comfort, support, and well-being, and your need for belonging feels consistently fulfilled.

Score 5: Profound Sense of Belonging and Interconnectedness

You almost constantly experience a profound, unwavering sense of belonging and interconnectedness, not just with specific groups, but with humanity or even the world at large. You feel deeply accepted, seen, and valued, and your relationships are consistently nurturing. Your need for belonging is not only met but also contributes to a deep sense of purpose and peace. You might actively foster belonging for others.

Reflection Prompts

1. What efforts do you make to connect with groups or individuals where you feel you belong?
2. How does your perceived level of belonging (or isolation) impact your self-esteem and emotional well-being?

5. Seeking Approval/Validation

'Don't wait for someone else's approval to feel valid. Your worth isn't up for a vote.' – **Anonymous**

Validation from others is fleeting. Validation from yourself lasts a lifetime.' – **Anonymous**

'People who want the most approval get the least and people who need approval the least get the most.' – **Wayne Dyer**

Scoring Guide

Here's a guide to help you score yourself on the quality of **Seeking Approval/Validation**:

Score 0: Overwhelming, Debilitating Need for Approval

You are almost constantly driven by an intense need for external approval and validation. Your **self-worth is entirely dependent on what others think of you**. You frequently modify your opinions, behaviours, or choices to gain acceptance, leading to significant distress, a lack of authenticity, and an inability to make independent decisions. Criticism or disapproval can be devastating.

Score 1: Severe, Frequent Need for Approval

You frequently seek validation from others, and your mood and self-esteem are significantly affected by their opinions. You often hesitate to express your true self or make independent decisions due to fear of disapproval. You might over-perform or people-please regularly, and perceived criticism causes substantial anxiety or self-doubt.

Score 2: Moderate, Noticeable Need for Approval

You periodically find yourself seeking approval, especially in new social settings, with authority figures, or concerning important decisions. While you can sometimes act independently, a noticeable part of your motivation comes from wanting others to think well of you. You might feel discomfort or self-consciousness when you don't receive positive feedback.

Score 3: Mild, Occasional Need for Approval

You experience mild, fleeting moments where you might desire approval, typically in specific situations (e.g., presenting a major project, meeting new, important people). However, these feelings are manageable, don't last long, and you are generally able to base your actions on your own values and judgment without being overly swayed by others' opinions.

Score 4: Rare, Brief Need for Approval

You very rarely seek external approval or validation. When you do, it's a brief, mild, and quickly resolved thought, perhaps a natural desire for positive reinforcement, but it doesn't impact your behaviour or self-worth. You are largely self-assured and trust your own judgment.

Score 5: Minimal or Absent Need for Approval/High Self-Validation

You almost never seek external approval or validation to define your worth or guide your actions. Your self-esteem is derived from within, based on your own values, integrity, and accomplishments. You are highly authentic, make independent decisions with confidence, and are genuinely unconcerned by others' opinions, focusing instead on internal standards and genuine connection.

Reflection Prompts

1. What are the underlying fears or insecurities that fuel your need for external validation?

2. How does relying on others' approval impact your authentic expression, decision-making, or sense of self-worth?

6. Conflict Resolution – The Story of *Ranchor*

The Rise of a Tyrant

Jarasandha, the mighty king of Magadha, was the sort of ruler who collected kingdoms the way children collect marbles. His daughters were married to Kamsa, the infamous tyrant of Mathura and Krishna's uncle. When Krishna ended Kamsa's reign of terror, Jarasandha took it personally – like a vendetta carved into his pride. He vowed to destroy Krishna and the Yadavas, no matter how many battles it took.

The 17 Battles of Mathura

What followed was nothing short of obsession. Jarasandha marched on Mathura 17 times with vast armies – so vast that the Kurukshetra War would look like a college skirmish in comparison. Each time, Krishna and Balarama defended Mathura with brilliance and valour. And each time, Jarasandha's forces were shattered.

Yet, Krishna never killed Jarasandha. Why? Because Jarasandha had become a magnet for demoniac forces. Every defeat he suffered was another opportunity for Krishna to cleanse the earth of destructive powers that kept joining his cause. What looked like a cycle of repeated wars was actually Krishna's way of reducing evil one wave at a time.

But there was a cost. The people of Mathura lived in constant fear. They never knew when the next horn would blow, when the next siege would come. Their homes rattled with anxiety long after the battle drums had stopped.

The Eighteenth Invasion

On the eighteenth assault, Jarasandha came back with even more fury. This time, he wasn't alone – he brought with him Kalayavana, a

Yavana king blessed by Lord Shiva with a peculiar boon: no weapon could kill him. Imagine having to fight a man who came with an inbuilt insurance policy against weapons!

Krishna assessed the situation. Facing Jarasandha's mammoth army and Kalayavana's invincibility meant only one thing: devastation. Innocent lives would pay the price for someone else's ego.

So, Krishna did something that looked unthinkable. Instead of marching out for the eighteenth time, he quietly moved his entire city. With the divine architect Vishwakarma, Krishna built Dwarka – a fortified city on the western coast, surrounded by the ocean's protection. Overnight, Mathura was empty.

When Jarasandha and Kalayavana arrived, they found silence where they expected screams. And when Kalayavana challenged Krishna to battle, Krishna smiled, turned his back, and walked away.

The Birth of *Ranchor*

Kalayavana, furious at being 'ignored,' chased Krishna as he ran. To the world watching, this was shocking. *'Krishna is fleeing the battlefield!'* the whispers spread. *'The so-called hero is a coward after all!'* That's when he earned the name ***Ranchor*** – the one who left the battlefield.

But what happened next was pure strategy wrapped in wisdom. Krishna lured Kalayavana into the cave of Sage Muchukunda, who slept under a unique boon: anyone who disturbed his slumber would be burned to ashes by his gaze. Kalayavana mistook the sleeping sage for Krishna, kicked him awake, and was incinerated instantly. Krishna, without lifting a weapon, had ended the invincible.

Meanwhile, by leaving Mathura, Krishna saved his people from destruction and gave them a new, safer home.

The Final Chapter with Jarasandha

Of course, Jarasandha wasn't done. Years later, his cruelty again blocked the Pandavas' path to dharma. That's when Krishna joined

Arjuna and Bhima in Magadha, not with an army, but with a plan. In a duel, Bhima – guided by Krishna's subtle signal – finally split Jarasandha in 2, ending his tyranny once and for all.

Key Takeaways

1. **Walking away is not a weakness.** Sometimes it takes more courage to leave than to fight. Krishna's 'flight' was not cowardice; it was strategy in action.
2. **Discernment is the highest strategy.** Bravery is not about entering every battle – it is about knowing which battles serve dharma and which only feed ego.
3. **Reputation is fleeting; intent is eternal.** Krishna did not care about being called 'Ranchor.' He cared about protecting lives and serving the higher good.
4. **Creative solutions trump brute force.** Where weapons failed, wisdom found a way – whether by relocating a city or guiding Bhima with a hand signal.
5. **Labels don't define you.** What others call you ('coward' or 'runner') matters less than living aligned with your purpose

Keshav's Take

'Sometimes the bravest act is to step away, not to strike.'
'True strategy is not about winning every fight, but about preserving what truly matters.'
'Do not let society's labels define you; let clarity of purpose guide you.'

Scoring Guide

Score 0: Debilitating Avoidance

You are overwhelmingly driven by an extreme fear of confrontation. You will sacrifice your own well-being, endure severe injustices, or tolerate significant discomfort rather than face direct conflict. This avoidance is debilitating, prevents you from advocating for yourself, and leads to chronic resentment, unresolved issues, and unhealthy relationships.

Score 1: Significant, Pervasive Avoidance

You consistently go to great lengths to avoid confrontation, even when it's clearly necessary. This leads you to suppress your true feelings, allow others to overstep your boundaries, or fail to address significant problems in relationships or at work. The thought of direct conflict causes you considerable anxiety or fear.

Score 2: Compliant Avoidance

You frequently avoid confrontation, often prioritizing peace over your own needs. You might feel anxious about direct conflict and tend to 'let things go' even when it causes you internal frustration or allows issues to fester.

Score 3: Moderate Engagement

You sometimes avoid confrontation, especially when you perceive it might disrupt peace or if you hope issues will resolve on their own. While you might experience mild internal discomfort, you generally address concerns eventually, albeit sometimes indirectly or after some delay.

Score 4: Consistent Engagement

You generally prefer direct communication and issue resolution, but may occasionally avoid confrontation in highly specific, high-stakes situations or with particularly challenging individuals. You typically reflect on these instances and might address them later if truly necessary.

Score 5: Healthy, Direct Engagement

You consistently engage with disagreements, address issues head-on, and establish clear boundaries. You prioritize direct communication and resolution, even when it might lead to tension, and never shy away from necessary confrontations. You handle conflict calmly and constructively, focusing on finding solutions.

Reflection Prompts

1. **Impact on Self:** When you avoid a confrontation, what happens to your feelings and thoughts afterwards? Do you feel relief, or does it lead to resentment, anxiety, or frustration?
2. **Impact on Others:** Think of a recent situation where you chose to avoid conflict. How do you think your decision impacted the other person and the relationship in the long run? Did the problem resolve on its own, or did it fester?

7. Aggression

'Aggression is different from anger. Anger is an emotion; aggression is a behaviour. There are better ways to deal with anger than behaving aggressively.' – **Gwen Randall-Young**

'Aggression unopposed becomes a contagious disease.' – **Jimmy Carter**

'Aggression should be replaced by assertiveness, anger by clarity, and conflict by dialogue.' – **Anonymous**

Scoring Guide

When assessing yourself, consider the **frequency, intensity, and expression** of your aggressive impulses. Think about how often you feel angry or hostile, how strongly those feelings manifest (verbally or physically), and their impact on your relationships and daily life.

Score 0: Overwhelming, Debilitating Aggression

You are almost constantly consumed by intense, uncontrollable aggressive impulses, leading to frequent outbursts of anger, hostility, or even physical or verbal abuse. You struggle to manage your temper, react explosively to minor provocations, and often regret your aggressive behaviour, which significantly harms your relationships and reputation.

Score 1: Severe, Frequent Aggression

You frequently experience strong aggressive urges and often react with anger, defensiveness, or hostility in stressful situations. You might regularly engage in yelling, blaming, or other forms of verbal aggression, and sometimes struggle to de-escalate conflicts, leading to strained relationships and a confrontational reputation.

Score 2: Moderate, Noticeable Aggression

You periodically display aggressive tendencies, particularly when provoked, frustrated, or under pressure. You might sometimes raise your voice, become argumentative, or show impatience. While you generally manage to contain outright outbursts, your aggression is noticeable to others and can create tension in your interactions.

Score 3: Mild, Occasional Aggression

You experience mild, fleeting moments of aggression from time to time, usually in response to significant stressors or perceived injustices. These might manifest as brief irritation, passive-aggressive behaviour, or sharp words. You generally have good control over your reactions and these moments don't typically lead to lasting negative consequences.

Score 4: Rare, Brief Aggression

You very rarely experience aggressive impulses. When you do, they are extremely mild and quickly managed, often only as a brief internal feeling of irritation that doesn't translate into outward behaviour. You consistently choose peaceful, calm, and assertive responses even in challenging situations.

Score 5: Minimal or Absent Aggression

You almost never experience aggression. You possess a profound sense of inner peace, patience, and self-control, approaching even the most challenging situations with a calm and non-confrontational demeanour. You are adept at de-escalation, empathy, and seeking harmonious resolutions, truly embodying a peaceful approach.

Reflection Prompts

1. Recall a recent situation where you felt or expressed aggression (verbally, physically, or passively). What triggered this feeling or behaviour?
2. What are the underlying emotions or unmet needs that might be fuelling your aggression (e.g., fear, frustration, a sense of powerlessness)?
3. What impact does your aggressive behaviour have on your relationships, your goals, and your own inner peace?

8. Overthinking

Yash's friend Neel was on an H1B visa in the USA. With the sudden buzz about changes in US visa rules, Neel's company had asked him to immediately cut short his India trip and return before the new regulation kicked in. The irony? The government had already clarified that the rules applied only to fresh applicants, not existing visa holders. But companies, like cautious parents during exam season, didn't want to take chances. So, Neel had to pack his bags and buy a ticket at *triple* the usual fare.

Neel sighed, 'Yash! Ever since I got this email from my company, my mind is playing endless 'what-if' scenarios. Professionally, I'm doing fine. But with this changing geopolitical drama, it feels like my American dream is hanging by a thread.'

Yash said gently, 'But the government has clarified there's no immediate threat to you.'

'Maybe,' Neel replied, 'but my mind has become a broken record. I can't switch it off. It's affecting my sleep, my productivity, and honestly, my peace of mind. Can your spiritual trainer help me clear this mental traffic jam?'

Yash smiled, 'Of course. I'll connect you to my spiritual trainer. Additionally, I can connect you to Keshav Uncle as well, who can help you with his perspective.'

Soon, Yash arranged a video call. Keshav Uncle listened patiently, then said, 'Neel, your case is a classic example of overthinking.'

Neel defended himself, 'But Uncle, I need to plan for the future!'

'Of course, planning is necessary,' said Keshav, 'but planning and overplanning are not the same. Run a scenario 2 or 3 times, jot it down on paper, and then return to your routine. Otherwise, your brain becomes like a cow chewing the same grass endlessly.'

Neel admitted, 'Uncle, that's exactly how it feels – like a stuck record. My thoughts keep looping, and it's now affecting my work and my peace within. Please tell me how to deal with this.'

Keshav explained:

'Overthinking is when the mind refuses to stop chewing on a thought – replaying past mistakes, worrying about the future, or analysing every micro-detail. For example:

- Reading an email 10 times before sending it.
- Replaying a conversation because you or another person said 1 awkward line.
- Postponing decisions while hunting for the 'perfect' option.
- Predicting imaginary arguments that may never happen.'

Psychologically, it takes 2 forms:

- **Past focus (rumination):** 'Why did that happen? What if I had said this?'
- **Future focus (anxiety):** 'What if this goes wrong? What if I fail?'

It becomes a loop of 'what ifs' and 'should haves,' draining your energy. Research even shows that overthinking raises stress hormones, reduces productivity, and leads to decision paralysis.'

Neel asked softly, 'Where does this come from?'

'From a deeper lens,' Keshav said, 'When the heart isn't anchored, the mind hijacks the driver's seat, running in circles. Ancient wisdom says overthinking arises from attachment (*raga*) and fear (*dvesha*): wanting a particular outcome or dreading another. Introspection helps us step back and ask, 'Is this thought helping me, or is it just noise?' That question itself reclaims power.'

Neel leaned forward, 'Uncle, tell me how to handle it then.'

Keshav gave **5 tools**:

1. **Name it:** Say, 'I'm overthinking again.' Awareness breaks the cycle.
2. **Write it down:** Journaling clears the clutter.
3. **Time-box it:** Give yourself 10 minutes to think, then stop.
4. **Shift to body:** Walk, breathe, meditate – bring attention back to now.
5. **Ask 1 filter question:** 'Is this useful, or just fear dressed as logic?'

'And of course,' he added warmly, 'you can seek help from a spiritual trainer to clear the accumulated unwanted energy around such thoughts.'

He smiled, 'And by the way, overthinking is not always bad. Sometimes it's a hidden blessing:

- It shows you care about details.
- It reflects empathy (you replay conversations because people matter to you).
- It can even spark creativity when revisiting an idea polishes it.'

Yash reminded, 'Uncle, this is just like Raj's case we discussed in the Anxiety chapter – his overthinking eventually turned into months of stress and health issues.'

'Exactly,' Keshav nodded. 'Overthinking, left unchecked, breeds stress, which then grows into anxiety. Dr Bruce Lipton, in *The Biology of Belief*, beautifully explains how such thought patterns even affect our cells and health.'

Turning to Neel, he concluded: 'Think, plan, prepare – but after that, let go and enjoy. Once you've done your best, accept the outcome. In the worst case, if you had to return to India, do you think a talented professional like you wouldn't find his place here? India's ecosystem would absorb you in no time.'

Neel's shoulders finally relaxed. 'Uncle, this discussion has given me a new perspective. I'll work on it.'

Key Takeaways

1. **Overthinking is not planning.** Planning has an endpoint; overthinking loops endlessly like a stuck record.
2. **Past vs. Future:** Rumination clings to the past ('why did that happen?'), while anxiety imagines the future ('what if it goes wrong?'). Both drain energy.
3. **The deeper root:** Overthinking often arises from *attachment* (wanting a specific outcome) or *fear* (dreading another). When the heart is unanchored, the mind takes over.
4. **It affects health:** Left unchecked, overthinking fuels stress and eventually anxiety, impacting productivity and even cellular health.
5. **Freedom comes from acceptance:** Do your best, prepare well, but then let go of results. Life has a way of absorbing and supporting you wherever you are.

'Overthinking, also, best known as creating problems that are never there.' – **David Sikhosana**

'Don't get too deep, it leads to overthinking, and overthinking leads to problems that didn't exist in the first place.' – **Jayson Engay**

'Thinking will not overcome fear, but action will.' – **W. Clement Stone**

Scoring Guide

When scoring yourself, consider the **frequency, intensity, and impact** of your overthinking on your mental state, decision-making, and overall quality of life.

Score 0: Overwhelming, Debilitating Overthinking

Your mind is almost constantly consumed by excessive rumination, worry, and analysis. You find it nearly impossible to make decisions, sleep, or focus on the present moment due to an incessant loop of thoughts, worst-case scenarios, and replaying past events. This level of overthinking is debilitating, causing significant anxiety, stress in daily life.

Score 1: Severe, Frequent Overthinking

You frequently engage in intense overthinking, often getting caught in cycles of worry, analysis paralysis, and self-doubt. You struggle to let go of thoughts, replaying conversations or anticipating future problems. This significantly impacts your peace of mind, decision-making speed, and ability to relax, even though you might manage to function.

Score 2: Moderate, Noticeable Overthinking

You periodically find yourself overthinking, especially in stressful situations, when facing important decisions, or after social interactions. While you can sometimes break free from these thought patterns, they are a noticeable and recurring part of your mental experience, causing discomfort and occasionally delaying action or adding unnecessary stress.

Score 3: Mild, Occasional Overthinking

You experience mild, fleeting moments of overthinking from time to time, usually in response to significant events or when trying to solve a complex problem. These thoughts are manageable, don't last long, and you are generally able to recognize when you're doing it and redirect your focus without significant effort or negative consequences.

Score 4: Rare, Brief Overthinking

You very rarely engage in overthinking. When you do, it's a brief, mild, and quickly resolved instance of thoughtful consideration rather than excessive rumination. You generally approach situations with clarity and confidence, trusting your intuition and making decisions efficiently without getting bogged down in unnecessary analysis.

Score 5: Minimal or Absent Overthinking

You almost never engage in overthinking. Your mind is typically clear, focused, and present. You make decisions confidently, process information effectively, and let go of thoughts that don't serve you. You experience a profound sense of mental peace and are highly adaptable, responding to situations rather than getting lost in excessive analysis.

Reflection Prompts

1. How does overthinking manifest for you (e.g., sleeplessness, indecision, anxiety, replaying scenarios)?
2. How does excessive thinking impact your ability to act, to trust your intuition, or to be present in the moment?

9. Seeking Pleasure and Avoiding Pain

One Sunday afternoon, Vaibhavi and Yash walked into Keshav Uncle's garden carrying 2 boxes – one with mangoes, the other with cream rolls. Yash held them up like trophies and said, 'Uncle, we brought supplies – fuel for wisdom, dessert for courage.'

Keshav, half-buried in his favourite armchair, chuckled. 'Wisdom? I prefer the word *life-saving wisdom*, but fine – what's today's topic?'

Vaibhavi leaned forward. 'Uncle, why do people chase pleasure and avoid pain so much? Everyone knows we grow most during struggles, yet the moment difficulties appear, we start panicking or running away. Why?'

Keshav raised his eyebrows. 'Ah, the oldest human habit – remaining in the comfort zone. We like soft cushions and hate sharp edges. But think about it: when I ask anyone, **'When did you learn the most in the last decade**?' the answer is always: *during struggle.* Never on vacation, always in the storm. Yet when the next storm comes, the majority tries to escape again – forgetting it's just life saying, 'Upgrade available – install now?"

Yash laughed. 'So, **pain is like a software update – nobody wants it, but it makes us better**?'

'Exactly,' Keshav said, sipping his tea. 'But instead of learning, most people pour all their energy into changing circumstances – or people. If that fails, they try shortcuts, half-truths, zero-truths, or the Olympic sport of blaming others. Those with fewer means often show more acceptance – they know they can't control much outside, so they start adjusting inside.'

Vaibhavi nodded. 'I see that in our generation, too. The moment something feels unpleasant, people exit – change jobs, break up, or divorce. Switching partners or careers has become like switching Netflix subscriptions – cancel anytime.'

Keshav chuckled. 'Yes. But as we discussed before: the Almighty gave us 100 per cent freedom in our actions, and He doesn't interfere. But the results – those are 100 per cent His domain. Yet, when outcomes aren't to our liking, we throw tantrums like toddlers denied a candy bar.'

Yash leaned back. 'I have a friend who's been chasing happiness for decades. New job, new city, new partner – still not happy. It's like changing chairs in a furniture showroom – sit for a while, move on. But the discomfort never ends.'

'Because,' Keshav said, 'happiness depends less on the chair and more on the posture. If one introspects, reviews their actions, and submits them to the heart, the inner voice often suggests a wiser path. I am sharing in my words what Louise Hay said redundant beautifully: in any difficulty – relationship, career, finance, or health – just pray, ***'God, let me know what I need to learn in this time.'*** Once the lesson is learned, the same problem doesn't return. New challenges may come, yes, but not the same exam paper again.

And also one needs to ponder over – 2 samosas today or 1 healthy heart tomorrow?'

The garden fell into a reflective silence. Even the squirrels paused mid-scamper, as if digesting this lesson.

Vaibhavi finally broke it. 'So, Uncle, **next time life sends pain, we should stop asking, 'Why me?' and instead ask, 'What am I meant to learn?"**

Keshav smiled warmly. 'Exactly. Seek lessons, not escape routes. That's how pain becomes your teacher, not your jailer.'

Yash reached for the cream roll box. 'And in the meantime, can I learn how to avoid sharing dessert with squirrels?'

The group burst into laughter, as the cream rolls disappeared one by one – pain avoided, pleasure thoroughly embraced.

Key Takeaways

1. We prefer comfort, but **real growth happens during struggles.**
2. Avoiding pain often leads to blame, lies, shortcuts, or quick exits – but rarely to deep happiness.
3. We have 100 per cent control over our **effort,** but results are in God's domain. Accepting this truth prevents pain.
4. Escaping discomfort doesn't solve problems; **introspection and listening to the heart** do.
5. Asking, '*What am I meant to learn here?*' transforms challenges into evolution.

'Out of suffering have emerged the strongest souls; the most massive characters are seared with scars.' – **Kahlil Gibran**

'It is impossible to avoid pain while seeking pleasure. It is because pain and pleasure are 2 sides of the same coin.' – **Kahlil Gibran**

'When people are afflicted by pain and trauma, those with the strongest spiritual core emerge resilient. They use the pain to create a new version of themselves.' – **Daaji**

Scoring Guide

When assessing yourself, consider how often your daily decisions and long-term choices are influenced by the desire for immediate comfort or pleasure versus your values, goals, or a willingness to endure difficulty for a greater good.

Score 0: Overwhelmingly Driven by Pleasure/ Pain Avoidance

Your actions are almost constantly dictated by the immediate pursuit of pleasure or the avoidance of discomfort. You struggle significantly to delay gratification, endure any form of pain (physical, emotional, mental), or engage in activities that are challenging but beneficial. You prioritize comfort and ease above all else, often to the detriment of long-term goals, growth, or deeper purpose.

Score 1: Highly Driven by Pleasure/Pain Avoidance

You frequently make decisions based on what feels good right now or what helps you avoid immediate discomfort. You find it very difficult to push through challenges, engage in difficult conversations, or stick with tasks that are tedious or painful. While you might occasionally try to prioritize other things, the lure of pleasure and avoidance of pain often win out.

Score 2: Noticeably Driven by Pleasure/Pain Avoidance

You periodically find yourself swayed by the desire for pleasure or the urge to avoid pain, especially when under stress or facing difficult choices. You might procrastinate on uncomfortable tasks or seek quick fixes for emotional distress. While you can sometimes choose a harder path, this drive is a noticeable influence on your behaviour.

Score 3: Moderately Driven by Pleasure/Pain Avoidance

You experience a natural inclination towards pleasure and away from pain, but you are generally able to manage these impulses. You can delay gratification when necessary and tolerate some discomfort for the greater good. However, you might still struggle with consistently choosing the more challenging path over the easier one, or with embracing discomfort as part of growth.

Score 4: Minimally Driven by Pleasure/Pain Avoidance

You very rarely allow the immediate pursuit of pleasure or avoidance of pain to dictate your significant actions. You are adept at tolerating discomfort, embracing challenges, and delaying gratification when it aligns with your values or long-term goals. You see pain and pleasure as transient experiences, not ultimate motivators.

Score 5: Almost Undriven by Pleasure/Pain Avoidance (Highly Purpose-Driven/Resilient)

Your actions are rarely dictated by the immediate pursuit of pleasure or avoidance of pain. You are profoundly driven by purpose, growth, and intrinsic values, willingly embracing discomfort, challenges, and delayed gratification as essential parts of your journey. You possess exceptional resilience and a deep understanding that true fulfilment often lies beyond immediate comfort.

Reflection Prompts

1. How does the drive to seek pleasure or avoid pain influence your choices, particularly in areas like diet, procrastination, or challenging conversations?
2. Are there instances where your pursuit of immediate pleasure or avoidance of discomfort might lead to negative long-term consequences for yourself or others?

10. Responding to Stress

'Stress can result in anxiety if handled poorly, or achievement if handled well.
Instead of thinking about your worries as problems, think of them as challenges –
and if possible, as opportunities.' – **Chelsea Erieau**

'It's not stress that kills us, it is our reaction to it.' – **Hans Selye**

'You can't always control what goes on outside. But you can always control what goes on inside.' – **Wayne Dyer**

Scoring Guide

When scoring yourself, consider the **emotional, mental, and behavioural impact** of stress on you. Think about how consistently you can maintain calm, clear thinking, and effective action when under pressure. Here, **Score 0 means responding with maximal distress/dysfunction,** and **Score 5 means responding with maximal calmness/effectiveness.** A higher score indicates a more composed and effective reaction to stressful situations.

Score 0: Overwhelmed and Dysfunctional

When faced with stress, you consistently become overwhelmed, leading to significant emotional distress (e.g., panic, extreme anger, despair) or complete functional breakdown. Your ability to think clearly, make decisions, or take effective action is severely impaired. Stressors often feel catastrophic.

Score 1: Highly Reactive and Impaired

You frequently react to stress with intense emotional outbursts (e.g., yelling, significant anxiety, withdrawal) or noticeable impairment in your ability to cope. While you might eventually function, your initial response is often chaotic, and you struggle to regain composure, leading to prolonged periods of distress or poor performance.

Score 2: Noticeably Stressed and Less Effective

You periodically feel significantly stressed, which noticeably impacts your mood, concentration, and effectiveness. You might become irritable, restless, or find it harder to manage tasks. While you usually get through stressful situations, you often feel drained, and your responses are not consistently calm or optimal.

Score 3: Generally Resilient, Occasional Strain

You generally respond to stress in a controlled manner, but you'll experience noticeable strain during significant stressors. You might feel increased tension or worry, and your calm demeanour might be tested, but you typically manage to push through and recover without major long-term impact on your functioning.

Score 4: Highly Composed and Proactive

You very rarely feel overwhelmed by stress. When faced with challenges, you typically maintain your composure, think clearly, and proactively seek solutions. You might experience a brief spike in tension, but you quickly self-regulate and remain effective, often inspiring confidence in others.

Score 5: Profoundly Calm and Effective

You consistently approach stress with remarkable calm, clarity, and effectiveness. Even in highly challenging or crisis, you remain poised, think strategically, and respond thoughtfully rather than react emotionally. You see stressors as opportunities to adapt and innovate, maintaining inner peace and optimal performance regardless of external pressure.

Reflection Prompts

1. Describe a recent stressful situation you faced. What was your immediate, automatic response (emotional, mental, physical)?
2. Think of a time when **you responded to stress in a way you were proud of** (e.g., calmly, proactively, with resilience). What enabled that response?
3. What are your typical **'go-to' coping mechanisms for stress,** and how do they **impact your long-term well-being and relationships**?

11. Impulsiveness

'Acting without thinking is like shooting without aiming.' **– B.C. Forbes**

'Impulse decisions, like sharp knives, often cut deeply.' – **Anonymous**

'Impulsiveness is the enemy of deep thinking.' – **Harvey F. Silver**

'Free the self from impulsive actions and watch yourself become truly free.' – **Jay Kumar Singh**

Scoring Guide

Here, **0 means Maximal Impulsiveness** and **5 means Minimal Impulsiveness.** A higher score indicates greater self-control and thoughtful decision-making. When scoring yourself, consider the **frequency, intensity, and impact** of your impulsive behaviours or thoughts. Think about how often you act without forethought and what consequences (positive or negative) arise from those actions.

Score 0: Overwhelming, Debilitating Impulsiveness

You are almost constantly acting on urges or whims without thinking through the consequences. This leads **to frequent regrettable decisions, financial instability, relationship damage, or risky behaviours.** You find it nearly impossible to pause, plan, or control your immediate reactions, often feeling completely at the mercy of your impulses.

Score 1: Severe, Frequent Impulsiveness

You frequently act impulsively, often making quick decisions without sufficient consideration, speaking without filtering, or engaging in spontaneous actions that later cause problems. You struggle significantly with self-control, leading to regular stress, missed opportunities for better outcomes, or needing to clean up after impulsive choices.

Score 2: Moderate, Noticeable Impulsiveness

You periodically display noticeable impulsiveness, especially when excited, stressed, or under pressure. You might sometimes blurt things out, make purchases on a whim, or jump into activities without full planning. While you can sometimes rein yourself in, your impulsiveness is a recurring pattern that others, and you, might notice.

Score 3: Mild, Occasional Impulsiveness

You experience mild, fleeting moments of impulsiveness from time to time, usually in less critical situations or when you're feeling particularly carefree. These instances are generally harmless and don't lead to significant negative consequences. You are typically able to pause and think, but occasionally a quick decision slips through.

Score 4: Rare, Brief Impulsiveness

You very rarely act impulsively on important matters. When you do, it's a brief, mild, and quickly managed urge. You are generally thoughtful, deliberate, and proactive in your decisions and actions, preferring to consider outcomes before proceeding.

Score 5: Minimal or Absent Impulsiveness

You almost never act impulsively. You consistently demonstrate high levels of self-control, patience, and thoughtful decision-making. You carefully consider consequences, prioritize long-term goals over immediate urges, and **respond to situations with clear intention rather than unexamined reactions**. You are a highly disciplined and deliberate individual.

Reflection Prompts

1. What were the short-term and long-term consequences of your impulsive action, both for yourself and for others involved?

2. In what specific areas of your life (e.g., spending, speaking, decision-making) do you notice your impulsiveness most frequently?
3. What might be the underlying emotions or unfulfilled needs that drive your impulsive behaviours?

12. Addiction, Including Screen Time

'Addiction is the process of looking outside ourselves to fill an inside void.' – **Anne Wilson Schaef** (psychologist)
'I realized that I was worth more than my addiction.' – **Macklemore**
'Checking WhatsApp every 2 minutes is the new chain-smoking.'

Scoring Guide

When assessing yourself, consider the **frequency, intensity of urges/ cravings, loss of control, and negative impact** that any substance or behaviour has on your life. This includes things like alcohol, drugs, gambling, gaming, excessive shopping, pornography, food, etc.

Consider the **total duration** you spend on screens (phones, computers, TV for leisure), the **awareness** of that usage, and the **impact** it has on your well-being, relationships, productivity, and engagement with the physical world.

Score 0: Severe, Debilitating Addiction

You are almost completely controlled by an addiction (substance, behaviour, etc.). Your life revolves around it, causing profound negative consequences across all areas: health, relationships, work/ finances, and mental well-being. You have tried to stop or reduce usage multiple times unsuccessfully and feel powerless over the addiction.

You are almost constantly on screens, feeling a compulsive need to check devices, browse, or consume digital content. You feel a loss of control over your usage and frequently neglect other aspects of your life due to screens.

You might recognize the problem but struggle to reduce usage despite negative consequences.

Score 1: Significant, Disruptive Addiction

You frequently engage in addictive behaviours or substance use, which significantly impacts your life. You experience strong cravings and withdrawal symptoms (physical or psychological) when attempting to stop. Your addiction regularly interferes with responsibilities, causes noticeable problems in relationships, sleep time and leads to feelings of shame or regret, though you might still maintain some areas of functioning.

You spend a significant portion of your waking hours on screens, often feeling drawn to them even when you intend to do other things. Your screen time regularly disrupts your sleep, focus, and engagement in non-digital activities.

Score 2: Moderate, Problematic Addiction

You periodically engage in addictive behaviours, and while you might not have daily or constant use, your engagement is problematic. You might experience occasional loss of control, neglect minor responsibilities, or have recurring negative consequences (e.g., financial strain, minor health issues, arguments). You often think about reducing or stopping but struggle with consistency.

You are aware that you spend a lot of time on screens, sometimes more than you'd like. Your screen time is noticeable and occasionally interferes with your tasks, hobbies, or social interactions. You might have periods of heavy use interspersed with attempts to cut back, but consistency is a challenge.

Score 3: Mild, Habitual Engagement with Risk

You engage in a habit or behaviour that *could* become addictive, or you occasionally use a substance in a way that approaches problematic levels. You might sometimes use it as a coping mechanism, but you generally maintain control, can abstain when needed, and the negative consequences are rare or minor. You are aware of the potential for it to escalate.

You use screens regularly, but generally feel in control of your usage. You can often put devices away when needed and engage in other activities. While you might occasionally get engrossed, your screen time doesn't typically disrupt important aspects of your life, and you find a reasonable balance.

Score 4: Very Low Risk of Addiction

You rarely engage in potentially addictive behaviours or substance use, and when you do, it is in a controlled, mindful, and infrequent manner. You do not experience cravings or withdrawal, and the behaviour does not interfere with any aspect of your life. You use discretion and moderation consistently.

You spend relatively little time on screens, and your usage is primarily intentional and purposeful (e.g., for work, specific learning, meaningful connection).

Score 5: Minimal or Absent Addiction

You have no current or past struggle with addiction. You possess strong self-control and healthy coping mechanisms. You engage in behaviours and substance use (if at all) in a fully controlled, mindful, and non-dependent way, or you abstain completely without difficulty. You feel completely free from any compulsive urges or reliance on external substances/behaviours.

You use screens as tools when necessary, but they hold little sway over your attention or time.

Reflection Prompts

1. **How does your addiction impact your daily life, your relationships, your health,** or your personal goals?

2. How much time do you estimate you spend on screens (phone, computer, TV) daily, and for what primary activities (e.g., work, social media, entertainment, learning)?
3. How does your screen time affect your sleep, attention span, mood, productivity, and in-person relationships?

4

HABITS AND CONDUCT

'Our habits are the footprints of our inner conditioning.'

If key attributes are the roots and emotions, the flowing sap, then **habits and conduct** are the fruits people see and taste. They are the outward evidence of our inner landscape – sometimes sweet, sometimes sour, often mixed, but always revealing.

Habits – The Invisible Architecture of Life

'Habits' are those **routine behaviours we perform almost on autopilot**, without pausing to reflect. They are the tiny drops that hollow the stone of our character – repeated often enough, they carve deep grooves in our daily life. Some habits are **constructive**: waking up early, exercising, reading, or listening attentively. Others, however, can quietly **impede progress**: constant scrolling, postponing work, interrupting conversations, or neglecting gratitude.

The tricky part is that habits often **hide in plain sight**. We brush our teeth without thinking – good. But we may also criticize without thinking – harmful. Both are habits; only one sustains harmony. Introspection helps us **shine a light on these automatic routines** and ask: ***Do they serve me, or do they limit me?***

Through self-awareness, you gain the ability to:

- Spot habits that quietly undermine growth or relationships.
- Reinforce those that support health, productivity, and kindness.
- Replace unhelpful loops with heartful alternatives.

Reclaiming agency over habits means you no longer let life happen in default mode – you begin to **live with intention**.

Conduct – The Mirror Others See

While habits often play out privately, **conduct** is public. It is the sum of your observable behaviours – how you speak, how you treat others, how you carry yourself in daily life. Conduct is the **translation of the inner circuit into outer performance**.

Every raised eyebrow, every word spoken in anger or affection, every promise kept or broken – these small expressions reveal the alignment (or misalignment) between our values and our actions. Conduct is where attributes, emotions, tendencies, and habits converge to form our **professional, social, and personal identity**.

By revisiting your conduct, you gain insight into:

- Whether your **actions reflect your values**.
- How others experience you in relationships, workplaces, and communities.
- The consistency between your inner world and your outer expression.

Good conduct is not about rigid conformity; it is about **authentic alignment**. When your behaviour consistently mirrors the person you aspire to be, you create trust, respect, and harmony in your environment.

The Interplay of Habits and Conduct

'Your conduct is your billboard; your habits are the ad agency behind it.'

Habits feed conduct, and conduct reinforces habits. A habit of gratitude creates conduct that radiates warmth. A habit of criticism produces conduct that distances others. By observing both together, you gain a **holistic picture of your growth journey**.

Ultimately, this chapter invites you to take a gentle yet honest look: *What do my daily habits reveal? What does my conduct communicate to the world?* The answers may surprise you, but they also offer the power to reshape your life from the inside out.

1. Ability to Listen

The banyan tree stretched its arms wide, ancient and rooted like time itself, overlooking the ghats of the Ganga. Evening lamps flickered along the stone steps as priests chanted, and the river flowed on, carrying both ashes and prayers with the same serene indifference.

Keshav sat quietly beneath the banyan, his cousin Arun beside him. For a while, words felt unnecessary. The stillness was so complete it felt like a prayer in itself, the chants from the ghats rising like incense, stronger with each passing minute. Speaking would only have disturbed the silent dialogue between earth, water, and sky.

In their hands, warm *kulhads* (earthen cups) of tea sent up faint wisps of steam. The earthy taste of clay mingled with the sweetness of the brew, grounding them in the present. Each sip felt less like tea and more like tasting the soil, the river, and the very air of Banaras.

They had come to visit their *Badi Mausi* (elder aunt), whose house stood tucked away in the winding lanes of the old city. She was famous in the family for her wit, sharp tongue, and endless tales – qualities that made every visit lively, unpredictable, and always memorable.

As they walked through the narrow alleys, Banaras unfolded in all its layered life – temple bells clanging, hawkers calling, cows meandering lazily through the crowd. The cousins reached their aunt's house, expecting the usual welcome: snacks, stories, and her famously unfiltered opinions.

And so it began. Their aunt launched into her animated tales – temples, neighbours, the milkman's daughter's wedding, the unmatched glory of Banaras silk, why Banaras paan was the crown jewel of civilization, and how the local chai at Godowlia was enough to cure heartbreak.

Arun leaned toward Keshav and groaned, 'If she mentions *paan* one more time, I'm finding an escape route.'

But Keshav sat still, eyes steady, listening not out of duty but with presence.

Then, like the Ganga shifting its current, her tone changed. The chatter slowed, grew fragile. Stories dissolved into confessions. She spoke of missing her sisters, of the silence that filled her house after her children left for faraway jobs. Festivals, she admitted, no longer carried the same sparkle – they had become rituals without laughter, without warmth.

Her voice broke when she whispered how some nights she left the radio on, not for music, but so the silence wouldn't feel so heavy. 'All I want,' she sighed, 'is for someone to ask me genuinely, How are you, really? Not just to be polite, but because someone truly cares.'

Arun froze mid-bite of *samosa*, startled. He wasn't used to hearing their aunt sound vulnerable. Keshav leaned in gently. He didn't interrupt, didn't rush her. He only listened – giving her the one gift she hadn't known she was yearning for.

'There is a deep connection between being listened to and feeling loved,' Keshav thought. 'She doesn't need fixing, or advice, or even words in return… only the assurance that her voice matters, her heart is worth their time.'

When she finally fell silent, her eyes shimmered with tears. 'Keshav… people say I talk too much. But tonight… I feel lighter. Tonight, I feel heard.'

Arun coughed, sheepishly smiling. '*Arre Mausi*, I tried too. Give me some credit! But the hot samosas were… a slight distraction.'

She smiled gently, her eyes softening. 'No, *beta*. I'm just glad you both came all the way to see me. Tonight I wasn't telling stories. Tonight, I was sharing lost pieces of myself.'

Later that night, under the same banyan tree, watching diyas drift across the Ganga's current like floating prayers. Arun nudged Keshav, whispering, 'You're right. Listening isn't small talk. It's a kind of love, isn't it?'

Keshav didn't answer with words. His silence said enough. Banaras itself seemed to echo the truth… sometimes, the deepest conversations are not spoken….they are simply heard with an honest heart.

'Listening is not about having answers; it is about creating space where the other person feels safe enough to bring out their hidden truths. When we truly listen, we are not just hearing words – we are honouring a soul. And in that moment, love quietly takes the shape of silence.'

Key Takeaways

1. True listening is not waiting for your turn to speak; it is presence without interruption.
2. Listening creates space where vulnerability can safely emerge.
3. To be listened to deeply is to feel loved – words may fade, but presence is remembered.
4. **Silence, when filled with attention, can heal more than advice ever could.**
5. Listening is an act of love, not just a conversational skill.

'Most of the successful people I've known are the ones who do more listening than talking.' – **Bernard Baruch**

'Listening is often the only thing needed to help someone.'
– **Anonymous**

'You cannot truly listen to anyone and do anything else at the same time.' – **M. Scott Peck**

Scoring Guide

When scoring yourself, consider how consistently you give your full attention to speakers, how well you understand their messages (both spoken and unspoken), and how effectively your responses demonstrate that understanding.

Score 0: Minimal or Absent Listening Ability

You rarely, if ever, genuinely listen to others. You might frequently interrupt, form your reply before someone finishes speaking, or dismiss what's being said. You struggle to absorb information or understand perspectives different from your own, often leading to misunderstandings and frustration in conversations.

Score 1: Limited Listening Ability

You sometimes listen, but your attention is often fleeting, or you easily get distracted. You might hear words but struggle to grasp the full meaning or emotional context. You often miss important details, require frequent repetition, and your responses might feel off-topic or superficial.

Score 2: Moderate, Situational Listening Ability

You can listen effectively in specific situations or with people you are highly comfortable with. However, your listening skills can be inconsistent, especially when tired, stressed, or when the topic is not of immediate interest. You might nod along but still miss nuances or deeper messages.

Score 3: Consistent, Active Listening

You regularly demonstrate active listening skills. You generally pay attention, allow others to finish speaking, and try to understand their message. You might ask clarifying questions and remember key points, leading to productive conversations and a sense of being heard by others.

Score 4: Deeply Attentive Listening

You possess a strong ability to listen deeply and attentively. You not only hear the words but also pick up on non-verbal cues, underlying emotions, and unspoken concerns. You **make others feel truly understood and valued,** and you can recall detailed information from conversations with ease.

Score 5: Profound, Empathetic Listening

Listening is a profound and consistent strength for you. You actively seek to understand others' perspectives, feelings, and intentions at a deep level, creating a safe space for them to express themselves fully. You absorb information comprehensively, reflect understanding accurately, and respond with exceptional insight and empathy, making others feel profoundly heard and genuinely connected.

Reflection Prompts

1. Describe a situation where you realized you weren't fully listening. What distracted you (e.g., internal thoughts, external environment, desire to speak)?
2. How does **your ability (or inability) to listen actively impact your relationships**, your understanding of others, and your capacity to offer support?
3. What specific behaviours indicate to you that someone else is truly listening to you? How can you emulate these behaviours more consistently?

2. Speaking with Love

'Speak with love and compassion, not with judgment and criticism. Words can heal or hurt, choose carefully.' – **Anonymous**

'Words are powerful. They can build up or tear down, encourage or discourage, motivate or defeat. Speak from the heart with love.' – **Anonymous**

'The words of kindness are more healing to a drooping heart than balm or honey.' – **Sarah Fielding**

Key Takeaways

St. Lalaji: The style of speech should be:

- Remove the rise and fall in the voice while talking (sharpness).
- Flow of speech should not carry any kind of weight on it, devoid. of: excitement or emotional outburst, rapid, short, tempered, and moody reaction.
- The voice may be modulated to avoid a high pitch or any variation of the tone.
- Whatever is spoken goes on touching the hearts of persons.

If someone follows the above, only those words will flow out during conversation that are intended, are right, and do not hurt anybody's heart.

*__Lala Ji__ (Shri Ram Chandra of Fatehgarh was the first guide of Heartfulness meditation)

Scoring Guide

When scoring yourself, consider the **tone, content, and impact** of your words across various interactions. Think about how often your communication expresses genuine warmth, kindness, empathy, and respect, and whether it builds up or tears down those you speak to.

Score 0: Minimal or Absent Loving Communication

Your communication style rarely, if ever, conveys love, kindness, or compassion. You might frequently use harsh, critical, sarcastic, or dismissive language. Your words often create distance, hurt, or misunderstanding, and you struggle to express warmth or positive regard, even to those you care about.

Score 1: Limited Loving Communication

You occasionally express love or kindness through your words, but it's often overshadowed by criticism, negativity, or indifference. You might struggle to find the right words to comfort or affirm others, and your communication can sometimes feel abrupt, leaving others feeling unappreciated or misunderstood.

Score 2: Moderate, Situational Loving Communication

You can speak with love and kindness periodically, especially when you are feeling positive or in very specific, comfortable situations. However, your ability to do so can be inconsistent, and you might struggle to maintain a loving tone when stressed, disagreeing, or facing conflict.

Score 3: Consistent Loving Communication

You regularly communicate with a noticeable degree of love, kindness, and respect. You generally choose your words carefully to avoid unnecessary hurt, offer support when needed, and express appreciation. Even when disagreeing, you strive to maintain a respectful and caring tone, fostering positive connections.

Score 4: Deeply Loving Communication

You consistently and intentionally speak with profound love, empathy, and compassion. Your words are often affirming, encouraging, and soothing, even in challenging conversations. You are adept at communicating difficult truths with grace and kindness, making others feel deeply heard, valued, and understood.

Score 5: Profound, Transformative Loving Communication

Speaking with love is a core and intrinsic aspect of your communication style. Every interaction is infused with deep empathy, unwavering compassion, and a genuine desire to uplift and connect. Your words have a transformative effect, fostering healing, understanding, and profound connection, regardless of the topic or situation. You embody the power of loving communication.

Reflection Prompts

1. How does speaking with love manifest in your words, tone, and body language? What specific qualities does it embody (e.g., patience, compassion, understanding)?
2. Think of a time when your words lacked love, perhaps causing hurt or distance. What emotions or thoughts might have prevented you from speaking lovingly?
3. What impact does speaking with love have on your relationships, both in moments of harmony and in times of conflict?

3. Humour During Difficult Conversations

The air in the office was heavier than the HR manual – thick with what nobody wanted to say. Arun, the team lead, sat across from Maya, his star developer. He had to deliver the kind of news that usually came with sterile corporate jargon and enough sighing to qualify as a wind tunnel: her cherished project, 'Horizon,' was being shelved due to budget cuts.

'Maya,' Arun began, voice gentle but cautious, 'I've got some difficult news about the Horizon project.'

Maya's shoulders dropped instantly. She didn't need a PowerPoint to know what was coming. 'It's getting cut, isn't it?' she said softly, disappointment etched across her face.

'I'm afraid so,' Arun admitted, bracing himself for the storm of frustration. He saw her eyes glisten as silence filled the room. Then – unexpectedly – Maya let out a short laugh through her tears.

'Well,' she said, dabbing her eyes with the back of her hand, 'I guess my Horizon is a lot closer now than I thought.'

Arun blinked. 'I'm not sure I follow.'

'You know…' she brightened, 'the project was called *Horizon* – always just out of reach. Well, now it's not out of reach. It's right here.' She pointed dramatically toward the office dustbin. 'In the dumpster.'

This time, a real laugh escaped Arun. Not the polite chuckle of a manager but a full-bodied laugh that loosened his tie and melted the stiffness from his shoulders. 'That,' he said, shaking his head, 'is the most brilliant and terrible pun I've heard in years. And I've heard a lot of bad puns.'

Maya smiled. 'Humour is my emotional airbag. Without it, I'd crash in meetings like this.'

That single moment of shared laughter didn't change the fact that the project was gone. But it transformed the tone. What could have been a painful, sterile conversation became a bridge to something more human. They spoke candidly about her future, her strengths, and the lessons from Horizon – proof that a joke, in the right moment, can hold more power than a 100 corporate consolations.

Key Takeaways

1. Humour is not about dismissing pain but about softening it – like a cushion against a hard fall.
2. A well-timed joke creates a bridge from despair to dialogue.
3. Leaders who allow humour in tough conversations show not weakness, but emotional intelligence.
4. Even dark humour, when self-directed, can transform tears into connection.

'Humour is mankind's greatest blessing.' – **Mark Twain**

'A sense of humour is a major defence against minor troubles.' – **Mignon McLaughlin**

Scoring Guide

Score 0: Avoids or Worsens with Humour

You either completely avoid using humour during tough talks or, when you try, it often backfires, making the situation more tense or misunderstood.

You **might use inappropriate jokes, sarcasm, or humour that dismisses the seriousness of the issue.**

Your attempts at humour are perceived as insensitive or defensive.

You don't see humour as a valuable tool in these situations.

Score 1: Tries, but Inconsistently or Awkwardly

You might attempt to use humour to lighten the mood, but it feels forced, out of place, or lands flat.

Your humour might be too self-deprecating, distracting, or off-topic, not truly serving to ease tension.

You struggle to gauge the room and the other person's receptiveness to humour during sensitive topics.

You might use humour as a nervous tic rather than a thoughtful intervention.

Score 2: Occasionally Effective, but Unpredictable

You sometimes manage to use humour successfully to break tension or make a point, but it's not consistent.

You might rely on pre-planned jokes or general light-heartedness rather than organic, situation-specific humour.

While your humour doesn't usually make things worse, it doesn't consistently make them better either.

You're still learning to recognize the right moments and types of humour to employ.

Score 3: Generally Skilful and Appropriate

You are generally adept at using appropriate, **well-timed humour to defuse tension or introduce a new perspective** during challenging discussions.

Your humour is typically gentle, relevant, and helps to humanize the conversation without trivializing the issue.

You can use light humour to build rapport or encourage a more relaxed, open dialogue.

You **know when *not* to use humour** and prioritize the seriousness of the conversation when needed.

Score 4: Highly Effective and Thoughtful

You consistently and skilfully weave humour into difficult conversations in a way that truly benefits the interaction.

Your humour is insightful, empathetic, and helps others feel more at ease, understood, or open to solutions.

You use humour to highlight shared experiences, reframe challenges, or gently point out absurdities, all while maintaining respect for the seriousness of the topic.

You are excellent at reading the room and tailoring your humour to the specific individuals and context, ensuring it always lands well.

Score 5: Masterful and Transformative

You are a master at using **humour as a powerful tool to navigate and transform even the most emotionally charged or complex conversations.**

Your humour is not just effective; it's often memorable, creating breakthroughs in understanding or diffusing intense conflict with remarkable grace.

You can use a wide range of humorous techniques (wit, self-deprecating humour, observational humour) with precision and empathy.

You genuinely **make difficult conversations less daunting for everyone involved, fostering connection and mutual respect** even when discussing tough subjects.

Others look to you to set a positive tone and **navigate sensitive discussions with your unique blend of insight and humour.**

Reflection Prompts

1. Recall a recent difficult conversation where you or someone else effectively used humour. What was the context, and how did the humour impact the interaction?

2. What kind of humour do you find appropriate and helpful during challenging discussions, and what types might be counterproductive?

4. Gossiping

Suparnakha, Manthara, and Shakuni were restless for a while. In one of their meetings, Shakuni sighed, 'Friends, I feel we're facing an existential crisis. Are we even required on Earth anymore? Our unique talents have been copied endlessly, and nobody respects intellectual property rights – let alone gives us credit! Honestly, I'm bored. I don't know what to do with my life.'

Manthara nodded. 'You've stolen my very thoughts, Shakuni.'

Suparnakha, forgetting even her latest nail-beautification plans, sighed, 'Now I see so many copying my methods – and some even outshining me. I often wonder if it's time for a role change.'

Manthara smirked. 'Don't tell me you're planning to join the likes of Kaushalya or Sita. Come on!'

Shakuni leaned back with a sly grin. 'Shall we add more dimensions to our gossiping?'

Suparnakha, looking utterly dejected, muttered, 'Even here, I don't see much scope. From our times, gossiping has taken a giant leap. I'm seriously considering applying for *Moksha*.'

But Shakuni, never one to give up, declared, 'Let's go to Consultant Keshav and seek his views on the subject.'

The troika descended into Keshav's dream – a safe haven where they could speak freely. Keshav, long accustomed to dreams filled with unexpected guests, calmly sipped his tea and asked, 'So, what brings the 3 legends to my doorstep today?'

Shakuni adjusted his invisible dice and sighed dramatically. 'Keshav, in our times, gossiping was an art form. We strategized, whispered, twisted, and spiced it up until kingdoms trembled! Now look – social media does in 5 seconds what I perfected over decades. Memes, hashtags, and even AI-generated rumours do my job. Honestly, I feel unemployed.'

Manthara, never to be left behind, interjected, 'Exactly! In Ayodhya, I worked hard – spending years massaging Kaikeyi's ego before she agreed to send Rama to the forest. Today, one push notification or a WhatsApp forward can create more chaos than I ever managed in my lifetime. Where's the recognition? Where's the craft?'

Suparnakha rolled her eyes. 'At least you 2 had some legacy. I've been reduced to a footnote! Earlier, I could spark a war by batting an eyelid and filing my nails. Today's generation has dating apps, reality TV, and influencer scandals. They don't need me at all. Even my nail designs get copied shamelessly on Instagram without credit!'

Keshav chuckled, trying hard not to spill his tea. 'My dear friends, you sound like start-up founders cribbing about competition after their idea went public. Times change, methods evolve. But tell me, do you realize the real cost of gossip?'

The 3 leaned in, curiosity momentarily silencing their theatrics.

Keshav continued, 'When gossip is harmless, it entertains. But when it becomes a way of life, it steals trust. Relationships crumble, workplaces get toxic, and inner peace runs away faster than Arjuna's arrows. You 3 may be at the verge of retiring, but gossiping is alive and thriving – only now, it's turbocharged by technology. People don't even need a palace corridor; they carry gossip factories in their pockets!'

Suparnakha, suddenly reflective, sighed. 'So, are you saying our legacy continues… but in distorted ways?'

'Precisely,' Keshav replied. 'Your methods were the training wheels. Humanity has taken them on a reckless joyride.'

Shakuni asked, 'Do you think what we did in our time had no value?'

Keshav smiled. 'The Mahabharata and Ramayana may never have unfolded without you 3. For a good script, opposite sides are necessary. Yes – you each had a role, and I thank you, for humanity gained invaluable lessons from those epics.'

'But here's the twist – you can redeem yourselves! Instead of fuelling gossip, why not teach people to pause, to listen deeply, to replace idle chatter with heartful conversation? Imagine – Shakuni running a workshop on 'Non-violent Communication,' Manthara leading a retreat on 'Listening Without Judgement,' and Suparnakha launching a salon called 'Nails and No Gossip."

The 3 looked horrified, then burst into laughter. 'That,' Shakuni declared between chuckles, 'would truly be an existential crisis!'

As dawn broke, Keshav woke with a smile. He whispered to himself, 'Even the greatest gossipers are tired of gossiping.'

But the troika was still not satisfied – they began searching for the legendary Narada...

Key Takeaways

1. Gossip entertains briefly but destroys trust if made a habit.
2. Modern technology has amplified gossip, making it instantaneous and far-reaching.
3. Even the most notorious gossipers have roles in history, but redemption lies in transforming chatter into heartful communication.
4. Conversations can either corrode relationships or create understanding – it depends on how we use them.

'Strong minds discuss ideas, average minds discuss events, weak minds discuss people.' – **Socrates**

'Words are free. It's how you use them that may cost you.'
– KushAndWizdom (as attributed on the internet)

'The tongue has no bones, but it is strong enough to break a heart. So be careful with your words.' – **Anonymous**

Scoring Guide

When assessing yourself, consider the **frequency, content, and impact** of your discussions about others. Think about how often your conversations involve sharing private or negative information about people who aren't present, and how that affects your relationships and reputation. This means a higher score indicates less gossiping and a greater ability to maintain discretion and focus on positive or constructive communication.

Score 0: Overwhelming, Debilitating Gossiping

You almost constantly engage in gossiping, often spreading rumours, negative information, or judgmental opinions about others. This behaviour is a central part of your conversations, causes significant harm to relationships, erodes trust, and often reflects a pervasive critical or negative mindset towards others.

Score 1: Severe, Frequent Gossiping

You frequently find yourself engaging in gossiping, discussing others' private lives, or sharing negative opinions about them, even when you know it's not constructive. This behaviour is a regular part of your interactions and often contributes to a negative or distrustful atmosphere in your social circles.

Score 2: Moderate, Noticeable Gossiping

You periodically engage in gossiping, especially when in certain social settings or when a topic of others' affairs arises. While you might sometimes catch yourself, it's a noticeable pattern that can lead to moments of regret or contribute to a less positive conversational dynamic.

Score 3: Mild, Occasional Gossiping

You experience mild, fleeting moments where you might engage in gossiping, perhaps in a moment of weakness or when feeling stressed or provoked. These instances are rare, usually involve less significant information, and you generally recognize and stop yourself, preferring more constructive conversations.

Score 4: Rare, Brief Slip-Ups

You very rarely engage in gossiping. If you do, it's an isolated and brief slip, perhaps sharing a minor piece of information without malicious intent, and you quickly correct yourself or shift the conversation. You are generally known for your discretion and respectful communication.

Score 5: Minimal or Absent Gossiping

You almost never engage in gossiping. You consistently maintain discretion regarding others' private lives and actively steer conversations away from negative or unverified discussions about people. You choose to focus on constructive topics, respectful communication, and building trust, embodying a highly positive and discerning approach to interaction.

Reflection Prompts

1. What underlying motivations or feelings might have led you to participate in gossip (e.g., a desire for connection, a feeling of superiority, boredom, insecurity)?
2. How does engaging in gossip impact your own sense of integrity, the trust in your relationships, and the atmosphere of your social environment?

5. Punctuality

'I could never think well of a man's intellectual or moral character if he was habitually unfaithful to his appointments.' – **Nathaniel Emmons**

'Punctuality is not just being on time, it's about respecting your own commitments and the time of others.' – **Anonymous**

'If I have made an appointment with you, I owe you punctuality. I have no right to throw away your time, if I do my own.'
– **Richard Cecil**

Scoring Guide

Score 0: Chronically Late

You are consistently late for appointments, meetings, and deadlines. You rarely arrive on time, regardless of the situation. You don't factor in travel time or potential delays.

Score 1: Frequently Late

You are often late, though not always. You might have a pattern of being late for certain types of events or with specific people. You underestimate travel time or have poor time management.

Score 2: Sometimes Late

You are usually on time, but occasional lateness occurs due to unforeseen circumstances. You might be late for less formal events but punctual for important ones.

Score 3: Generally Punctual

You make a conscious effort to be on time and are punctual in most situations. You plan ahead and allow for buffer time.

Score 4: Very Punctual

You are almost always on time, demonstrating respect for others' time. You prioritize punctuality and take steps to ensure it.

Score 5: Exceptionally Punctual

You are consistently early, demonstrating exceptional time management and respect. You factor in potential delays and strive to be prepared.

Reflection Prompts

1. What are the common reasons you are punctual, and conversely, what factors typically lead you to be late?
2. How does **your level of punctuality impact your personal reputation, your relationships**, and your ability to manage your time effectively?
3. What emotions do you experience when you are running late, or when others are late for you?

6. Argumentative

'The more arguments you win, the fewer friends you'll have.'
– Anonymous

'An argument is always about what has been made more important than the relationship.' – **Hugh Prather**

'Do not argue for, whenever you do, you tear apart the essence. Truth is lost in arguments.' – **Daaji**

Scoring Guide

When scoring yourself, consider the **frequency, intensity, and impact** of your tendency to initiate or engage in arguments. Think about how often you find yourself in a dispute and whether you prioritize being right over maintaining harmony and understanding.

Score 0: Overwhelming, Debilitating Argumentativeness

You are almost constantly engaging in arguments, debates, or contradictions, often for the sake of being right or having the last word. You find it extremely difficult to accept differing opinions, compromise, or let go of disagreements. This pervasive argumentativeness severely damages your relationships, creates constant tension, and prevents peaceful resolution.

Score 1: Severe, Frequent Argumentativeness

You frequently initiate or escalate arguments, even over minor points. You often feel a strong need to challenge statements, correct others, or assert your opinion forcefully. This behaviour is a prominent part of your interactions, leading to strained relationships, frequent conflicts, and a reputation for being confrontational.

Score 2: Moderate, Noticeable Argumentativeness

You periodically find yourself becoming argumentative, especially when you feel strongly about a topic or when your opinions are challenged. You might get drawn into debates more often than you'd like, and sometimes struggle to disengage or agree to disagree, leading to noticeable tension in conversations.

Score 3: Mild, Occasional Argumentativeness

You experience mild, fleeting moments where you might become argumentative, typically in response to a genuine disagreement on an important topic. These instances are rare, usually brief, and you are generally able to express your viewpoint respectfully and move on without escalating into prolonged conflict.

Score 4: Rare, Brief Argumentativeness

You very rarely engage in argumentative behaviour. If you do voice a strong disagreement, it's typically done assertively but respectfully, without malice or a desire to 'win.' You easily accept different viewpoints and focus on understanding rather than contention.

Score 5: Minimal or Absent Argumentativeness

You almost never engage in argumentative behaviour. You consistently approach discussions with an open mind, respect for diverse opinions, and a focus on understanding or collaboration rather than debate. You easily find common ground, **agree to disagree gracefully**, and actively foster harmonious and constructive communication environments.

Reflection Prompts

1. What emotions or underlying beliefs tend to fuel your argumentative tendencies (e.g., a need to be right, feeling unheard, insecurity, enjoying debate)?
2. **How does being argumentative impact your relationships,** your ability to truly listen, and the overall atmosphere of your interactions?
3. What might be a more constructive way to approach disagreements or differing opinions, allowing for mutual understanding rather than conflict?

7. Prejudice

Keshav's Take

Prejudice is never a one-way street. We think it's about others – their colour, background, habits, or beliefs – but in truth, every external bias hides a subtler inner bias. When we label others as 'too loud,' 'too ambitious,' or 'too emotional,' what we're often revealing is our own discomfort with those traits within us. It's like disliking a mirror for showing what we'd rather not see.

A truly self-aware person begins to notice that prejudice outside dissolves when judgment inside softens. External discrimination and inner criticism share the same root – separation. The moment we see the sameness beneath difference, both vanish quietly, like fog when the sun rises.

'It's curious – we spend years learning how to avoid being judged by others, yet forget to stop auditioning for our own inner critic.'

'Prejudice is a burden that confuses the past, threatens the future, and renders the present inaccessible.' – **Maya Angelou**

'Prejudice, not being founded on reason, cannot be removed by argument.' – **Samuel Johnson**

'When there is peace, we can be creative. We can be even more creative when we are joyful, and joyfulness will come when there is the absence of adamance, prejudice.' – **Daaji**

Scoring Guide

When scoring yourself, consider your **internal thoughts, automatic reactions, and overt behaviours** towards people from different backgrounds than your own. Reflect on how consistently you approach everyone with an open mind, respect, and a lack of preconceived negative notions. A higher score indicates less prejudiced thinking and a more open, accepting, and equitable mindset.

Score 0: Overwhelming, Debilitating Prejudice

You consistently hold strong, negative, and often irrational preconceived opinions or biases against individuals or groups based on their identity (e.g., race, gender, religion, sexual orientation, nationality). These prejudices deeply influence your thoughts, words, and actions, leading to discriminatory behaviour, exclusion, and a profound inability to connect with or empathise with those outside your preferred groups.

Score 1: Severe, Frequent Prejudice

You frequently exhibit prejudiced thoughts, beliefs, or subtle discriminatory behaviours towards certain individuals or groups. While you might not always act overtly, your biases often surface in your conversations, judgments, and discomfort with diversity. You struggle to overcome ingrained stereotypes and may contribute to environments where others feel unwelcome or devalued.

Score 2: Moderate, Noticeable Prejudice

You periodically notice prejudiced thoughts or biases arising, especially in certain situations or when interacting with individuals from groups you are less familiar with. You might catch yourself making assumptions or feeling uncomfortable. While you generally try to be open-minded, these biases are a recurring internal struggle that sometimes influences your reactions or quiet judgments.

Score 3: Mild, Occasional Prejudice

You experience mild, fleeting moments where a subconscious bias or an old stereotype might surface. These thoughts are quickly recognized, challenged, and dismissed. You are generally open to learning about and connecting with diverse individuals, but occasional unexamined assumptions might momentarily cross your mind.

Score 4: Rare, Brief Unconscious Bias

You very rarely experience overt prejudiced thoughts or behaviours. If an unconscious bias surfaces, you immediately recognize it and actively work to counter it through conscious effort and a commitment to fairness. You are generally seen as open, inclusive, and equitable in your interactions and judgments.

Score 5: Minimal or Absent Prejudice

You consistently demonstrate a profound lack of prejudice. Your thoughts, words, and actions are driven by genuine acceptance, equity, and an unwavering belief in the inherent dignity of all individuals, regardless of their background or identity. You actively seek to understand and celebrate diversity, and you challenge injustice or bias wherever you encounter it, both within yourself and in the world.

Reflection Prompts

1. Reflect on any preconceived notions or judgments you might hold about individuals or groups based on limited information (e.g., appearance, background, social status).
2. How might these hidden prejudices inadvertently influence your interactions or decisions?
3. What is the source of these prejudices (e.g., upbringing, media, past experiences)?

8. Truthfulness

'Truthfulness really implies the sense of presenting one's own self in its true colours. This is the state at which a man exclaims spontaneously, 'It is as it is.' – **St. Babu Ji**

'If you tell the truth, you don't have to remember anything'. – **Mark Twain**

'Whoever is careless with the truth in small matters cannot be trusted with important matters.' – **Albert Einstein**

Scoring Guide

When scoring yourself, consider the **frequency, intent, and impact** of your honest communication. Reflect on how consistently you speak your truth, even when it's difficult, and how much others rely on your words as an accurate representation of reality.

Score 0: Minimal or Absent Truthfulness

You frequently or habitually distort the truth, tell outright lies, or intentionally mislead others for personal gain, to avoid consequences, or simply out of habit. Honesty is rarely a guiding principle in your communication, leading to a reputation for unreliability and eroded trust in your relationships.

Score 1: Limited Truthfulness

You often stretch the truth, tell white lies, or omit crucial information to paint a better picture for yourself, avoid discomfort, or manage others' perceptions. While you might not tell outright fabrications all the time, your communication lacks consistent transparency, and others may find it hard to fully trust your words.

Score 2: Moderate Truthfulness with Notable Exceptions

You generally aim to be truthful, but you **periodically find yourself bending the truth, exaggerating, or being evasive**, especially when under pressure, to avoid minor conflicts or when it feels more convenient. You might rationalize these instances, but there's a noticeable gap between your stated intention and consistent practice.

Score 3: Consistent Truthfulness

You regularly prioritize telling the truth in most situations. You strive to be honest and direct, even when it's uncomfortable. While you might occasionally omit a minor detail or choose silence to avoid unnecessary hurt, your overall communication is reliable, and people generally perceive you as trustworthy.

Score 4: High Truthfulness and Integrity

You consistently uphold truthfulness as a core value. You are direct and honest in your communication, even when it's challenging, and you proactively correct misunderstandings. You rarely engage in dishonesty, and your words are highly reliable, **fostering deep trust in your relationships**.

Score 5: Profound, Unwavering Truthfulness

Truthfulness is an absolute and unwavering principle that guides all your communication and actions. You are committed to complete honesty, transparency, and integrity in every situation, regardless of personal cost or convenience. Your words are a direct reflection of reality and your inner values, earning you a reputation for exceptional trustworthiness and authenticity.

Reflection Prompts

1. Recall a recent situation where you had an opportunity to be completely truthful, even if it was challenging or uncomfortable. What was the situation, and what was your decision?
2. Are there **specific situations or relationships where you find it more difficult to be fully truthful**? What fears or reasons might contribute to this?
3. What is the **difference for you between speaking the truth and speaking the truth with kindness or compassion**?

9. Willpower

'Willpower is the key to success. Successful people strive no matter what they feel by applying their will to overcome apathy, doubt or fear.'
– Dan Millman

'In the absence of willpower the most complete collection of virtues and talents is wholly worthless.' **– Aleister Crowley**

'The difference between a successful person and others is not a lack of strength, not a lack of knowledge, but rather a lack in will.'
– Vince Lombardi

Scoring Guide

When rating yourself, try to think about your typical behaviour over an extended period (e.g., the last few months), rather than just a single good or bad day.

Score 0: Minimal Willpower/Easily Swayed

You consistently struggle to resist impulses or immediate gratification.

You rarely follow through on intentions, especially if they require sustained effort or discomfort.

You often give in to temptations (e.g., unhealthy snacks, procrastination, distractions) even when you know it's not in your best interest.

Starting new habits is extremely difficult, and maintaining them is almost impossible.

You frequently abandon tasks or goals at the first sign of difficulty or boredom.

Score 1: Very Low Willpower/Sporadic Effort

You recognize the need for self-control but frequently fail to exercise it.

You might make a strong effort for a very short period, but quickly revert to old patterns.

Temptations are often too strong to resist, leading to regret later.

You find it very challenging to stick to a routine or discipline yourself without external accountability.

Your motivation is highly dependent on your mood or external circumstances.

Score 2: Developing Willpower/Inconsistent

You can exercise willpower in some situations, but it's inconsistent or requires a lot of conscious effort.

You might successfully resist minor temptations but struggle with stronger, more habitual ones.

You sometimes follow through on commitments, but often with delays or significant internal struggle.

Starting new habits is possible, but maintaining them long-term is a significant challenge.

You are aware of your weaknesses and might feel frustrated by your lapses.

Score 3: Moderate Willpower/Generally Reliable

You generally demonstrate good self-control in most daily situations.

You can resist common temptations and stick to your plans most of the time.

You usually follow through on your commitments and complete tasks, even when they are challenging or unpleasant.

You are capable of building and maintaining positive habits with consistent effort.

You might have occasional slips, but you usually get back on track without too much difficulty.

Score 4: Strong Willpower/Highly Disciplined

You consistently demonstrate strong self-control and discipline across various areas of your life.

You can easily resist most temptations and stay focused on your long-term goals.

You are highly reliable in following through on your intentions, even when faced with significant obstacles or discomfort.

You excel at establishing and maintaining beneficial habits, often making them feel effortless over time.

You can defer gratification effectively and maintain focus on challenging tasks for extended periods.

Score 5: Exceptional Willpower/Unwavering Discipline

Your willpower is an outstanding strength; you are remarkably disciplined and self-controlled.

You rarely give in to impulses or distractions, consistently prioritizing your highest goals.

You are an expert at setting and achieving challenging objectives through sheer determination.

You can maintain focus and effort even in the face of extreme adversity, discomfort, or long-term challenges.

You embody consistent self-mastery and inspire others with your unwavering commitment to your principles and goals.

Reflection Prompts

1. Recall a specific situation when your willpower felt weak or gave out. What were the circumstances, and what internal or external factors contributed to that?
2. How does your level of willpower impact your ability to achieve personal goals, resist temptations, and maintain healthy habits?
3. What strategies or conditions help you strengthen your willpower (e.g., clear goals, removing temptations, accountability, sufficient rest)?

10. Praising Others

'Every time you praise something, every time you appreciate something, every time you feel good about something, you are telling the Universe, 'More of this, Please." – **Abraham Hicks**

'The deepest principle in human nature is the craving to be appreciated.' – **William James**

'Sincere praise is not flattery; it is the oxygen that helps people breathe easier in their efforts.' – **Anonymous**

Scoring Guide

You use praise as a powerful tool for development, helping individuals see their strengths and build on them. You make others feel seen and truly appreciated.

Score 0: Rarely or Never Praises

You almost never offer praise, even when someone performs exceptionally well.

You might believe good work is simply expected and doesn't require acknowledgement.

You may focus more on what's missing or what needs improvement.

You find it awkward or unnecessary to verbally appreciate others.

Score 1: Reluctant Praiser

You rarely praise, and when you do, it feels forced or generic.

You might struggle to find specific things to commend.

You may only praise under direct prompting or when it's absolutely unavoidable.

You might think praise makes people complacent or doesn't contribute to real progress.

Score 2: Occasional Praiser

You offer praise sometimes, especially for significant achievements.

Your praise might be general ('Good job') rather than specific.

You appreciate good work internally but don't always vocalize it.

You might praise colleagues or team members, but less frequently for those you manage or family members.

Score 3: Consistent Praiser

You regularly recognize and praise others for their efforts and achievements.

You try to be specific in your praise, pointing out what was done well.

You understand the value of positive reinforcement and its impact on morale and motivation.

You're comfortable giving praise in various settings, both private and public.

Score 4: Enthusiastic and Specific Praiser

Your praise is frequent, genuine, and highly specific, highlighting *why* their contribution was valuable.

You make an effort to connect the praise to the person's strengths and positive impact.

You understand how effective praise can boost confidence, foster growth, and strengthen relationships.

You might also offer constructive feedback alongside praise to balance it out effectively.

Score 5: Inspiring and Developmental Praiser

You consistently and authentically praise others in ways that uplift, motivate, and inspire them.

Your praise is not just specific to a task, but often ties into a person's character, growth, or potential.

You create an environment where others feel valued and recognized for their contributions.

You naturally celebrate successes, big and small, and encourage others to do the same.

Reflection Prompts

1. What prevents you from praising others more frequently, even when you feel it internally (e.g., shyness, fear of it being misconstrued, not wanting to draw attention)?
2. What **impact does sincere praise have on your relationships**, the morale of those around you, and your own sense of connection?

11. Humility

'Humility is the most sublimated state of ego. Humility is not flattery or servility.
Instead, humility is a sign of great self-awareness. Such awareness gives you a feeling of insignificance that helps you grow.' – **Daaji**

'One rises to prominence only when he thinks himself to be humble and low.

Humility brings forth what arrogance cannot.' – *Complete Works of Ram Chandra Vol-II* by **St. Babuji**

'Humility, so far as it serves as a safeguard against pride and vanity, is a virtue.

But when it leads us to underrate our talents and inner capacity, it is harmful.'

– *Complete Works of Ram Chandra Vol-I* by **St. Babu ji**

'It was pride that changed angels into devils; it is humility that makes men as angels.' – **Saint Augustine**

Scoring Guide

When assessing yourself, consider how you behave in various contexts – at work, with family, among friends, and especially when challenged or successful.

Score 0: Arrogant/Self-Aggrandising

You consistently believe you are superior to most others in knowledge, skill, or importance.

You **rarely admit mistakes** or acknowledge your own limitations.

You frequently boast about your achievements and seek constant recognition.

You dismiss others' opinions or contributions, especially if they differ from yours.

You struggle to learn from others, especially those you perceive as less experienced or knowledgeable.

Score 1: Proud/Defensive

You find it very difficult to accept criticism or feedback without becoming defensive.

You often highlight your contributions and might subtly downplay others' contributions.

You are reluctant to ask for help or admit when you don't know something.

You tend to **attribute successes primarily to yourself and failures to external factors.**

You might listen to others, but often with the intent to counter or assert your own view.

Score 2: Self-Conscious/Inconsistent Humility

You understand the concept of humility but struggle to practice it consistently, especially when your ego is challenged.

You might admit mistakes, but it often feels grudging or with justifications.

You can sometimes appreciate others' contributions but might still seek more personal credit than due.

You are open to learning but might hesitate to step outside your comfort zone or expose your vulnerabilities.

Your humility can waver depending on the situation or who you are interacting with.

Score 3: Generally Humble/Open to Learning

You are generally open to feedback and consider constructive criticism thoughtfully.

You willingly acknowledge the contributions of others and share credit appropriately.

You are comfortable admitting when you don't know something and are willing to ask for help or seek advice.

You celebrate the successes of others genuinely.

You recognize that you have areas for growth and are willing to learn from anyone, regardless of their position or experience.

Score 4: Deeply Humble/Growth-Oriented

You actively seek out feedback, even when it's challenging, as a means for growth.

You are quick to give credit to others and frequently highlight their strengths and contributions.

You naturally put others at ease and make them feel valued, regardless of your own accomplishments.

You **view mistakes as learning opportunities** and openly share your own lessons learned.

You demonstrate a **genuine curiosity and eagerness to learn from everyone around you,** regardless of their background or expertise.

Score 5: Exemplifies Humility/Inspiring

Your humility is a defining characteristic, consistently evident in your words and actions.

You are comfortable being a student, even as a teacher, and constantly seek new knowledge and perspectives.

You genuinely uplift others, empowering them and drawing out their best, often putting their needs and growth before your own recognition.

You possess a profound self-awareness of both your strengths and limitations, allowing you to act with authenticity and grace.

Your presence inspires others to be more humble and collaborative. You embody true wisdom that comes from recognizing one's place in the larger scheme of things.

Reflection Prompts

1. Recall a time when a lack of humility (e.g., arrogance, needing to be right) created a challenge in a relationship or a learning opportunity.
2. How does cultivating humility impact your ability to learn from others, admit mistakes, receive feedback, and connect authentically?
3. What is one specific instance this week where you could practice humility by listening more than speaking, acknowledging someone else's contribution, or admitting you don't know something?

12. Respect

'I speak to everyone in the same way, whether he is the garbage man or the president of the university.' – **Albert Einstein**

'When we respect others, we pave the way for them to respect us in return.' – **Friedrich Nietzsche**

'By honouring differences we express our respect.' – **Daaji**

Scoring Guide

When rating yourself, consider your behaviour across various relationships and contexts – with family, friends, colleagues, superiors, subordinates, and even strangers.

Score 0: Disrespectful/Demeaning

You frequently interrupt, dismiss, or talk over others.

You often make sarcastic, condescending, or belittling remarks.

You disregard others' opinions, feelings, or boundaries.

You might use derogatory language or engage in discriminatory behaviour.

You show little regard for rules, property, or privacy.

Score 1: Often Disregardful/Inconsistent

You sometimes interrupt or speak without considering others' turns.

You might make light of serious concerns or dismiss feelings.

You occasionally disregard boundaries or make assumptions about others.

You might be respectful towards some but not others (e.g., those in lower positions).

You might struggle to accept differing viewpoints or opinions.

Score 2: Developing Respect/Reactive

You generally try to be respectful, but might struggle when under stress or disagreeing.

You sometimes forget to acknowledge others' contributions or efforts.

You might become defensive or argumentative when challenged.

You respect rules when convenient, but might bend them if it serves your immediate purpose.

You're learning to listen, but might still formulate your response while others are speaking.

Score 3: Consistently Respectful/Aware

You consistently listen actively and allow others to finish speaking before responding.

You acknowledge and value diverse opinions, even if you don't agree with them.

You are generally courteous and considerate in your interactions.

You adhere to rules and boundaries and treat others' property and privacy with care.

You offer constructive feedback while maintaining a respectful tone.

Score 4: Highly Respectful/Empathetic

You go out of your way to ensure others feel heard, valued, and safe in your presence.

You proactively **seek to understand different perspectives** and cultural nuances.

You tailor your communication to be respectful of individual preferences and sensitivities.

You are a **strong advocate for fair treatment and inclusivity**, challenging disrespect when you see it.

You consistently demonstrate respect for time, resources, and trust.

Score 5: Exemplifies Respect/Inspiring

Your interactions are characterised by deep empathy, genuine regard, and unwavering respect for every individual.

You create an environment where all voices are not just heard, but celebrated and integrated.

You embody respect through your actions, words, and non-verbal cues, making others feel profoundly seen and appreciated.

You model **respectful behaviour even in highly challenging or confrontational situations.**

Your presence fosters trust, collaboration, and psychological safety, inspiring others to act with similar levels of respect.

Reflection Prompts

1. Think of a situation where you felt disrespected, or where your own actions might have inadvertently shown a lack of respect for someone else. What happened, and what was the impact?
2. How does your consistent demonstration of respect (or lack thereof) influence the trust, psychological safety, and quality of your relationships across various contexts (family, friends, colleagues, strangers)?
3. What specific behaviours or attitudes do you believe are essential for modelling respectful behaviour, even in challenging or confrontational situations?

13. Sacrifice

This story is from the icy heights of the Siachen Glacier – home to the world's longest, coldest conflict since April 1984. At the trijunction of Karakoram Pass, Nubra Valley, and Shaksgam, Siachen anchors India's strategic flank in Ladakh.

Until 1984, Siachen was remote and largely unoccupied. Ambiguity beyond NJ-9842 and cartographic claims turned ice into geopolitics, prompting **Operation Meghdoot** – India reached the glacier and the Saltoro Ridge before Pakistan could.

Since 1984 the Army has manned Siachen at heavy material and human cost. Two major spikes preceded 1998 – initial combat in 1984 and **Op Rajiv (May–June 1987)**, when the Bana Post (erstwhile Quaid

Post) on the Saltoro was retaken. This story unfolds during the **third spike** (Apr–Oct 1998), when Pakistan tried to claw back **Bana Post**.

Four air warriors drive this story: **Manish–Anand** and **Pavitra–Bhanu** – IAF helicopter crews at Siachen Base. Manish was the longest-serving, most experienced **Glacier Captain; Pavitra** was the detachment commander.

Since April, the enemy action had been brutal, and as all knew intuitively, it was building up to something big. Amar and Sonam Posts, forming the left and right shoulders of the Bana Top (Post) on the Soltoro Ridge, and holding the notorious distinction of being the highest and most abused (in terms of deadly accurate Mortar fire by the Pakistanis) operational helipads anywhere in the world. These posts were being battered continuously by the Pakistanis for the last 2 months. The conditions at Amar were especially precarious. The Pakistani Post, which was situated on the other side at the base of the ridge that had the Amar helipad, and sheltered in the shadow of a huge rocky outcrop, could actually hear the Indian helicopter coming into land at Amar, and possibly even see the snow kicked up by the landing helicopters.

By the first week of June, Manish had inducted **6 Company Commanders ('Tigers')** into Amar and evacuated all as casualties – **4 in body bags**. 1 was hit by a splinter while disembarking and had to be pushed back into the chopper – he survived. The only workable tactic was a **first-light, terrain-masked dash**. Often, just the lead bird could dump supplies and bolt. Reception parties stayed bunker-bound – stepping out drew fire. The co-pilot had to kick loads out on short finals at **~20,000 feet**, where every kilo feels like 15 (who needs a gym at that altitude?). When gravity becomes your personal trainer, you don't need a fitness app.

Suggestions: At midnight on 1 July, the Base Commander called: **Amar had run out of salt.** A week of bad weather had choked Air Maintenance; morale was cracking. De-induction loomed – a humiliation from post to HQ. Manish, jolted awake, briefed Pavitra at once. In Siachen, running out of salt is the culinary equivalent of a national emergency.

In the ensuing discussion, it was suggested by Manish that they should get airborne with the salt a few minutes before sunrise time at Base Camp, as that would allow them to make the Amar helipad just in the minimum required lighting conditions to safely execute the approach and landing there, considering the 20 minutes flying time. Manish also suggested that because Pavitra had just arrived at the Base Camp the previous morning after a considerable break and was less situationally aware of the current conditions in the Glacier, therefore, Manish should be leading the 2-helicopter formation and the first one to land at Amar. Pavitra immediately overruled the suggestion. No amount of reasoning from Manish would convince Pavitra to change his stance.

Col Singh, the Base Commander, was at the operations hut at 0430h and waiting for the helicopter crew. He looked disturbed and desperate. A thorough and stoic gentleman, he again anxiously narrated the whole situation at Amar. In the briefing, it was planned that on reaching the huge Glacier bowl that had the Soltro ridge at its western end, Manish would orbit at the eastern edge of the bowl while Pavitra would continue with the approach and landing onto the helipad – the sound of just 1 helicopter approaching Amar would be heard by the Pakistanis much later than 2 helicopters approaching the helipad in quick succession, thereby increasing substantially, their reaction time.

As planned on reaching the glacier bowl, Manish kept observing Pavitra as he continued on the approach to Amar, becoming a progressively distant speck in the dim daybreak greyness.

'Echo Fox'!! Manish was rudely jolted by Pavitra on the radio and saw him sharply turn right and discontinue the approach. Manish was filled with a sinking feeling. He knew that they had lost perhaps the only chance to deliver sustenance to the Bravehearts manning Amar that day. As Pavitra got closer to Manish's on the eastern side of the Glacier bowl, he piped up on the radio to convey that they had observed enemy mortar shells fall across the Amar helipad onto the base of the Soltoro ridge in the bowl. It was Manish turn now but the milk was spilled already – the Pakistanis were wide awake and ready. It was all quiet till Manish approached short finals and then they lit up the helipad with all sorts of mortar shells – air bursts, ground bursts, tracers, and burrow bursts.

'Dump collective – left rudder – one-eighty!' The ridge flashed past the rotor tips. Two prayers sprinted through Manish: *Bajrangbali, spare the tail; spare us the airbursts.* Through oxygen hiss came Anand's thin call: **'TERRAIN!'**

They bottomed out **<50 feet** above the bowl, dropping at **>1000 fpm,** then clawed away and rejoined. Debrief note: **Bhanu (Pavitra's co-pilot) hadn't seen shells** on their approach. 3 more tries failed – the enemy's plan was working. That evening, Manish again requested the lead; Pavitra rebuffed him.

The next morning was a new day. Again, Col Singh was at the Ops hut at 0430h and waiting for the helicopter crew to arrive. The same routine was repeated and Col Singh was more positive today – 'surely we can't fail 2 days in a row', he said cheerfully. Later, in the glacier bowl, working to the same plan as the previous day, Manish heart was heavy with premonition.

Again, Pavitra aborted early. Manish pressed in; enemy fire began mid-approach – too late for a landing. Debrief déjà vu: **Bhanu saw no rounds**. Two more failed tries. As they spooled for a third, Col. Singh ran in: 'Abort. **Amar Tiger** says his men can't leave bunkers – not even for nature's call due to enemy fire.'

Evening turned heavier than the air. Manish told **Bhanu** (senior-most officer): 'Sir, this can't continue. Either we fix it now, or I call the CO. I won't fly under Pavitra tomorrow.' Confrontation followed; Pavitra yielded – **Manish would lead; co-pilots swapped** (Bhanu with Manish; Anand with Pavitra).

The next dawn felt different. Col. Singh arrived with the **Northern Glacier CO**, who offered to fly along. Manish declined – too risky, too distracting. As they reached the chopper, the CO gripped his shoulder: **'Beta, my *Naam, Namak, Nishan* are in your hands.'** ' Sir, now I carry 2 of them today. Yours and mine. I promise I'll do my best'.

Later, at the Glacier bowl spanning out from the Eastern rim of the Soltoro ridge, Manish descended westwards towards Amar while Pavitra orbited at the Eastern entrance to the bowl. As planned between Manish and Bhanu, they descended to 17,500 feet, almost 2000 ft below the helipad elevation. They were working on a randomly decided radio frequency to prevent the Pakistanis from accidentally catching their radio chatter. Pavitra was alarmed to see Manish descend so low into the bowl – ' What are you doing?'

Manish: 'Ops Normal – R/T silence please'.

They were now more than halfway through the approach and more than double the normal approach speed. As they entered the last third of the approach, Manish reduced the Collective setting and gently eased up on the Cyclic Stick, establishing a gentle climb of about 500 ft/min. They were still way below the helipad, and now Manish could clearly see the burn marks of exploded enemy mortar shells on the ice ledge in front. Less than a 100 feet from the helipad, Manish sharply raised the collective and eased the Cyclic Stick further back to climb up to be level with the helipad and gently eased the helicopter onto the helipad. It was easily the best 'No Hover Landing' he had accomplished in his lifetime.

To his surprise and that of Bhanu, ghostly human figures jumped out of the snow around the helipad and opened the right door. Before they could react, Manish saw the door being closed with the load gone. They could see the first of the airbursts beginning to arrive already. There was only one thing to do now – in one sweeping motion, Manish picked up the helicopter without the required right rudder, and it swung away to the left sharply as it dipped into the bowl behind. The first day's prayer to 'Bajrangbali' was still current. They could actually hear the airburst shrapnel whizzing past them randomly, but the elation of having 'done it' allowed no heed to fear.

'Mission accomplished. Let's go home.'

At base, Col. Singh and the NG CO received them with **sweets** – salt delivered, sweetness deserved. The CO had radioed **Amar Tiger** to keep the reception party ready. It likely saved lives. There was no debrief; some days, silence performs the salute.

P.S.: The next week, Pakistanis made their boldest attempt at regaining control of Bana Top (Quaid Post), since they lost it to Subedar Bana Singh and his team in June 1987,. The Amar Tiger and his boys played a stellar role in foiling this attempt, as the slope on the western approach to Bana Top is in the line of sight to Amar. More than 15 Pakistani SSG Commandos were killed in the Operation. They have never attempted to re-take Bana Top since.

Keshav's Take

Duty without theatre, courage without noise – that's Manish, Bhanu, Pavitra, and Anand. Their readiness to trade breath for ***Naam, Namak, Nishan*** is the quiet grammar of sacrifice. Service above self isn't a slogan here; it's standard operating procedure.

Key Takeaways

1. **Sacrifice is quiet precision.** At 20,000 feet, a clean no-hover landing can feed morale more than a hundred speeches.
2. **Small things carry big meaning.** Salt on a ridge can hold a post – and a formation – together.
3. **Trust is a force multiplier.** Aircrew, helipad party, and commanders aligned in intent make miracles routine.
4. ***Naam, Namak, Nishan*** – identity, loyalty, and the flag – are lived, not laminated.
5. Sacrifice isn't always dramatic – it can be as simple as parents skipping dessert so their child can have a second helping.

'True heroism is remarkably sober, very undramatic. It is not the urge to surpass all others, at whatever cost, but the urge to serve others at whatever cost.' – **Arthur Ashe**

'Duty, Honour, Country.' – **Douglas MacArthur**

'There is no success without sacrifice. If you succeed without sacrifice, it is because someone has suffered before you.' – **Adoniram Judson**

Scoring Guide

Here, a higher score indicates a greater willingness and ability to make personal sacrifices for others or for a greater cause.

Score 0: Minimal or No Sacrifice

You rarely, if ever, make sacrifices for others or for principles. Your decisions are almost always driven by personal convenience, immediate gratification, or self-interest, even if it means neglecting the needs of others or a greater good. You expect others to accommodate you.

Score 1: Limited Sacrifice

You occasionally make minor sacrifices, typically when it's easy or directly benefits you in some way. However, you often shy away from situations requiring significant personal cost, effort, or discomfort, prioritizing your own needs above almost all else.

Score 2: Moderate, Situational Sacrifice

You can make sacrifices periodically, especially for close family or friends, or when there's a clear, tangible benefit. However, your **willingness to sacrifice is often conditional**, and you might struggle with it when it involves significant personal discomfort, financial cost, or a long-term commitment.

Score 3: Consistent Sacrifice

You regularly demonstrate a willingness to make sacrifices for those you care about or for causes you believe in. You understand that personal give-and-take is necessary for healthy relationships and collective well-being. While it might sometimes be challenging, you generally prioritize the needs of others or the greater good when it truly matters.

Score 4: Deeply Sacrificial

You possess a strong and pervasive capacity for making significant personal sacrifices. You frequently put the needs, well-being, or advancement of others or a cause before your own, often enduring considerable personal cost (time, comfort, resources) without resentment.

This is a core part of your character.

Score 5: Profound, Selfless Sacrifice

Sacrifice is an intrinsic and almost effortless part of your being. You consistently demonstrate extreme selflessness, readily making profound personal sacrifices for the benefit of others, community, or humanity, often without expectation of reward or recognition. You embody a deep commitment to service and the welfare of something larger than yourself.

Reflection Prompts

1. Recall a time when you made a significant sacrifice for a person, a cause, or a long-term goal. What was it, and what motivated you?
2. What did you give up or endure as part of that sacrifice, and what emotions (both positive and challenging) did you experience during the process?
3. What was the outcome or impact of your sacrifice on yourself and on others involved? Do you have any regrets, or do you feel a sense of fulfilment?

5

SCORE CARD AREAS FOR FURTHER ENHANCEMENT

Growth is gradual but visible to the honest eye.

Chapter 1: Key attributes

This scorecard is not judgment; it's awareness.

S. No.	Areas for further enhancement	Score Date:	Score Date:	Remarks
1	**Introspection**			
2	**Courage**			
3	**Clarity**			
4	**Strong Likes and Dislikes**			
5	**Acceptance**			
6	**Peace Within Myself**			

7	**Reaction or Response**
8	**Expectations**
9	**Selfishness**
10	**Anger**
11	**Dealing with Criticism**
12	**Patience**
13	**Forgiveness**
14	**Procrastination**
15	**Adaptability and Flexibility**
16	**Comparing Yourself with Others**
17	**Ego**
18	**Resisting Change**
19	**Love**

Note:

1. Please add additional attributes as per your requirement.
2. You may repeat the assessment after a fixed interval: 12/ 06/ 03 months to get the full benefit.

Chapter 2: Emotional quotient

This scorecard is not judgment; it's awareness.

S. No.	Areas for further enhancement	Score Date:	Score Date:	Remarks
Primary emotions:				
1	**Fear**			
2	**Sadness**			
3	**Disgust**			
4	**Irritation**			
5	**Guilt**			
6	**Shame**			
7	**Gratitude**			
8	**Compassion**			

9 **Happiness**
10 **Joy**
11 **Empathy**

Secondary (Complex Emotions):

12 **Jealousy**
13 **Pride**
14 **Embarrassment**
15 **Anxiety**
16 **Loneliness**

Positive Emotions:

17 **Confidence**
18 **Hope**
19 **Excitement**
20 **Admiration**
21 **Satisfaction**
22 **Contentment**

Negative Emotions:

23 **Despair**
24 **Frustration**
25 **Resentment**
26 **Regret**
27 **Bitterness**

Neutral and Mixed Emotions:

28 **Curiosity**
29 **Victim thoughts**

Emotional States:

30 **Boredom**

Notes:

1. The following attributes pertaining to emotions have been covered in Chapter 1-Key attributes: Anger, Love, Calmness (similar to Peace within myself)
2. You may also consider attributes: Nostalgia (as fond remembrance), Nostalgia (as a negative longing/ sadness) if applicable.

Chapter 3: Tendencies

This scorecard is not judgement; it's awareness.

S. No.	Areas for further enhancement	Score Date:	Score Date:	Remarks
1	**Harbouring Hurt**			
2	**Complaining**			
3	**Tendency to Find Fault**			
4	**The Need for and Sense of Belonging**			
5	**Seeking Approval/ Validation**			
6	**Conflict Resolution**			
7	**Aggression**			
8	**Overthinking**			
9	**Seeking Pleasure and Avoiding Pain**			
10	**Responding to Stress**			
11	**Impulsiveness**			
12	**Addiction, Including Screen Time**			

Notes:

The tendencies 'Reaction or response', 'Procrastination' have been covered in Chapter 1, Key attributes.

Chapter 4: Habits and Conduct

This scorecard is not judgment; it's awareness.

S. No.	Areas for further enhancement	Score Date:	Score Date:	Remarks
1	**Ability to Listen**			
2	**Speaking with Love**			
3	**Humour During Difficult Conversations**			

4	**Gossiping**
5	**Punctuality**
6	**Argumentative**
7	**Prejudice**
8	**Truthfulness**
9	**Willpower**
10	**Praising Others**
11	**Humility**
12	**Respect**
13	**Sacrifice**

Notes: The habit 'Reaction or Response' has been covered in Chapter 1, Key attributes.

Indicative Attributes Applicable for Spiritual Seekers

This category is designed for those on a conscious spiritual path, focusing on indicative attributes that are particularly pertinent to deeper spiritual growth and self-realization. These 'Qualities for Spiritual Seekers' delve into more subtle aspects of consciousness, inner experience, and one's relationship with the divine or higher truths. While these attributes are universally beneficial, their specific framing here aims to support individuals actively engaged in spiritual practices, helping them to assess their progress and areas for further cultivation on their inner journey.

The self-assessment (awareness) guide is not being provided for this section since its an advanced subject. To understand these qualities better, seekers may reflect, write observations in a diary and also may refer to the book *Complete Works of Ram Chandra Vol-I, Spiritual Anatomy* by Daaji for a comprehensive understanding.

S. No.	Areas for further enhancement	Score Date:	Score Date:	Remarks
1	Acceptance			Covered in Chapter-1
2	Peace			Covered in Chapter-1
3	Love			Covered in Chapter-1
4	Courage			Covered in Chapter-1
5	Clarity			Covered in Chapter-1
6	Selflessness			Opposite attribute Selfishness; has been Covered in Chapter-1
7	Stillness			
8	Peace			Covered in Chapter-1
9	Insignificance, Surrender and humility			
10	Belongingness			
11	Restlessness, Vision of reality			
12	Settledness			
13	Omnipresence, Omniscience, Omnipotence			
14	Simplicity			
15	Character			
16	Devotion			
17	Practice with an Open Heart			

18	Response on Being Wronged
19	Response on Being Abused
20	Response on Being Scolded, Taunts and Scoffs
21	Response on Tests During Spiritual Journey

6

THE WAY FORWARD

I hope that by now, you've clearly identified the attributes you wish to enhance. Congratulations – you've crossed a major milestone in your life journey!

Now begins the next exciting phase: exploring tools for managing change in the areas you've recognized. While you're encouraged to design your own personal growth plan, a simple, step-by-step guide is offered here to help you get started.

As the revered Saint Babuji Maharaj wisely said:

> *'If you are able to see the snake* (your attribute),
> *then 50 per cent of the job of change and course correction is done.'*

Spotting our inner 'snake' is not an occasion for panic, but for celebration – awareness itself is half the victory!

However other half of the process is managing the change.

Change Management

'Change Management' is a familiar phrase in the professional world – usually reserved for meetings, flowcharts, and PowerPoint slides.

In organizations, it's about altering processes. In relationships, it's about altering *people* – particularly one's partner (an even more challenging process!).

The truth is, processes and relationships don't change by themselves – *people* do. What if we applied those same structured, step-by-step 'change management' tools to our own lives? Before improving our teams, partners, or friends, why not begin **the pilot project right here – with ourselves?**

In professional settings, we gladly pay consultants to tell us what's wrong – and sometimes even thank them for it! But on the personal front, when our 'consultants' (spouse, family, or friends) offer feedback for free, our willingness mysteriously drops. The real question is: 'Am I ready to listen to them, and more importantly, to my inner consultant, the Heart?'

Here is a step-by-step guide for managing the change. You have already completed Step 1, 2 so far.

Step 1 – Identify the Attributes Ready for Change

Growth begins with honesty – knowing exactly which parts of ourselves need fine-tuning. Awareness is the spark; readiness is the flame.

Step 2 – Introspection

With the self-assessment (awareness), you've just completed your second step towards recognizing patterns in your behaviour and tendencies. Introspection is one of the most powerful tools of transformation – it helps us tune in to the quiet counsel of the Heart, our wisest inner advisor.

A short prayer to God (if you believe) before introspection can open the door to honesty and help us notice the areas where light needs to enter.

Step 3 – Acceptance and Willingness

With the help of the scorecard, once the need for change is felt, acceptance and willingness become the 2 sturdy wings that help you move forward. And if you truly feel 'Life is Good' and nothing needs to change – that's wonderful! Still, read on… You may discover a few surprise guests hiding under that calm surface.

Step 4 – Listening to Critics

The next best option – when introspection feels like climbing Everest without oxygen – is to simply **listen**. Our family, friends, and colleagues have likely dropped hints about our rough edges more times than we care to admit. The key skill here is the *art of listening without interruption or reaction*.

As Saint Kabir beautifully said:

'निंदक नियरे राखिए, ऑंगन कुटी छवाय,
बिन पानी, साबुन बिना, निर्मल करे सुभाय।'

Keep your critic close; give them space in your courtyard.
Without soap or water, they cleanse your character.

Holding your reactions while someone critiques you requires courage and conscious restraint. The sequence is simple: first listen, then introspect, and only then decide if the given input makes sense to you and change is needed. The choice remains entirely yours – no one else holds that pen.

If Kabir ji's logic makes sense, then please, resist the ancient reflex to *shoot the messenger*.

And if you find that your own thoughts drown out the speaker halfway through their sentence, take a leaf from **Dale Carnegie's** classic *How to Win Friends and Influence People*.

'Listening without interruption is not passive – it's an active skill. It requires patience, humility, and focus.

Dale Carnegie emphasises that being a good listener is often more powerful than being a good talker. People love to feel heard, and giving your full attention – without interrupting – is one of the greatest compliments, validating their worth.

The patient listening reduces defensiveness and avoids arguments. Even in disagreement, hearing others out communicates respect. Most people are absorbed in their own thoughts, so genuine listeners stand out as rare, trustworthy, and likeable – winning both friends and influence.'

Being aware

Once we have followed Steps 1–4, we become more aware. Once we know with Introspection, where we stand. It also means that we are able to identify our own filters such as judgments, prejudices, fear, etc. Once we become aware of the filters, we start our journey to be free from them.

The next question is How to change?

Step 5 – Finding a Comprehensive Method for Change

5.1 Developing Understanding with Self-help Books
Books are wonderful teachers that don't argue back. They gently point out our blind spots, and we usually accept their feedback more calmly than when the same truth comes from our spouse or boss!

They can definitely enhance self-awareness and offer handy quick fixes – like counting to 10 or sipping water when angry. While this technique undeniably helps in preventing immediate fireworks, the root cause – underlying anger often remains, merely being controlled or on pause.

5.2 Root Cause Cure and Everlasting Results
Our real goal isn't just to control symptoms but to reach the **root cause** – the very source where thoughts are born. If we can prevent the source of the thought that leads to anger from arising, peace automatically follows, saving time, relationships and sanity.

We have already discussed how accumulated impressions, including *samskaras,* cloud the capacity of the mind to act in a balanced way. As we have seen in the anecdote of clarity and anxiety, the moment our impressions are cleaned – permanent change starts in us. We have also discussed, in case of anxiety, how health gets impacted when emotional balance is disturbed

Practices like **Meditation and Cleaning** offer precisely such depth. Cleaning removes the unwanted impressions of the day and the deeper *samskaras* gathered over lifetimes.

On a personal note, I have practised **Heartfulness meditation** for over 16 years. Earlier, self-help books helped me spot my patterns, but lasting transformation came only through Heartfulness meditation and cleaning. The process gently worked for me, where words could not – within the heart itself.

A gentle reminder: results bloom fully only when the method is followed completely. Half-hearted practice delivers half-baked change; full commitment to the method for a period of 3–6 months may bring a feast of transformation.

Step 6 – Diary Writing – The Mirror That Expands You

Diary writing may appear like a simple act of recording events – what happened, who said what, and how we felt. But underneath this ordinary habit lies a profound instrument for transformation. The moment we begin to write, something magical happens: *we start to observe*.

When we pick up a pen and describe our day, we are compelled to notice the details we often overlook – the tone of a conversation, the tension in a thought, the joy in a small success, or the heaviness that quietly settles in our chest. Writing slows the mind's restless pace and asks, '*Wait, what really happened here?*' That pause is where observation begins.

Observation is the bridge between experience and awareness. Without observing, life rushes past us in a blur; with observation, we begin to *see* ourselves in action – our patterns, impulses, and inner narratives. This simple act of seeing has an extraordinarily beneficial side effect: it *increases our consciousness*. The more we write, the more we notice; the more we notice, the more conscious we become.

Over time, diary writing becomes less about events and more about *essence*. We begin to notice not only what we did, but *why* we did it – the subtle motives behind our choices, the recurring emotions that colour our days. These realizations are not available in the noise of ordinary thought; they appear only when the pen slows us down enough to meet ourselves on the page.

Post-introspection journaling is a force multiplier in this process. After a meditation, self-reflection, or a difficult day, journaling helps to anchor insights before they dissolve into forgetfulness. It gives structure to the formless – turning fleeting awareness into living wisdom. The page becomes a sacred meeting point between our conscious and subconscious selves, a space where lessons settle and clarity emerges.

Every entry is a quiet dialogue with the Self. It requires honesty, patience, and a gentle courage to look at oneself without judgment. Over time, this daily dialogue builds emotional resilience, sharper self-understanding, and deeper authenticity. We stop reacting to life and start responding to it – thoughtfully, calmly, consciously.

So, if growth is your pursuit, diary writing is your silent ally. It is the mirror that does not lie, the friend who listens without interruption, and the teacher who helps you observe – not to criticize, but to evolve. In observing yourself, you begin to shape yourself. And in shaping yourself, you begin to live consciously.

Step 7 – Observing Results and Course Correction

As the saying goes, 'The proof of the pudding is in the eating' – though in our case, it's the pudding of *practice!* There are many good methods out there; choose the one that speaks to your heart, but measure its effect honestly.

However, consistently observing the results is crucial. Any method that doesn't provide incremental positive results within 3–6 months should be re-evaluated or changed.

In this regard, re-evaluation of the desired attributes and recording it in the Scorecard could be a great help.

Results must continue to improve incrementally forever – truly, until our last breath. If incremental change ceases, it indicates that something is amiss with either the method itself, our own effort, or perhaps even our guide.

Summary

If there's only 1 timeless quality to learn – and to pass lovingly to the next generation – it is **Introspection.**

True introspection means looking within with calm neutrality, seeing without judging, and learning without blaming.

Through this, our observation deepens, awareness expands, and consciousness blossoms. Step by step, we identify our gaps, close them with will and grace. By applying willpower and committing to consistent self-improvement, this approach empowers us to become better human beings.

The journey of self-refinement can be summarized as:

Introspection → Enhanced Observation → Heightened Awareness → Enhanced Consciousness → Identifying Gaps → Change Management → Becoming a Better Human Being.

When seeking to understand the Purpose of Life, most philosophical traditions emphasise learning, evolution, and self-realization. This prompts the question: **What should we learn, and what should we aspire to become**? While individual goals vary, the most fundamental aspiration could be to become a good human being. From there, the journey can extend to becoming a balanced individual, a *Stithaprajna* * (one with steady wisdom in all circumstances), and ultimately, a truly wonderful, loving being – someone everyone cherishes being around.

* The *Stithaprajna* is not a monk in a cave but a master within movement – one whose peace is portable, whose joy is independent of events. He responds, never reacts. He feels deeply yet remains inwardly free. In modern terms, he lives **'externally dynamic, internally still.'** To know more about the term *Stithaprajna*, you may refer to Gita Chapter 2, Sloka 54–72.

'It is in the stillness of the mind that we perceive the heart with clarity.
By constantly observing the inner weather,
we steer through life wisely, steadfastly, sans regrets.' – **Daaji**

EPILOGUE

It had been some time since those long, heartfelt discussions on various attributes with the many characters in this book took place.

In Year 2026, Damini proposed that everyone – including Keshav's circle of friends – gather in Hyderabad to share their further journey.

The chosen venue was Kanha Shanti Vanam, about 29 kilometres from Hyderabad airport – the global headquarters of Heartfulness Meditation.

It was the perfect place for reflection. The world's largest meditation hall stood serenely at its centre, vast enough for 80,000 seekers to sit together in silence. Around it, lush gardens spread like living mandalas – each with a theme of its own – but the *Yatra Garden* was the crown jewel, where every turn felt like a step deeper into the heart, mind and beyond.

When the group arrived at Kanha, they were greeted by a silence so alive it felt like music between breaths. The years had changed them all – not dramatically, but deeply. The young participants had grown – professionally, emotionally, and spiritually – carrying a calm that came only from inner work.

Damini was now married and managing her own startup with quiet confidence. Vaibhavi and Yash had risen steadily in their careers, and something about their composure reflected Keshav's subtle influence.

As they gathered near the meditation hall, Vaibhavi turned to Keshav Uncle, her eyes warm with gratitude.

'Uncle, our sessions have made me so much more aware. During team meetings, I sometimes hear myself speaking like you – helping others with their professional and personal challenges. These days, many colleagues approach me when they're struggling. I think I'm turning into a mini version of you!'

Damini laughed, nudging her friend playfully.

'Correction – she's becoming a *relationship aunt*! But honestly, I find myself echoing her thoughts too.'

Their laughter drifted into the open air – light, sincere, and full of affection. Keshav smiled quietly, letting their joy speak louder than advice ever could. The leaves above rustled gently, as if approving their growth.

Yash: 'I wish I had been made aware of these attributes when I was younger. I feel that this needs to be added to the course curriculum of all the streams in Colleges. Probably then we can emulate our ancient education system where education included the subjects pertaining to the professional as well as our own evolution'.

Later that evening, they walked through the tree-lined pathways of Kanha, where the scent of jasmine mingled with the earthy fragrance of dusk. The sun melted into the horizon, spilling gold across the ponds. The Meditation Hall shimmered in the twilight – vast, luminous, still.

Standing near the water's edge, Keshav said softly, 'You see, life isn't about changing others.

It's about understanding yourself so deeply that others begin to feel safe in your presence.'

No one replied. They didn't need to. The silence said everything.

That evening, as they watched the sky fade from amber to indigo, something subtle shifted within them. The lessons of the past years – all those stories, reflections, and self-assessments (awareness) – had taken root. The teachings were no longer just in the book; they were living through each of them.

REFLECTION BEYOND THE REUNION

As you turn the last page of this workbook, pause for a moment – not to mark an ending, but to acknowledge a beginning that is quietly unfolding within you.

You have walked through anecdotes, emotions, and perhaps a few gentle confrontations with your own patterns. If you've reflected honestly, smiled at your follies, and felt even a flicker of understanding for yourself or someone else – then you've already succeeded. Introspection doesn't need applause; it just needs sincerity.

The purpose of this book was never to cast judgment, but to help you *see* who you already are – with greater clarity, compassion, and courage. Growth, after all, isn't about adding layers; it's about shedding what no longer serves.

You may notice, as days pass, that your responses soften, your patience deepens, and your understanding of others widens. That's the quiet power of inner work. It rarely announces itself; it simply begins to express through how you listen, how you pause, and how you choose response over reaction.

When you look back at your relationships – personal or professional – you might realize that they weren't obstacles on your path; they *were* the path. Each person who irritated you, challenged you, or loved you deeply was a chapter in your own evolution story.

There will still be days of restlessness, of doubt, of fatigue. On such days, just remember what Keshav might say with a smile:

'Don't fight the storm. Just clean your windshield and keep driving.'

Keep practising introspection as a periodical act of care – like brushing your inner world clean. Reflect each night. Forgive quickly. Respond gently. And never underestimate the quiet miracle of a well-timed pause.

If you ever feel lost, return to your heart. It is your truest compass.

May this workbook be your companion in those in-between moments – between stimulus and response, between hurt and healing, between self-judgment and self-acceptance.

And as you walk forward, may your journey be guided by this simple truth:

'We don't become better than others by introspection; we become better with others, through introspection.'

ACKNOWLEDGEMENTS

This workbook is the result of many quiet moments of reflection and the grace that guides them.

My deepest gratitude to my spiritual guides, **Revered Chari ji** and **Daaji,** whose teachings have illuminated every page of this work. Their wisdom has been the compass that steers my journey.

I remain thankful to the **Heartfulness community** for creating an environment where inner work becomes a living practice. Every conversation, every observation, and every silence has added depth to these reflections.

Many thanks to the contributors of 14 Anecdotes: Shiva Faridi, Mudit Dikshit, Shailesh Vickram Singh, Ajay Darbari, and Manoj Kumar.

Gratitude to Gp Capt. MVM Prasad (retd.) for helping in finalizing the attributes and review the idea of the book.

To my friends, mentors, and early readers – thank you for your honest feedback and encouragement. Each of you helped refine this workbook into something that can reach hearts across all walks of life.

And finally, to **you, the reader** – for your willingness to pause, look within, and grow. This book finds its purpose only through your practice.

With gratitude and warmth,
Vinay Singh
March 2026

ANECDOTES CONTRIBUTION

1. **Anecdotes by Shiva Faridi on: Love, Gratitude, Jealousy, Resentment, Victim Thoughts, Complaining, Ability to Listen, and Satisfaction.**
   Shiva Faridi is a seeker, storyteller, and social catalyst whose journey spans social sector education, international development, and corporate leadership. She coordinated Project Shiksha Kendra, bringing learning and hope to underprivileged children, and later led Asia-wide initiatives in girl-child education and UN-based development projects. In recent years, she has headed international programs in Public Relations, Business Development, and Administration. She has taught Drama and Speech at the London School of Music and written and directed several plays. A writer and playwright at heart, she believes stories are the soul's way of leaving footprints on the world.
2. **Anecdotes by Mudit Dikshit on: Sacrifice, Empathy, and Hope**
   Mudit Dikshit is a Pilot (Captain) for Canada Airlines and lives in Canada. He is also a spiritual practitioner and a Heartfulness spiritual trainer. He also served in the IAF.

3. **Anecdote by Shailesh Vickram Singh on: Adaptability and Flexibility**
   Shailesh Vickram Singh is a Venture Capitalist focused on Climate tech. Apart from investing, he also writes on startups/economy in leading publications.
4. **Anecdote by Ajay Darbari on: Guilt**
   Ajay Darbari is a spiritual practitioner and poet who lives in Greater Noida. He volunteers for public programs for spiritual aspirants. He also served in the IAF.
5. **Anecdote by Manoj Kumar on: Admiration**
   Manoj Kumar is a spiritual practitioner, an artist, and offers consulting services for security agencies. He also volunteers for public programs for spiritual aspirants. He also served in the IAF.

To discuss more on introspection or for any queries related to this book, you can write to the author at vinaysingh.books@gmail.com.

NOTES

RAISING READERS

Books Build Bright Futures

Dear Reader,

We hope you enjoyed reading this book and we'd love your attention for one more page, to share with you what's going on with children and books.

The number of children reading in their leisure time and for fun is in rapid decline. Young people have a lot of competition for their time, and a worryingly high number have only a few or no books at home.

If this is not a crisis already, it soon will be.

Studies have shown that reading for fun is the **single biggest predictor of a child's future success** – more than family circumstance, parents' educational background or income. It improves academic results, mental health, wealth, communication skills and ambition.

Our business works committedly to create books that are well-researched, engaging, and enduring, but here are some ways we can all raise more readers:

- Reading to children for just 10 minutes a day makes a difference
- Don't give up if children aren't regular readers – it's not just about the number of books they have or read but about encouraging interest and engagement
- Encourage them to listen to audiobooks
- Support schools and other libraries
- Give books as gifts

Thank you for reading: there's a lot more information about how to encourage children to read on our website.

www.hachetteindia.com